UNBECOMING
NATIONALISM

UNBECOMING NATIONALISM

FROM COMMEMORATION TO REDRESS IN CANADA

HELENE VOSTERS

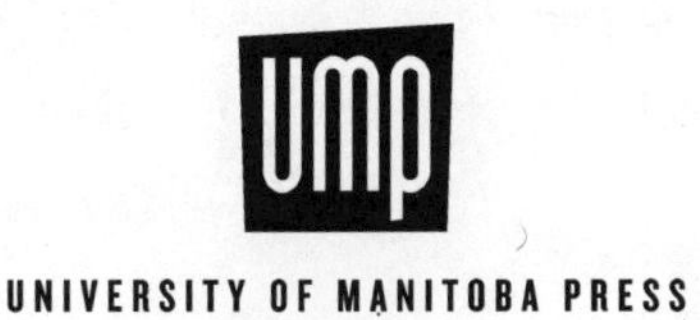

UNIVERSITY OF MANITOBA PRESS

23 22 21 20 19 1 2 3 4 5

University of Manitoba Press
Winnipeg, Manitoba, Canada
Treaty 1 Territory
uofmpress.ca

Cataloguing data available from Library and Archives Canada
ISBN 978-0-88755-841-2 (PAPER)
ISBN 978-0-88755-585-5 (PDF)
ISBN 978-0-88755-583-1 (EPUB)

Cover image: Detail from *Flag of Tears: Lament for the Stains of a Nation.*
Photo by Helene Vosters
Cover and interior design by Jess Koroscil

Printed in Canada

This book has been published with the help of a grant from the Federation for the Humanities and Social Sciences, through the Awards to Scholarly Publications Program, using funds provided by the Social Sciences and Humanities Research Council of Canada.

The University of Manitoba Press acknowledges the financial support for its publication program provided by the Government of Canada through the Canada Book Fund, the Canada Council for the Arts, the Manitoba Department of Sport, Culture, and Heritage, the Manitoba Arts Council, and the Manitoba Book Publishing Tax Credit.

Funded by the Government of Canada | Canada

CONTENTS

LIST OF ILLUSTRATIONS

INTRODUCTION

LEST WE FORGET

THE CONTESTED TERRAIN OF CANADIAN SOCIAL MEMORY

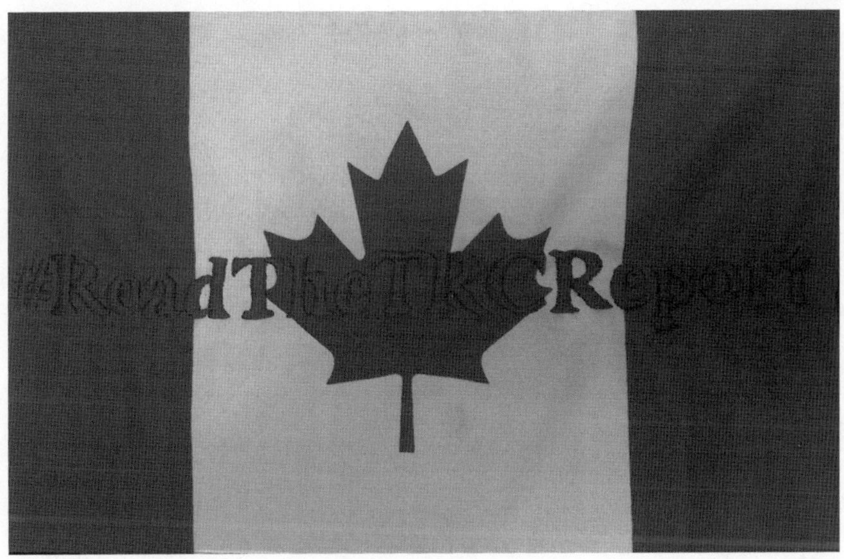

Figure 1. Canadian flag with #ReadTheTRCReport embroidery.[1]

> The best way to heal is to move forward together. Not to blame, not to point fingers, not to live in the past.
> — Senator Lynn Beyak, speaking about Canada's residential schools[2]

> A century later, we continue to honour the service and sacrifice of the brave young men and women, at home and abroad, during the First World War. . . . The Canadian victory at Vimy Ridge is considered a historic moment that helped define Canada and the people we are today.
> — Kent Hehr, Minister of Veterans Affairs and Associate Minister of National Defence[3]

> 2017 is here! The 150th anniversary of Confederation! Let the celebrations begin! . . . Let's all embrace this opportunity to celebrate the rich heritage and cultural diversity that make Canada such a great place to live.
> — Mélanie Joly, Minister of Canadian Heritage[4]

> This year, the federal government plans to spend half a billion dollars on events marking Canada's 150th anniversary. Meanwhile, essential social services for First Nations people to alleviate crisis-level socio-economic conditions go chronically underfunded. Not only is Canada refusing to share the bounty of its own piracy; it's using that same bounty to celebrate its good fortune. Arguably, every firework, hot dog and piece of birthday cake in Canada's 150th celebration will be paid for by the genocide of Indigenous peoples and cultures.
> — Pamela Palmater, Mi'kmaw lawyer and activist[5]

It's March 2017, and I'm hosting a Stitch-by-Stitch sewing circle and reading group at Winnipeg's Tallest Poppy restaurant.[6] For two days, participants gather around tables strewn with mugs of coffee and tea, embroidery hoops, red embroidery floss, scissors, a copy of the Truth and Reconciliation Commission (TRC) of Canada's Summary Report, and fifty-eight Canadian flags inscribed with the text of the TRC's ninety-four Calls to Action.[7] Eighteen of the flags—thirty-three of the calls—are completely embroidered; an additional dozen flags are in varying stages of progress. With each new arrival to the circle there are introductions, an orientation to the project, and, for those new to embroidery or in need of a refresher, a hands-on skill-sharing session. Then, we stitch, we read, we talk, heads bent to the tasks at hand—embroidery and critical reflection—both necessarily care-filled and time-demanding labours.

Those with embroidery experience share their technical skills. Likewise, those with greater knowledge of Canada's residential schools, the TRC Report, and the terms and concepts it engages also generously share information and resources. "Jason," a young man who arrives in the final hour of the two-day circle, tells us he has been hovering outside for half an hour trying to build the nerve to join us. At first, I assume it's the embroidery that daunts him. I'm wrong. It's the Report, or more precisely, his lack of knowledge of the history of residential schools in Canada, that intimidates him.

Jason is not alone. Many if not most non-Indigenous Canadians—including many of us in the circle—are only beginning to learn about the history of Canada's residential schools and their role in the larger context of settler colonialism. This is the point of the Stitch-by-Stitch circle. This is at least one of the points of the TRC. As the Report states, "Ongoing public education and dialogue are essential to reconciliation."[8]

Just as Jason is not alone, neither is Senator Lynn Beyak. On 7 March 2017, during a meeting of the Senate's Standing Committee on Aboriginal Peoples, Senator Beyak spoke "in memory of the kindly and well-intentioned men and women and their descendants . . . whose remarkable works, good deeds and historical tales in the residential schools go unacknowledged for the most part and are overshadowed by negative reports," and went on to assert that an "abundance of good" has come out of the residential school system.[9] Beyak's statement was immediately met with calls for her to resign from the Committee on Aboriginal Peoples and to educate herself about residential schools. Refusing to voluntarily step down, Beyak claimed: "I don't need any more education."[10]

In his response to Senator Beyak's refusal and her insistence that "the best way to heal is not to live in the past," Senator Murray Sinclair drew national attention to the double standard that is endemic within dominant social memory practices: "Why can't you always remember this? Because this is about memorializing those people who have been the victims of a great wrong. Why don't you tell the United States to 'get over' 9/11? Why don't you tell this country to 'get over' all the veterans who died in the Second World War, instead of honouring them once a year?"[11]

Although Senator Beyak was removed from the committee on 5 April 2017, it would be a mistake to view her statements as isolated or the issue as resolved—as was all too evident in the racist letters of support the senator later posted on her official Canadian Senate website.[12] Beyak's ignorance belongs to a vast, institutionally manufactured and maintained process of settler-Canadian forgetfulness. A myriad of government-funded social memory projects—monuments, museums, ceremonies and celebrations, educational programs and materials, media representations, and so on—shape our collective memory by directing Canadian civilian attention toward who and what to remember, and by omission, who and what to forget.

On 9 April 2017, just one month after Senator Beyak's infamous comments, over 20,000 Canadians made a pilgrimage to France to commemorate the 100th anniversary of the Battle of Vimy Ridge. Additional tens of thousands attended commemoration ceremonies in cities across Canada, while hundreds of thousands tuned in to watch the coverage on CBC (Canadian Broadcasting Corporation) television. Canadian participation in Vimy Ridge commemoration ceremonies at home and abroad was funded, in part, through Operation Distinction, a Canadian National Defençe program launched during former prime minister Stephen Harper's Conservative administration. In a 2014 *Globe and Mail* article on the administration's increased spending on military history projects, Steven Chase reported: "The initiative spans all the way to 2020, which will mark the 75th anniversary of the Second World War's victory in Europe Day and Victory over Japan Day."[13]

The upsurge in government spending on the promotion of and participation in overseas military commemorations during Stephen Harper's almost decade-long term as prime minister was part of a larger multi-million-dollar military commemoration budget that also included "$32-million for the Department of National Defence over seven years and nearly $50-million over three years at the Departments of Veterans Affairs for public education, ceremonies, events and remembrance partnerships. [An additional] several million dollars [was channelled] through the Department of Canadian Heritage."[14]

As Canadian studies scholars A.L. McCready, Ian McKay and Jamie Swift, Jerome Klassen and Greg Albo, and Howard Fremeth (among others) note, increased government spending on military memory projects during the Stephen Harper administration was part of a broader ideological investment in shifting Canadian national identity away from peacekeeping and toward an increasingly militarized nationalism. Speaking to the pervasive effects of this shift on national consciousness, A.L. McCready writes: "Militarization is the process by which non-military social institutions from education, to the workplace, to the media and entertainment industries and the economy as a whole become conscripted into militarism and wedded to military purposes and objectives."[15]

I concur with McCready (and others) that the Harper government contributed significantly to the militarization of multiple spectacular and everyday aspects of Canadian culture, and will return to this in my discussion of the Highway of Heroes and Remembrance Day (Chapter 1) and the Canadian War Museum (Chapter 2). However, it is also important to note that Canada's ideological and fiscal commitments to Canadian military commemoration precede and exceed any particular administration's term of office. A key difference between Stephen Harper's Conservative and Justin Trudeau's Liberal governments has been not so much in the amount of fiscal resources budgeted to Canada's military, but in how that support is administered and ideologically managed. As an avowed anti-militarist, I believe that one of the only (perhaps *the* only) "hopeful" aspects of the Harper administration's aggressive support for a more militarized national image was that it engendered debate. My concern with Prime Minister Trudeau's return to the soft sell of peacekeeping is that it has allowed the government's actual fiscal investments—such as the commitment to a $62 billion increase in funding to the Canadian Armed Forces over the next twenty years[16]—to fly under the radar of public debate.

Senator Beyak suggested that the best way for Canadians to heal from historical violence is to stop living in the past, but as Senator Sinclair so poignantly noted, when it comes to the nation's officially recognized military history—as opposed to the overlooked perpetration of state violence against Indigenous peoples—Canadian governments across administrations have invested heavily in the memorialization of historical violence. Whether through commemoration ceremonies, immersive military re-enactments, memory projects, or military history teaching guides, Canadians—Canadian youth in particular—are enlisted to step into the trenches of past wars, and into the combat boots of those who served in them.[17]

In contrast to the obligatory reverentiality of military commemoration, Canada 150 events called forth a more celebratory nationalism. In place of the sombre call of the bugle's Last Post or the reverberating roar of the cannon's twenty-one-gun salute, spectacular jubilation marked the federal government's recognition of Canada's year-long sesquicentennial birthday party. In Ottawa alone, the fireworks that lit up the sky for the inaugural Canada 150 New Year's Eve bash cost over $200,000.[18] On one hand, Canadians are called to reverentially recall historic battlefield moments that "define Canada and the people we are today"; on the other hand, they are encouraged to "celebrate the rich heritage and cultural diversity that make Canada such a great place to live."

The Canada 150 Fund's mandate "is to create opportunities for Canadians to participate in local, regional, and national celebrations that contribute to building a sense of pride and attachment to Canada."[19] For many in Canada's Indigenous and settler ally communities, the national invitation to "celebrate" the 150th anniversary of Canadian Confederation was, in the words of Michif (Métis) artist and activist Christi Belcourt, "an insult."[20] The government's half-billion-dollar investment in the national birthday celebrations added injury to insult by perpetuating an attitude of indifference, as Mi'kmaw lawyer, scholar, and activist Pamela Palmater writes, to the "crisis-level socio-economic conditions" of Indigenous peoples in contemporary post-Confederation Canada.[21]

Looked at in this light, Conservative Senator Beyak's call for Canadians to "move on" is not so different from Liberal Canadian Heritage Minister Mélanie Joly's enthusiastic hailing of Canadians to celebrate "the 150th anniversary of Confederation!" Both Beyak and Joly were official representatives of the nation-state at the time of their statements. Both implored Canadians—Beyak by blatant admonition, Joly by celebratory omission—to focus on the good that is Canada while turning a blind eye to the ongoing violence of settler colonialism.

Despite its previous criticisms of the Canada 150 Community Infrastructure Program as a "slush fund," Canada's newly elected Liberal government added $150 million to the program's coffers in March 2016. With over $500 million in federal funds invested in its commemoration, Canada's sesquicentennial anniversary of Confederation loomed large on our national budgetary and cultural horizons from 2015 through 2017—the period in which I was writing this book. In fact, I submitted my first draft of this manuscript to the University of Manitoba Press in the early months of 2017, when the sesquicentennial celebrations had just begun, with Chapter 5—on Canada 150—as a work in progress.

Like many, I felt trepidation over how the year would unfold. By the time 2017 had reached its Canada Day zenith, it had become apparent that the story the celebrations were meant to perpetuate—that of a beneficent Canadian nation committed to equity and multicultural inclusivity—had been significantly eclipsed in mainstream and social media by critiques of the sesquicentennial's ahistorical premise and its disregard for the ongoing violent effects of settler colonialism. In retrospect, it appears that Canada 150 was somewhat of a miscalculation on the part of Prime Minister Justin Trudeau's public relations–savvy government. Despite the hefty $500 million price tag, Canada 150's spectacles of celebratory nationalism may well have proved more effective in mobilizing and invigorating political resistance than in evoking pride and attachment to the nation (more on this in Chapter 5).

Far from an anomaly—and despite its limited success as a national celebration—Canada 150 was merely the latest in a long, steady procession of increasingly spectacular Canadian cultural memory projects that have included (among others) military commemoration ceremonies, Canada Day celebrations, and multi-million-dollar national museums like the Canadian War Museum (Chapter 2) and the Canadian Museum for Human Rights (Chapter 4). Taken together, these national memory projects construct a becoming image of Canada as a model of an enlightened, equitable, and multi-ethnic nation while simultaneously obscuring (or assimilating) unbecoming acts—past and present—that do not support dominant notions of Canadian national innocence and geopolitical moral exceptionalism.

Through an investigation of how Canadian social memory is simultaneously performed and produced, *Unbecoming Nationalism: From Commemoration to Redress in Canada* points to the precariously thin lines between reverential military commemoration, celebratory cultural nationalism, and white settler-colonial nationalism. Against the backdrop of Canada's burgeoning government-funded social memory industry, *Unbecoming Nationalism* combines a critical inquiry into state-sponsored performances of social memory with readings of counter-memorial performances and projects that work to *un*become popular narratives of benevolent Canadian nationalism and advance the work of social memory beyond the official mandates of elegiac or celebratory national commemoration, toward a praxis of redress.

Like military commemoration, celebratory performances of Canadian cultural nationalism rely on the naturalization of the becoming nation and the masking of the violence of its originary and ongoing becoming. For

Canadian settler nationalism to function and for its unbecoming acts to appear justifiable, the nation-state—with its imposed political, economic, and legal structures—must be perceived by the dominant population as a normalized (and ethical) entity whose existence goes without question. But like all nations, this land called Canada is an "imagined community."[22] As Benedict Anderson asserts, nationalism and its construction of imagined communities was integral to colonial expansion and contributed to the naturalization of European colonial rule and settler colonialism. Alongside performances of Canadian military commemoration, cultural nationalist productions can serve to affirm and normalize the Canadian settler-colonial nation-state.

Lest we forget—as dominant national memory projects would have us do—the work of Indigenous studies and anti-colonial scholars reminds us that Canadian settler colonialism is not a thing of the past. As Yellowknives Dene political scientist Glen Sean Coulthard argues, "A settler-colonial relationship is characterized by a particular form of *domination*; that is, it is a relationship where power—in this case, interrelated discursive and nondiscursive facets of economic, gendered, racial, and state power—has been structured into a relatively secure or sedimented set of hierarchical social relations that continue to facilitate the dispossession of Indigenous peoples of their lands and self-determining authority."[23] Canada 150 was emblematic of Canadian settler-colonial nationalism, both in its normalizing denial of settler colonialism's historical "overtly coercive means" as well as in its more contemporary form of colonial governmentality, wherein, as Coulthard asserts, naked aggression is replaced by "the asymmetrical exchange of mediated forms of state recognition and accommodation."[24]

Using performance as both a lens and a practice-based research methodology, *Unbecoming Nationalism* brings readings of institutional, aesthetic, and activist performances of Canadian commemoration and counter-memorialization into conversation with literature that examines the relationship between memory, violence, and nationalism from the disciplinary arenas of performance studies, Canadian studies, Indigenous studies, feminist historicism, queer and gender studies, critical memory studies, and critical race and anti-colonial studies. With its multidisciplinary scope, its readings of cultural performances as texts, and its use of embodied inquiry as a method, *Unbecoming Nationalism* works across disciplinary vocabularies as well as the disparate lexicons of written scholarly work and aesthetic and embodied practice.

Glossary Break

I want to pause to clarify several terms that appear throughout the book, and to explain how and why I use them. I begin with *becoming*. In one sense, becoming speaks to a process of coming into being. As a descriptive term, it evokes something that is appealing or pleasing. I use becoming in both senses: on one hand, to gesture toward the way nationalist performances work to become—or construct—the imagined Canadian nation; on the other, to name the idealized national identity they produce. In spite of the increase in performances of militarized national memory as part of the concerted efforts of former prime minster Stephen Harper's administration to rebrand Canada into what Ian McKay and Jamie Swift have dubbed a "Warrior Nation," Canada's friendly, or more becoming, image continues to be the hallmark of settler-Canadian national identity. Often positioned in contrast to what many Canadians characterize as our belligerent, war-mongering, impenitent southern neighbours, our becoming national identity casts us as ever-humble, polite global peacekeepers and proud multiculturalists who are not afraid to say "sorry."

Harper's official apology on behalf of Canadians to Indigenous survivors of Canada's Indian residential school system, issued on 11 July 2008, can be seen as a quintessential example of a politically instrumentalist performance of becoming Canadian humility. A little over a year later, on the international stage of the 2009 G20 summit, Harper went on to state that Canada had "no history of colonialism." As Coulthard writes: "There is no recognition of a colonial past or present, nor is there any mention of the much broader system of land dispossession, political domination, and cultural genocide of which the residential school system formed only a part. Harper's apology is thus able . . . to comfortably frame reconciliation in terms of overcoming a 'sad chapter' in our shared history."[25]

This brings me to *unbecoming*. Used as a descriptor, unbecoming refers to that which detracts from or renders less attractive one's image or reputation. Attention to the violence of settler colonialism or the not-so-altruistic motivations and actions of Canada's military risks marring Canada's beloved becoming image of national innocence, and thereby rendering the nation unbecoming. Used to refer to a process, unbecoming gestures toward the multiply situated practices and projects that work to unsettle, decolonize, dismantle, or *un*become Canadian settler-colonial nationalism.

Similarly, I use unbecoming both in my examination of the less-than-attractive practices on which Canadian militarism is based as well as in discussing counter-memorial performances that work to undo Canada's prevalent narrative of humanitarian militarism. One thing that became increasingly apparent during the time I researched this book, however, is that while there are numerous inspiring examples of activist and aesthetic projects that work to unbecome narratives of settler-colonial nationalism taking place in Canada at this moment in history—most notably by Indigenous cultural producers—the number of visible projects that work to unbecome Canadian narratives of benevolent militarism are, in contrast, extremely limited (a point I will return to in the book's final chapter).

I use the term *white Canadian settler-colonial nationalism* to explicitly mark the Canadian nation's European settler-colonial origins—with its ongoing differential distribution of both privileges and violent effects—*and* the continuing primacy of whiteness within dominant constructions of the Canadian nation. This is not to deny the multicultural makeup of Canada's populace. Rather, it is intended to resist Canada's popularized narrative of multiculturalism that works to project a national identity that glosses over internal difference and, as critical race and anti-colonial scholar Sherene Razack asserts, "de-rac[es]" violence, in support of an idealized notion of national innocence.[26] Throughout the book I alternate terms—Canada, Canadian nationalism, white Canadian settler-colonial nationalism, and so on. Always, however, when I write of Canada or Canadian nationalism, the reader should assume I am speaking of Canada as a settler-colonial nation that continues to operate through a myriad of institutionalized mechanisms of white privilege.

I use the words *commemoration* and *performance* in concert to describe a broad range—popular, institutional, repertorial, aesthetic, archival, architectural, and so on—of enactments of social memory. Whereas the common definition of commemoration—a ceremony or service in memory of a person or event—conveys a kind of neutrality, there is nothing neutral about performances that commemorate the nation or its privileged subjects. "Nationalism," as postcolonial scholar Gayatri Chakravorty Spivak writes, "is the product of a collective imagination constructed through rememoration."[27] Who and what is memorialized or commemorated is intricately associated with who and what is forgotten or cast outside of social memory's national narrative. Canada's dominant national memory needs to be understood as a political performance, one that must be continuously re-performed in order to maintain its hold on the collective national—and international—imagination. By situating commemorative performances as political projects, I challenge the term's benign usage and instead direct attention to its pedagogical role in the construction of Canadian national identity. In particular, as a white settler Canadian, I am interested in how commemorative performances can produce narratives of national innocence that work to distract or blind settler Canadians from reflecting on the ongoing privileges of white settler nationalism, the ongoing violence of settler colonialism at home and of Canadian militarism abroad.

Finally, I use the phrase *praxis of redress* to describe counter-memorial performances that work to unbecome the dominant narratives of Canadian nationalism and the fictive innocence of our imagined nation. The term derives from and extends settler-Indigenous studies scholar Len Findlay's notion of "redress rehearsals."[28] Findlay proposes that as an organizing trope "rehearsal" allows for "the diverse pursuit of redress as a performance of... academic, cultural, and political *theatre* which functions as a necessary preliminary to the *big show of belated justice*."[29] Rehearsal in the context of redress foregrounds notions of practice, experimentation, refinement, and review, and resists containment within imposed institutional and structural mandates and timeframes. Rehearsal is improvisational. It generates fissures, leaks, and sticky impressions that make their way into unexpected cultural arenas. Rehearsal offers a frame for the ongoing and intergenerational labour of refusing the "structural forgetfulness" of Canadian nationalist narratives.[30]

Though Findlay uses the term "theatre" in his definition, throughout his application of rehearsal as an organizing trope he proposes an extra-theatrical framework. I call this rehearsal *praxis*. With this augmented naming, I distinguish rehearsal from its instrumentalist theatrical applications. In the context of professional theatrical production, rehearsal—though often productively experimental—remains the hidden labour that is the necessary precursor to the "show" as consumable product. Looking at rehearsal as a praxis resituates its productive potential, moving it from a behind-the-scenes process of preparation for audience consumption to the social arena, where performance of an experimental and fluid praxis of redress becomes part of a larger epistemological model for collective capacity building toward the unbecoming of Canada's settler-colonial nationalism. Categorizing counter-memorial performances as an ongoing praxis of redress refuses national reconciliatory discourses that bracket off "cultural" harm from processes of colonial land grabs, institutionalized racism, and cultural genocide.

THE DUELLING MANDATES OF CULTURAL FUNDING (THREAD 1): Securing the Cultural Defences of a Becoming Nation

> We must strengthen those permanent institutions which give meaning to our unity and make us conscious of the best in our national life . . . Our military defences must be made secure; but our cultural defences equally demand national attention; the two cannot be separated.
>
> — *Report of the Royal Commission on National Development in the Arts, Letters and Sciences*[31]

As a study of performances of Canadian social memory, *Unbecoming Nationalism* necessarily grapples with the duelling mandates and methodologies of government funding bodies and the cultural producers whose work contests the dominant narratives of Canadian nationalism. For their part, national funding bodies aim to balance mechanisms that exert sufficient control to ensure the production of a properly becoming image of Canada while simultaneously allowing for adequate critical engagement, so that notions of inclusivity, diversity, and acceptance of difference can be integrated into the overarching becoming image. The cultural producers, community groups, and activists who contest dominant nationalist narratives—or even the very legitimacy of the Canadian nation—have another challenge altogether. Since they are often dependent, at least to some degree, on government funding, they are called upon to employ an array of uncanny subversions in order to navigate, without capitulating to, the ever-shifting exigencies of government funding and the confines of national institutions and reverential and celebratory narratives of nationalism.

While Canadians rightfully pride themselves on belonging to a nation that supports the arts and culture, they have perhaps been less vigilant in interrogating the ideological underpinnings of Canada's cultural funding structures and institutions, or in tracking deteriorations of arm's-length principles in contemporary arts funding. Just as peacekeeping and multiculturalism provide ideological cover for Canadian militarism and dominant settler-Canadian nationalism, notions of arm's-length neutrality provide Canadians at large and, to a far lesser extent, Canadian cultural funders and producers with a means through which to construct a fictively objective distance between the managerial arm of the nation-state and the cultural products it finances. Despite (fluctuating) commitments to arm's-length principles and an abundance of performances by cultural producers whose work brilliantly unbecomes dominant narratives of settler-Canadian nationalism, it is important to recognize that from the outset, those responsible for Canada's overarching cultural funding structures have equated cultural nationalism with national security.

A critical event in the genesis of Canadian cultural funding was the 1951 publication of the Massey Report. With growing concern over the "anemic state of Canadian culture and the pervasive influence of American culture" in post–Second World War Canada, Prime Minister Louis St.-Laurent launched the Royal Commission on the Development of the Arts, Letters and Sciences, headed up by University of Toronto Chancellor Vincent Massey.[32] The resulting Massey Report is arguably one of the most significant events in the proliferation of Canadian cultural nationalism. Two of the report's more consequential outcomes for Canadian artists included the expansion of the National Film Board and the formation of the Canada Council for the Arts.

Investments channelled in and through organizations like the National Film Board and the Canada Council have contributed immeasurably to the production and promotion of a richly textured and diverse Canadian cultural landscape for consumption at home and abroad. They have also provided bread-and-butter funding for generations of Canadian artists, filmmakers, performers, writers, and other cultural producers. Despite the commitment of these institutional bodies to the principle of arm's-length funding, however, it would be naive to view them as neutral entities, capable of withstanding political pressures exerted by governmental and other stakeholder constituencies. Performances of Canadian cultural memory belong to a larger project of becoming and defending the Canadian nation. As Canadian theatre and performance studies scholar Alan Filewod argues concerning (English) Canadian theatre productions, these performances do not simply reflect the stories of a maturing Canadian nation—they are an essential part of the project of actively producing that nation. Likewise, the "pride and attachment to Canada" that the Canada 150 Fund mandates its projects to foster are feelings that are essential ideological and affective mechanisms for shoring up Canada's national borders.

Though it falls beyond the scope of this book to provide a comprehensive analysis of the historical and reciprocal relationship between cultural production and Canadian national sovereignty, I want to note a couple of twists and turns on the road of Canadian arts funding over the past several decades that are salient to a discussion about cultural memory projects that work to either become or unbecome dominant narratives of Canadian nationalism. In this first section on the duelling mandates of cultural funding, I will map some key factors that have influenced funding for the increased production of contemporary military memory projects in Canada. I will follow this with a section that looks at the vastly different influences on funding mandates that have helped facilitate a growing number of projects that work to unbecome or unsettle narratives of settler-colonial nationalism.

Many, and with good cause, point to the Harper administration as a key factor in the increase of Canadian military memory projects. Canadian studies scholar Howard Fremeth, however, looks to influences that predate the Harper government by at least a decade. In the early 1990s, Fremeth notes, there emerged in Canada a complex network of organizational and institutional stakeholders that became adept at using popular media forms and accessing infrastructural support to "canonize and archive Canadian military memory."[33] Stakeholder groups included military historians and scholars, Canadian Armed Forces representatives, veterans' organizations, organizations that represent military families, as well as a range of cultural producers.

Fremeth identifies the CBC's 1992 prime-time airing of the film series *The Valour and the Horror*, a three-part docudrama about Canada's military engagements in the Second World War, as a formative event in the emergence of this network of military stakeholders and the resulting expansion of Canadian military-cultural memory projects. Written by brothers Terence McKenna and Brian McKenna, *Valour* came to be seen as part of what General Rick Hillier, during his tenure as Canada's Chief of the Defence Staff, dubbed a "decade of darkness"[34] for the Canadian Forces—an era in which the Somalia Affair, the Canadian Airborne Regiment's initiation rites controversies, and Canada's failed attempt to halt the Rwandan genocide disrupted Canada's reputation as a peacekeeping nation and left the Canadian Forces with a deeply tarnished public image (Chapter 2).

Valour's most contentious episode, "Death by Moonlight: Bomber Command," challenged on both strategic and moral grounds the legitimacy of the allied bomber offensive campaign in which 50,000 Canadians participated and 600,000 German civilians were killed.[35] The series sparked a $500 million class action lawsuit by Canadian Royal Air Force veterans against the program's producers (the CBC and the NFB), a Senate committee hearing, and a nationwide public debate over who had legitimate rights to the control of Canada's social military memory, and by what means. Though the Senate committee did not contest the accuracy of the filmmakers' representation of the facts of the bombing, it raised questions about the "appropriate" use of public arts funds, and the legitimacy of arm's-length funding. Ultimately the Royal Air Force veterans were unsuccessful in their class action suit and in their efforts to have the McKennas' film series censored. Despite this loss, however, stakeholders in Canada's military memory network appear to have won two larger battles: the first, over control of the framing of Canada's military-cultural memory, and the second, over increased access to arts-based funds that were formerly deemed arm's-length.

Evidence of the reinvigorated and increasingly media-savvy military-cultural memory network in Canada that emerged in the post-*Valour* era can be seen in multiple arenas. In addition to increased spending on conventional memorials and museums dedicated to warfare and military commemoration, performances and arts-based projects began playing a more substantial role in the memorialization of Canadian military history. Examples include large-scale institutional projects like the $140 million Canadian War Museum, with its spectacular array of interactive multimedia displays; the CBC's popular radio drama series *Afghanada*; the Harper administration's $28 million funding package earmarked for War of 1812 Bicentennial Commemoration events, which included the first professional production of the late James Reaney's opera libretto *Taptoo* (2012); two Canadian war film epics, *Passchendaele* (2008) and *Hyena Road* (2015), both starring and directed by Paul Gross; and a plethora of historical re-enactments, multimedia interpretive programming and tours, documentary films, theatrical, musical, and dance performances, and visual artworks.

In a 2008 *Globe and Mail* article, James Bradshaw argued that a key mechanism through which the mandate of arm's-length funding in Canada was being shifted to "socially appropriate" funding was the funnelling of arts and culture funding dollars into "branches of the Department of Canadian

Heritage that focus on the department's social mandate."[36] This move away from arm's-length funding principles, as Barbara Jenkins notes in her study of Canadian cultural spending, corresponded with an overall decline in arts funding across Canada throughout the 1990s. These combined changes to arts funding had a profound effect on artists and cultural producers across Canada, who found themselves either vying for fewer truly arm's-length dollars or being compelled to frame works in terms that met the nationalist, and often military, mandates of heritage project selection committees. Even popular public arts programs like *Dusk Dances* climbed on the War of 1812 bandwagon during the 2013/14 funding season when emcee Dan Watson took on the persona of "the Colonel" to lead audience "troops" through Toronto parks from one "dance battle" to the next. While Watson's portrayal of the Colonel was whimsically tongue-in-cheek, I nevertheless found it troubling how—as with the growing presence of military display at sports and community events—it contributed to a ubiquitous normalization of militarism.

The eulogizing narratives propagated through performances of Canadian military commemoration are particularly well-suited to the production of a nationalist discourse since they are adept at homogenizing the dead while simultaneously silencing the living with the imposition of overt and covert protocols of obligatory reverentiality. Recent works by historians, journalists, and Canadian studies scholars—Teigrob, Klassen and Albo, McCready, McKay and Swift, and Fremeth (among others)—offer unsettling accounts of how Canada's long embrace of elegiac military commemoration, alongside Canadians' attachment to a peacekeeping ideology, contributes to what historian Robert Teigrob refers to as an absence of "thorough-going criticisms of Canadian military exploits."[37] *Unbecoming Nationalism* extends this body of research in several ways. First, it bridges an investigation of how Canadian nationalism becomes itself through performances of military memorialization that construct narratives of benevolent Canadian militarism with a critical analysis of celebratory commemorative performances of Canadian cultural nationalism that similarly work to disavow the nation-state's unbecoming settler-colonial characteristics and actions. Second, this book examines the effects that two disparate stakeholder assemblages have had, and continue to have, on contemporary narratives of Canadian nationalism. The first, discussed above, is the network of military-cultural memory stakeholders; the second, discussed below, is the "assemblage" of Indigenous artists, activists, and scholars who are working to unsettle the narratives and corresponding practices of Canadian settler-colonial nationalism through an ongoing, intergenerational praxis of redress.[38] To be clear, I am not suggesting that these are the only constituencies who are exerting pressures on cultural funding mandates that in turn impact larger discourses of Canadian nationalism, only that they are the two groups that presently hold the greatest influence in relation to the two threads that are the focus of this book, performances of Canadian militarism and of settler-colonial nationalism.

THE DUELLING MANDATES OF CULTURAL FUNDING (THREAD 2): Unbecoming Settler-Colonial Nationalism under Multicultural Skies

Whereas evidence of the success of military memory stakeholders can be seen in the proliferation of projects that work to shore up becoming narratives of Canadian military humanitarianism, the success of a broad-based assemblage of Indigenous (and settler-ally) artists, activists, and scholars who are working toward a praxis of redress is perhaps most immediately and dramatically evidenced in the plethora of counter-memorial performances by Indigenous artists, activists, and public figures that crashed Canada's $500 million sesquicentennial party. The message of Canada as a nation of multicultural inclusivity that the multi-million-dollar celebration sought to propagate was repeatedly interrupted, contested, and subverted. Despite and because of its insulting and ahistorical premise—that Canada is a nation with a 150-year history—Canada 150 mobilized immense, and immensely effective, political resistance.

Indigenous artists were at the forefront of the Canada 150 resistance, and in a broader sense, at the forefront of the growing movement to unsettle Canada's ideology of national innocence. Christi Belcourt began the year with the YouTube circulation of her impeaching lament "Canada, I can cite for you 150," and continued throughout the year to use the Canada 150 backdrop as a space from which to voice critiques of Canadian settler colonialism.[39] Two-spirit Cree multidisciplinary artist Kent Monkman brazenly commandeered the sesquicentennial celebrations with his monumental Canada 150 counter-memorial solo exhibition, *Shame and Prejudice: A Story of Resilience* (2017). And in lieu of homages to the Group of Seven, many art galleries across the country used Canada 150 funds to host exhibitions and activities that foregrounded works by artists who disrupt dominant narratives of Canadian nationalism.

Included among the many powerful exhibitions was *INSURGENCE/RESURGENCE* (2017). The largest exhibition of contemporary Indigenous artists ever produced at the Winnipeg Art Gallery, *INSURGENCE/RESURGENCE* was co-curated by the Winnipeg Art Gallery's Curator of Indigenous and Contemporary Art, Anishinaabe-British curator-artist Jaimie Isaac, and the Chair of the History of Indigenous Art at the University of Winnipeg, Métis scholar and artist Dr. Julie Nagam. Though *INSURGENCE/RESURGENCE* opened in the fall of 2017, the exhibition was not framed as part of or a response to Canada 150. As its name indicates, and as Isaac and Nagam point out, the exhibition pays homage to the ongoing practices of Indigenous political insurgence and how these have made, and continue to make, way for increasingly visible and vibrant practices of cultural resurgence. "We chose the term 'insurgence,'" write Isaac and Nagam, "to acknowledge past efforts and all the political work that fell on the backs of so many people, as well as to pay homage to the current political insurgencies Indigenous people enact on the front lines—as land and water protectors—for the future of Indigenous and non-Indigenous children alike."[40]

The long history of Indigenous assemblages engaged in practices of resistance to Canadian settler colonialism has in recent years manifested in prolific, highly visible movements of political insurgence and cultural resurgence. The Idle No More protest movement brought Indigenous issues, cultural practices, and public education on settler colonialism into streets and shopping malls across the nation. And while there was much concern that the TRC Report would become yet another shelved document—and it remains uncertain what effects the Commission and the communities it mobilized will have on material factors like control over lands and resources—the TRC has had an undeniable impact on public discourse and has significantly shifted practices and mandates across a range of Canadian cultural and educational institutions.

When I began my research for this book, my focus was on the role of Canadian military commemoration in producing hierarchies of grievability and narratives of national innocence and humanitarian militarism. As the project developed, I became interested in how Canadian cultural funding worked to shape discourses of Canadian nationalism, and how, in turn, stakeholder assemblages—like the military-cultural memory network—work to shape cultural funding mandates. As I encountered more works by Indigenous artists—many of whom operate under the mandates of Canadian cultural funding bodies and institutions—I became increasingly impressed by how effectively assemblages of Indigenous artists, activists, and scholars were in resisting, creatively subverting, and even reshaping the overarching nationalist mandate of Canadian cultural funding bodies and institutions. So while this book began as a critical investigation of *parallels* between the two threads of this project—performances that work to become or unbecome dominant narratives of benevolent Canadian militarism; and those that work to become or unbecome dominant narratives of Canadian settler-colonial national innocence—it has instead become a study in *contrasts* between these two threads.

While all cultural producers are, to varying degrees, beholden to funding bodies and institutions, their ability to successfully produce work that unbecomes dominant Canadian nationalist narratives also depends on non-governmental and non-institutional factors. In addition to working with funders, curators, and other institutional stakeholders, cultural producers operate within the context of broad and multiply situated assemblages of actors whose work takes place outside of gallery or museum spaces—activists, community organizations, and others. The relative presence or absence of these larger influencing assemblages is a critical factor in producing the cultural landscape where performances that work to engender processes of collective reckoning with the role of Canadian military and settler-colonial violence can take place.

In the case of Canadian military memory projects, there exists a powerful collection of stakeholders who have been extremely and increasingly effective in accessing and channelling government resources to present an elegiac narrative of Canadian humanitarian militarism. Correspondingly, there is a near absence of actors effectively working to *challenge* dominant narratives of Canadian humanitarian militarism. In the case of performances that work to become and unbecome narratives of Canadian settler-colonial nationalism, on the other hand, it could be argued that there are powerful assemblages on both sides. On the side of becoming narratives of Canadian nationalism there is, most notably, the Canadian nation-state and its representatives. Despite adjustments to the public image of the nation-state by different administrations, every Canadian government invests in constructing its notion of a becoming nation.

In contrast to the lack of a visible assemblage of stakeholders resisting dominant narratives of Canadian military benevolence, on the side of performances that work to unbecome narratives of Canadian settler-colonial nationalism there exists a powerful intergenerational assemblage of Indigenous actors whose ongoing praxis of political insurgence and cultural resurgence has been and is challenging dominant narratives of Canadian nationalism. One of the many arenas where this "insurgence/resurgence" is evident is in art galleries across the country. After decades of relegating Indigenous artists to "cultural museum" spaces, the practice of juxtaposing contemporary Indigenous art that is critical of settler colonialism alongside celebrated European-Canadian artists has become commonplace in mainstream Canadian galleries.

This move by galleries could be considered part of Canada's broader multicultural managerial strategy, which, as Coulthard and Razack (among others) argue, is deployed as a tactic for absorbing difference. It is also, however, the result of a long practice by Indigenous cultural producers in Canada in the art of creatively navigating the traps of multiculturalist ideologies and settler colonialism's toxic representations.

Borrowing from queer and performance studies theorist José Esteban Muñoz, I propose that Indigenous cultural producers who work to unbecome mythologies of Canadian nationalism use a "disidentificatory" approach wherein they are able to draw upon, while concurrently resisting, settler-Canadian nationalism's purifying, forgetful, and toxic representations. As a strategic approach to resisting dominant ideologies, disidentification departs from assimilationist and anti-assimilationist strategies and instead re-marks the unmarked dominant through a creatively queer array of performative infiltrations, subversions, amplifications, and distortions. While Muñoz developed the notion of disidentification to theorize performances by queers of colour as "a minority population whose identities are formed in response to the cultural logics of heteronormativity, white supremacy, and misogyny,"[41] with *Unbecoming Nationalism* I extend this use of disidentification to performances that work on, through, and against dominant narratives of Canadian humanitarian militarism and settler-colonial nationalism. The Indigenous artists who skillfully perform their acts of disidentificatory resistance are not alone. As Findlay, Isaac, and Nagam (among others) make clear, they belong to larger intergenerational assemblages that include artists, curators, cultural institutions, and funders, as well as activists, scholars, lawyers, policy makers, politicians, and educators who together exert pressure on institutional bodies and government administrations.

Just as Canadian cultural funding has proven malleable despite its overarching nation-building agenda, Canada's official policy of multiculturalism has engendered tangible positive effects despite its deployment as a managerial mechanism. This is a central paradox of the Canada-the-good mythology and Canada's multiculturalist policies. On one hand, as Mohawk anthropologist Audra Simpson asserts, "tolerance, recognition, and the specific technique that is multicultural policy are but an elaboration of an older sequence of attitudes toward 'the problem' of difference on acquired, some might argue *seized*, territories."[42] On the other hand, Canada's official multiculturalist policy has also been a mechanism whereby resources have been successfully, albeit insufficiently, channelled and accessed by Indigenous, non-white, and other institutionally marginalized cultural producers.

Though conceived in response to discourses on anglo-francophone bilingualism and a shift in immigration trends from majority European ancestry to majority non-European ancestry, Canada's multicultural policies have nevertheless been, as art historian Charlotte Townsend-Gault notes, instrumental to Indigenous cultural producers in gaining access to arts funding and other resources. Even while living in California during the early 1990s, I saw evidence of the difference Canadian arts funding makes for Indigenous filmmakers. At the 1993 American Indian Film Festival in San Francisco, a festival organizer directed the audience to pay attention to not only the content of the films but also their credits. As it turned out, Canada's National Film Board had funded the majority of the festival's films. By contrast, films produced by Indigenous filmmakers in the United States necessitated hundreds of individual and small-group sponsors.

Indigenous arts funding generated in response to Canada's official commitments to multiculturalism include policies adopted by CBC and the Canada Council that encouraged Indigenous hires and funding applicants, the development of an Indigenous arts program at the Banff Centre for the Arts, and the establishment of the Aboriginal Peoples Television Network (APTN).[43] Looked at from the historical perspective of Canada's settler-colonial timeline, funding for Indigenous cultural producers was painfully slow in coming. When it did come, however, it contributed to the accelerated development of a vibrant contemporary Indigenous arts movement that has made its way into national and international mainstream cultural arenas. Despite these increased funding opportunities, however, many of Canada's most renowned Indigenous artists still find themselves without a steady source of economic support, since arts funding is piecemeal.

In pointing to the blurry lines between Canadian cultural funding, Canadian militarism, and Canadian settler nationalism, I am not suggesting a cause-and-effect relationship. Nor am I suggesting that cultural projects funded through Canadian national funding bodies are necessarily serving a nationalist agenda. As examples throughout the book illustrate, counter-memorial projects that work to unbecome dominant narratives of Canadian nationalism are often supported by national funding bodies and housed within Canadian institutions. That said, it is important to note vast differences in the malleability of specific institutional mandates. For example, as I detail in my discussion on the Canadian War Museum, influence over the museum's content is fairly intractable, even for those who hold curatorial decision-making positions within the institution. At the Canadian Museum for Human Rights, on the other hand, Indigenous artists, curators, and community groups have been far more successful in building relationships and working productively together to use the museum's overarching narrative of indigeneity to foreground issues of concern to Indigenous communities.

Perhaps nowhere has the malleability of Canada's cultural funding and multiculturalist discourse been more evidenced than in the proliferation of creative subversions to Canada 150 by Indigenous artists and cultural producers. Despite its celebratory narrative, Canada 150 set the stage for a myriad of highly visible, vocal, and creative challenges to dominant notions of settler colonialism in the national consciousness. Whereas multiculturalism may well have provided the Canadian government with the ideological incentive for contributing to arts funding that supports Indigenous artists, and whereas Canada 150 may have inadvertently provided Indigenous cultural producers with a national platform, the real credit for the multiple enactments of cultural resurgence that was so evident during 2017 belongs to intergenerational assemblages of actors who have been engaged in the labour of Indigenous resistance to Canadian settler colonialism across the centuries. As Ojibwe cultural producer, critic, and newly appointed Director of Canada's Indigenous Screen Office Jesse Wente wrote as 2017 was coming to a close: "Activists, community leaders, and storytellers have called out the lack of movement on systemic and urgent issues—such as clean water, suicide and the underfunding of Indigenous children in their communities. Artists have refashioned the meaning of the sesquicentennial, disrupting the celebration at every turn, advancing the national dialogue even as that dialogue is steeped in the same antiquated ideas that bubble to the surface during moments of colonial anxiety."[44]

From the obligatory reverentiality of Highway of Heroes and Remembrance Day ceremonies (Chapter 1) to the vainglory of Canada 150 celebrations (Chapter 5), performances of national commemoration set out to reaffirm Canada as a becoming and unified nation. If Canadian peacekeeping might be considered a sacred cow of Canada-the-good nationalism, multiculturalism is the nation's golden calf. Where Stephen Harper worked to transform the cow into a bullish warrior and to slaughter the calf with a return to a more homogenous patriotic national identity grounded in the colonial nation's British roots, Justin Trudeau has re-imbued military commemoration with the halo effect of Canada's purifying peacekeeping mythology and returned multiculturalism to its revered national pedestal. Where Harper's Conservative administration shifted away from arm's-length arts funding and toward "heritage funding" to support its rebranding of Canada as a warrior nation, Trudeau and his Liberal administration have delivered on promises to increase funding to the arts.

It is critical to note, however, that while the Trudeau administration reinvested in arts funding, in a peacekeeping rhetoric, and in promoting a multiculturalist national identity that draws heavily on a reconciliatory discourse around Canadian-Indigenous relations, there has been no abatement in investment in military commemoration and the Canadian military budget. Nor has there been any divestment from pipelines or other incursions into Indigenous territories. Just as Stephen Harper's claim that Canada has no history of colonialism revealed the emptiness of his instrumentalist apology to residential school survivors, Justin Trudeau's insistence that "the Trans Mountain [Kinder Morgan pipeline] expansion will be built" and his invocation of "the rule of law" and "national interests" calls into question the sincerity of his commitments to Indigenous peoples in Canada and to the United Nations Declaration on the Rights of Indigenous Peoples. As Mi'kmaw lawyer Pamela Palmater writes, "Approval of the Kinder Morgan expansion is proof that even the most charming leader who is 'absolutely' committed to reconciliation with Indigenous peoples will ignore those rights in the name of corporate interests."[45]

While cultural producers in Canada applauded the Liberals' 2016 budget announcing a $1.9 billion boost in arts funding over five years,[46] far less attention has been paid to the government's commitment to increase the annual military budget by 70 percent over the next ten years—to bring it to almost $33 billion by 2026.[47] Prior to and throughout 2017, there was much vocal denouncement of the government's decision to invest $500 million in the celebration of Canada 150, and assertions were made that the monies should have been redirected to address some of the socio-economic conditions that Indigenous peoples experience as a result of Canadian settler colonialism. Surprisingly, however, there has been little discussion of how the billions of additional dollars that the Trudeau administration has earmarked for militarism might be redirected to alleviate the ongoing structural violence of settler colonialism.

Locating Self: Identity, Place, Practice

I am a white anglophone settler Canadian, born, raised, and currently living on Treaty One Territory—ancestral territory of Anishinaabe, Cree, Oji-Cree, Dakota, and Dene peoples, and the homeland of the Métis Nation (Winnipeg). I have also lived as an uninvited occupant of the territories of the Mississauga of the New Credit First Nation, the Anishinaabe, Haudenosaunee, Wendat, and Huron Indigenous Peoples (Toronto), and the Ohlone and Coastal Miwok (San Francisco Bay Area). My first encounter with the practice of territorial acknowledgement was in 2009, when I returned to Canada after living in the United States for over twenty years. After living for decades on the outskirts of belonging, as a queer anglo "alien," I imagined my return as a homecoming of sorts, a return to a place I had a "right" to be. Hearing the territorial acknowledgement in this context had a profound and productively destabilizing effect on me—one that unsettled my nostalgic notion of home and my melancholic longing for a place of belonging.

I grew up in Winnipeg in the 1960s, '70s, and early '80s, a place-time saturated with a naturalized and overt racism against Indigenous peoples (or "Indians"). The territorial acknowledgement jarred me into the realization that I knew very little about the land I lived on or the Indigenous peoples whose territory it was and is. Like Jason (the young man who joined our

Stitch-by-Stitch sewing circle) and like Senator Beyak, I was/am not alone in my ignorance. Nor was/is my ignorance an accident. It is an ignorance born of Canadian history lessons, of Eurocentric enlightenment and missionary narratives of "progress" and "civilization," of governmental archives, records, and documents, and of media representations. It is an ignorance inherited from my Dutch immigrant parents who, like generations of new Canadians that came before and after them, learned nothing from their Canadian citizenship study guides about the territory they arrived on or the Indigenous peoples whose traditional territory it was and is, who learned nothing about the treaties they/we are beholden to as settlers. It is the ignorance of an imagined national identity performed through a multitude of re-memoration practices that range from the spectacular to the mundane—commemoration ceremonies and celebrations, citizenship swearing-in rituals, museum displays, school recitations of the national anthem, and daily encounters with monuments and place names. It is an ignorance constructed of privileged memory and calculated omissions and lies.

To say that my ignorance is part of a national project of privileged memory and structural forgetfulness is not to disavow personal accountability. When the TRC first released its Calls to Action on 2 June 2015, I wanted to begin embroidering them onto Canadian flags, but I hesitated. I could give many reasons—excuses—for why. Perhaps the most honest explanation is that I was afraid. Afraid that as a white settler Canadian woman, my response was so woefully inadequate. Like Jason, I hovered at the threshold of my privileged settler forgetfulness, afraid of revealing my ignorance, afraid of making mistakes, until after almost a year of inaction—which is also a marker of settler privilege—the point of embroidering the Calls became less elusive. It was a way of taking them in hand, of labouring with them, of engaging them. Not an end, but a beginning. So on 2 June 2016—the one-year anniversary of their release—I began to embroider. After about eight months of embroidering alone, I put out a call to friends and community groups to see if anyone wanted to join me in embroidering or to host a TRC sewing circle and reading group that would combine the task of embroidering the Calls to Action onto flags with reading aloud from the TRC's 388-page Summary Report.

Embodied inquiry in the form of a series of task-based durational countermemorial performance meditations—like Stitch-by-Stitch—has been an integral component of my research for *Unbecoming Nationalism*. These durational projects act as both a metaphor and a way. Stitch-by-Stitch, for example, is a reminder that like embroidery, redress requires the ongoing and necessarily care-filled labour of collective reckoning. The time spent together discussing the Calls and the TRC Report, fingers busy with the task of inscribing in thread *this* word, *this* sentence, *this* Call onto Canada's familiar Maple Leaf mascot-flag, is a collective labour of learning—and unlearning.

My ongoing engagement in performing counter-memorial meditations has provided me with a means to ground my research in an embodied praxis of critical reflection. Some of the performance meditations that have made their way into this book include *Impact Afghanistan War* (Canada Day 2010–Canada Day 2011); *Unravel: A Meditation on the Warp and Weft of Militarism* (2011–14); *Flag of Tears: Lament for the Stains of a Nation* (2014–ongoing); and Stitch-by-Stitch (2016–ongoing). Reflections on Stitch-by-Stitch have appeared in this Introduction, the reflective remains of *Impact* and *Flag of Tears* are scattered throughout Chapter 1, and *Unravel* is discussed in Chapter 3. At times, as with Stitch-by-Stitch, these reflections are embedded into the narrative flow of the chapter. In other cases, as with *Impact*, *Flag of Tears*, and *Unravel*, reflections can take the form of in-the-moment fragments that are intended to give the reader a sense of my experience from within the performance meditations. Since all of my counter-memorial meditations are durational, involving task-based repetition over sustained periods of time, the reflections are not fixed or conclusive but rather are glimpses into an ongoing process. With each repetition of the task and with each performance, perceptions and understandings change, meanings multiply. In this way, I look upon my counter-memorial performance practice as a durational dance of unbecoming, becoming, and unbecoming, again, and again, and again.

These embodied meditations have also been a tactile means through which to resist what performance studies scholar Dwight Conquergood calls the "arbitrary" and "booby-trapped" binary of "the division of labour between theory and practice, abstraction and embodiment."[48] Too often, the theory-practice binary positions the academically articulated and archived theory that makes its way to the page as valued, while the day-to-day embodied theorizations of artists and workers, and of Indigenous, racialized, ethnic, and working-class communities are reduced to raw material in need of academic refinement in order to be rendered comprehensible or valuable.[49] When I speak of performance, I see it as a form of embodied theory. I mean this in two ways. First, performance and aesthetic practice can be used as methods of extending theoretical concepts by translating them into material lexicons and resituating them in public spaces. But just as significantly, I believe that performance and aesthetic practices—as well as all manner of physical labour and expression—are in themselves articulations of analytic conceptions. In other words, they are in and of themselves ways of knowing—and unknowing.

The writing of *Unbecoming Nationalism* has also been a way of knowing for me. As with my durational counter-performance meditations, I consider writing to be a vehicle for sustained engagement, more a way of knowing than an expression of expertise. What I like about the phrase "way of knowing" is its focus on the path or approach to learning, rather than emphasizing the acquiring of or arriving at a conclusive body of knowledge. As an interdisciplinary project, *Unbecoming Nationalism* has challenged me to venture across disciplinary thresholds that are relatively new to me. This is one of the gifts of durational work—research, writing, and task-based mediation: it requires that I confront, over, and over, and over again, my bias toward "knowing" as a fixed destination that I can arrive at and comfortably settle into, and instead prompts me to embrace learning as both a practice and a praxis. One of the troubling paradoxes of writing is the way the product risks masking the process of its always becoming, and unbecoming. In this sense, I view the printed word as a crossroads in which there is a collision between the dissonant logics of fixed product and embodied process, or in the words of performance studies scholar Diana Taylor, "the archive and the repertoire."[50]

Compositionally, *Unbecoming Nationalism* is organized in a contrapuntal fashion that also mirrors the meaning-making process of my performance practice. More than a deconstructionist critique, with this approach I seek to bring a diverse array of performances together in a polyphonic chorus of lament against the forgetfulness of dominant narratives of Canadian humanitarian militarism and settler-colonial nationalism. Throughout the book, my approach to writing about other people's—or institutions'—becoming and unbecoming performances shares some commonalities with my approach to writing about my own performances. Most notably, at times I use italicized sections to share my subjective in-the-moment perceptions of performances as I encounter them. These "performances" take many forms, including public commemoration ceremonies, museum architecture and displays, and aesthetic projects like Rebecca Belmore's *Trace* and Kent Monkman's *Shame and Prejudice*. The italicized sections are derived from journal writing I do either while viewing the piece or shortly thereafter, when the experience is fresh. With them, I seek to capture and share how these performance pieces impact me emotionally, physically, intellectually, and imaginatively in order to instigate and punctuate the broader discussions in which they are embedded.

Some of the durational labours that produced *Unbecoming Nationalism* and will continue after its text is fixed to the page are undertaken in the spirit of what Métis artist, curator, and scholar David Garneau calls "perpetual conciliation."[51] Whereas "*re*-conciliation refers to the repair of a previously harmonious relationship, [and is a] word choice [that] imposes the fiction that equanimity is the status quo between Indigenous people and Canada," writes Garneau, "conciliation is an ongoing process, the seeking rather than the restoration of an imagined agreement."[52] *Unbecoming Nationalism*, in this sense, is a reflection of my return as a settler to this land now called Canada and of my ongoing journey to unbecome my settler-colonial ignorance and acknowledge settler-colonial violence. It is also a reflection of my despair at the lack of a visible anti-militarist movement I found when I returned to Canada and an attempt to understand the underlying factors that contribute to this absence. In its investigation into the epistemological role of performances of Canadian settler-colonial and military nationalism, *Unbecoming Nationalism* looks both at how memorial projects operate as a means of "hailing" Canada's civilian populations into particular kinds of settler-colonial nationalism—with tangible and violent affects[53]—and at how performance might serve as a methodology toward the production of counter-memorial performances that resist Canadian nationalism's forgetful narratives.

CHAPTER ONE

BEYOND THE HIGHWAY OF HEROES

FROM REVERENTIAL SILENCE TOWARD A PERIPHERAL POETICS OF LAMENT[1]

20 February 2011
Christie Pits Park, Toronto
falls 23,400–23,500[2]
I drew a picture after falling today of one hundred fallen stick-figure bodies (Figure 2). *In some ways it's easier to fall one hundred times than to draw one hundred fallen stick figures. When falling, each fall is intact unto itself. Each fall comes before or after another. Like language. Like words on the page—meaning falsely ordered through linear progression. But as the number of fallen stick figures multiplied on the page, they began to fall on top of one another until the distinction between bodies became obscured. By the time I reached one hundred they were not only no longer recognizable as individual bodies, their very recognizability as bodies had become obliterated—they had been rendered an unknowable mass.*

Who do we mourn? Who do we remember? Who do we forget? Which bodies and populations do our national mourning practices make knowable to us? Which bodies and populations are rendered unknowable, unrecognizable? The politics of social memory—intricately entwined with the politics of social forgetting—is about *who* and *what* we remember. It is also about *how* we remember and *how* we forget. What are the mechanisms through which Canada's privileged national subjects are placed at the top of the nation's hierarchy of grievability, while entire populations of unknowable "others" are cast beyond the horizon of our collective grief? How are some historical narratives rehearsed and reiterated until they become fixed in collective memory, while others are qualified, contained, or allocated to the distant forgetful peripheries of national memory?

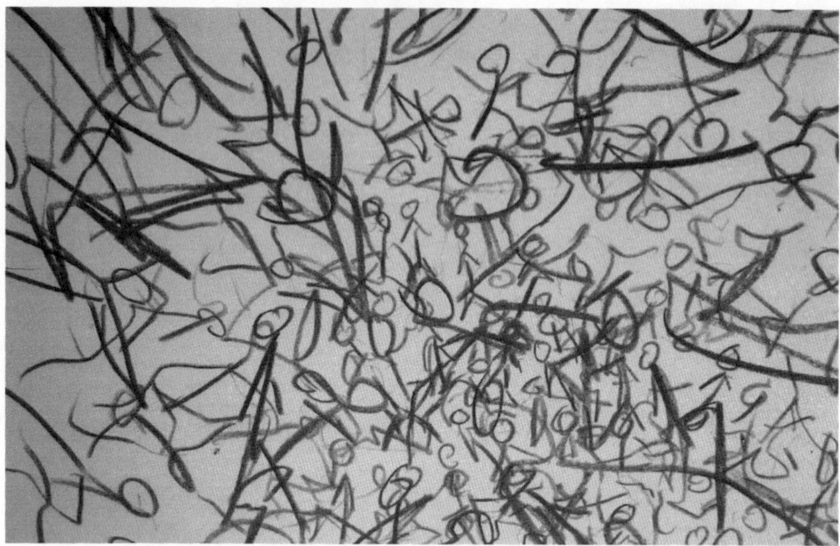

Figure 2. Drawing of fallen stick-figure bodies.

With the return of Canada's first combat fatalities from the war in Afghanistan in spring 2002, Canadians began to gather along the 172-kilometre repatriation route between the military base in Trenton, Ontario, and the Toronto coroner's office. As each new casualty returned home, the crowds on the roadsides and freeway overpasses of Ontario's Highway 401 grew. Veterans, police officers, firefighters, and residents waited—sometimes for hours—in heat and rain, in cold and snow, to pay tribute to the soldiers whose bodies were being transported in the passing motorcades. The phenomenon garnered positive media attention across Canada (as well as in the United States), led to the official renaming of sections of the repatriation route as the "Highway of Heroes" (2007) and "Route of Heroes" (2010), and inspired a host of songs, YouTube video tributes, books, and other institutional and popular cultural representations.

I learned of the Highway of Heroes memorials in 2009 when I returned to Canada after living for twenty years in the United States. I was immediately struck by the contrast between Canada's popular and widely publicized roadside mourning rituals and the U.S. government's (then) ban on media coverage that displayed images of caskets of repatriated U.S. soldiers. Initially, I was profoundly moved by the public display of mourning for Canada's military casualties. But as I witnessed the Highway of Heroes memorials through their prolific reiteration via Canadian mainstream and social media venues, two things stood out: first, the absence of any acknowledgement of Afghan deaths; and second, the extent to which the Highway of Heroes—though framed as a "spontaneous" and "grassroots" movement—resembled a host of other Canadian military commemoration ceremonies.

At first, I imagined the Highway of Heroes memorials to be a gesture of resistance to militarism and opposition to the war in Afghanistan (an assumption I attribute to my time in the United States, where military casualties are more commonly invoked in anti-war protests). But my imagined Highway of Heroes bore little resemblance to the roadside memorials. Like Remembrance Day and other government-sponsored ceremonies of military mourning, Highways of Heroes memorials embrace a militaristic and nationalist poetics of mourning that contributes to the production and dissemination of very distinct narratives of Canadian militarism and nationalism. These ceremonies act as public stages onto which Canada's military dead are cast as "just warriors" who heroically sacrifice their lives in acts of enlightened military intervention and selfless national loyalty. Where, I wondered, were the voices of lament of the mothers, fathers, children, lovers, friends, and civilians who dissent from the Canadian narrative of selfless sacrifice and humanitarian militarism? Where were the voices questioning the geopolitical conditions that resulted in the loss of those being mourned? And where were the voices of lament for the Afghan dead?

I did not attend any Highway of Heroes memorials. It was not an easy decision. I struggled with the tension between my desire to take part in a collective act of mourning for war's dead and my concern that participation would implicate me in a form of nationalist and militarist display. Instead, I began *Impact Afghanistan War*, a counter-memorial project in which I fell one hundred times a day in a public space for one year—each fall in recognition of a death in the Afghan war. Over the course of the year—from Canada Day 2010 through Canada Day 2011—I fell in parks and on campuses, in courtyards and public squares, in front of churches and political institutions, at festivals and conferences, in cities throughout Canada, the United States, and Europe.

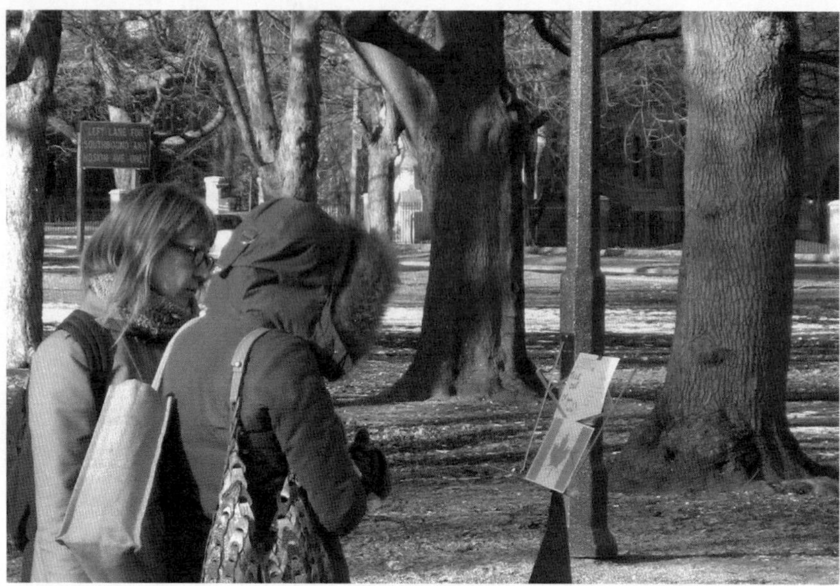

Figure 3. Witnesses looking at *Impact* display stand.

Each time I fell, I set up a small music stand onto which I attached a cloth flag and placed information flag-postcards. In addition to being signifiers of the nation, the flag and informational postcards (Figure 3) served a more didactic purpose as they bore the following message:

> Dear Witness,
> On July 1 (Canada Day) 2010 I began *Impact Afghanistan War*, a one-year project where I fall 100 times a day in a public space. Each fall represents a death in Afghanistan.

Since the onset of the post-9/11, US-led invasion of Afghanistan, 150 Canadian military personnel have been killed in Afghanistan.[3] I dedicate my first 150 falls to these dead. Each of these deaths has been memorialized through public repatriation ceremonies, the naming of the "Highway of Heroes," and more recently, the "Route of Heroes."

Unlike the Canadian military dead, there are no exact numbers for Afghans who have been killed or died as a result of war-related causes. The lack of an accurate accounting of Afghan dead is the result of US/NATO no body count policy.

Impact Afghanistan War is my attempt to reach beyond the numbness produced by abstract numbers, political debates, and media spectacularization.

Sincerely,
Helene

An investigation of the space between "us" and "other," between individual and social mourning, between personal ritual and public protest, *Impact* was an attempt to register, in and through the body, the impact of "our" (Canada's) engagement in Afghanistan. *Impact* was also a way for me to engage the Highway of Heroes in an embodied dialogue that though not proximal (or on-site), through its gestures (standing at attention before and after each fall) and its signifying symbol (the Canadian flag) had a recognizable association with the popular memorial. With its inscribed-upon flag as an unbecoming signifier of the nation and through its daily insinuation into the everyday present of the public sphere, *Impact* sought to question the confinement of social grief within national boundaries.

4 February 2011
Christie Pits Park, Toronto
falls 21,800–21,900
Stand. Fall. Stand. Fall. Stand. Fall. The impact of body with ground. The surprising accommodation of surfaces. The season's first snow was soft and embracing, but now, as winter wears on the ground has taken on the topography of a moonscape. Falling is the easy part—the curious architecture of body and limbs. It's standing, rising, that's difficult. Stand. Fall. Breathe. Traffic,

birdsong, distant or passing voices, circling hawk, tree limbs, plane slicing sky, snow. Falling. The ground becomes a between-space where I experience both the vastness of my distance from, and a closeness to, all those who have fallen, are falling, in Afghanistan. Distance, because I am acutely aware of the inadequacy of my gesture. I fall of my own accord. I have not been struck down. I am not injured. I can rise. Do rise. But it is precisely this awareness of distance that connects me. Each fall becomes an embodied meditation on the unequal distribution of vulnerability in our geopolitical landscape. With each fall I recognize—it "could" be me, it isn't me, and, the reasons it's not.

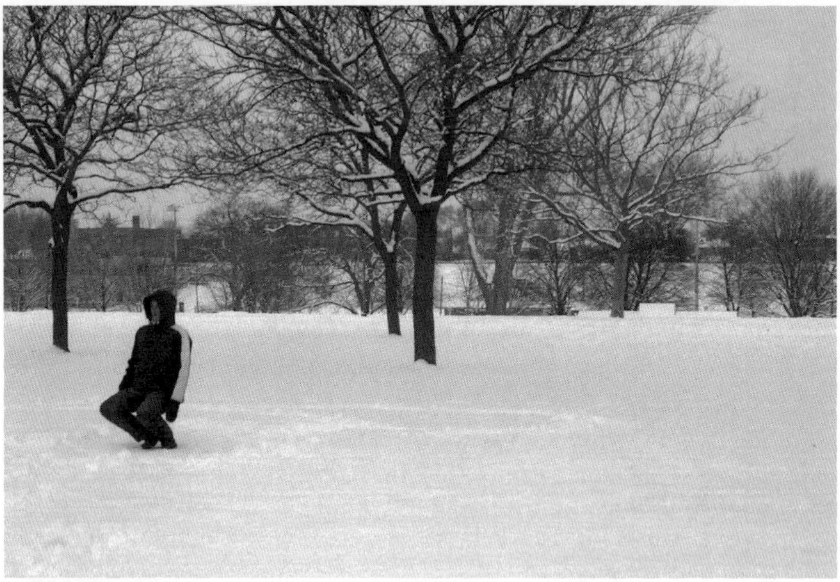

Figure 4. Falling in Christie Pits.

In *Frames of War*, Judith Butler extends Louis Althusser's notion of "modalities of materiality" to argue that the mechanisms through which war is framed need to be understood as "material instrumentalities of violence" that function as more than simple precursors to or commentaries on war, but as acts of war in and of themselves.[4] These frames function not only by legitimizing particular agendas and geopolitical world views through the selective placement of images and narratives within the frame but also through the "de-realization" of "enemy" populations by casting them outside of what is considered the normal realm of human values into an otherness that is consequently outside of the range of our compassion.[5]

While de-realization at its most overt is evident in the demonization of the "enemy," it also functions more subtly by placing entire populations outside of the range of our collective grief, thereby facilitating a large-scale empathetic detachment from the consequences of our nation's military actions. A primary mechanism through which this de-realization operates in the social sphere is through the "differential allocation of grief," wherein institutionally supported venues for "celebrated public grieving" are allotted to "grievable humans," while there is a corresponding "prohibition on the public grieving of others' lives."[6] In this sense, Canadian military memory projects need to be understood as more than simply commemorative events that function to memorialize Canada's fallen military personnel. They are also epistemological frames that work to focus participant and observer eyes on what is inside their foreclosing parameters.

Butler suggests that a more "egalitarian mourning" that insists on the grievability of all lives, a mourning that is based on the recognition that vulnerability is a primary (and shared) condition of life, could facilitate "an ethics of non-violence and a politics of a more radical redistribution of humanizing effects."[7] Writing in the context of the United States, she argues, however, that such mourning would destroy national self-perception and require that "the notion of the world itself as a sovereign entitlement of the United States must be given up, lost, and mourned, as narcissistic and grandiose fantasies must be lost and mourned."[8] Extending Butler's analysis north of the border, one can imagine that if Canadians were to adopt a more egalitarian approach to grieving Afghanistan war deaths, the collective identity we would have to give up and mourn is the (perhaps less narcissistic but equally grandiose) notion of ourselves as a benevolently becoming nation of global peacekeepers.

Despite Canada's involvement in the U.S.-led war in Afghanistan, and a concerted effort on the part of Stephen Harper's Conservative administration to give Canada's image a warrior makeover, it appears that Canadians were and are not ready to give up and mourn their national peacekeeper identity. As A.L. McCready notes, "in 2008 only a meager fifty-three percent of Canadians agreed that Canada's combat mission in Afghanistan was, in fact, a war, illustrating both confusion about the legal justification of the mission and the tenacity of peacekeeping myths."[9] As many Canadian studies and defence and foreign affairs scholars concur, Canada's contemporary military agenda bears little resemblance to its historical peacekeeping mandate. In the 1950s, Canada's minister of external affairs Lester B. Pearson helped shape prerequisites for early United Nations peacekeeping operations, which included such conditions as a "cease-fire agreement; consent of the parties; impartiality of the Force; use of force strictly limited to self-defense; and executive responsibility of the Security General." Today, as Jocelyn Coulon and Michel Liégeois note, "Canadian governments have preferred to commit Canada to military interventions outside the UN structure, and in the particular case of Afghanistan, in a counter-insurgency mission."[10]

Canadian military commemoration memorials, from formal Remembrance Day ceremonies to "spontaneous" Highway of Heroes gatherings, provide a powerful affective frame to sustain Canada's identity as a nation of benevolent militarists. Inside the popular Highway of Heroes memorial frame are the Canadian military personnel who died while serving in the Afghanistan war. These are lives that in death are simultaneously exalted and eclipsed. Sacrificed on the altar of national commemoration, the remembered and revered dead cease to exist for themselves, their families, and communities. Not only are they corporeally dead, in death their right to an identity in difference is also denied. However minoritarian, disavowed, dissenting, frightened, or even mundane they may have been in life, in death they are forever pressed into service as heroically patriotic representatives of the militarized nation-state.

And outside the frame? Cast outside of the frame are haunting legions of de-realized and disavowed "others": populations and histories—past, present, and in the making—whose inclusion within the frame would disrupt the patriotic and binary narratives of good and evil, Us and Them that supply nation-states, and their dominant and dominating populations, with their ideological foundation and moral justification. Cast outside of the frame of Canadian military commemoration are those whose visibility within the frame would interfere with the nation's capacity to hail its armies of enlisted soldiers and their civilian supporters, or to maintain a sense of national innocence.

However material we might understand the frame to be—and most certainly, its material effects are annihilatingly real—those outside its purview are not unreal, not unseeable. More than creating an inside and an outside, the frame trains the see-er by numbing their capacity to apprehend the lives that exist outside of the frame's construct.[11] As a nationalist spectacle, Canadian military commemoration constructs its frames of legitimization and grievability through the production of privileged subjects whose destructibility is rendered "*unthinkable*" while their acts of destruction are simultaneously rendered "*righteous.*"[12] Canada's just warriors are eulogized within nationalistically prescribed parameters, while "others" are banished to the peripheral realms of ungrievability and inapprehensiblility. Over time, the frame and the narratives it produces become normalized. Instead of being recognized as a construction, or even as a fragment of a more complex and troubling image of war, what is inside the frame becomes the whole picture while what is outside falls away.

What stories does the Highway of Heroes tell about Canada, about the Canadian Forces, about Canadian military engagements, and about those who line the roadsides and overpasses of the repatriation route? How does the oft-repeated tale of the Highway of Heroes "spontaneous" and "grassroots" emergence mask the extent to which the memorials are a logical extension of Canada's long history of institutionally supported military commemoration events, most overtly evidenced through Canada's annual Remembrance Day ceremonies? How did eulogy—or praise of the dead—come to replace more polyvocal expressions of grief and loss? What lives and motives are cast outside the popularized frame of Canadian military commemoration?

REFRAME 1: The Silencing Effects of Military Commemoration's Elegiac Poetics

5 January 2011
York University, Toronto
falls 18,800–18,900
Yesterday, while falling at York, an ambulance appeared on the horizon. It was travelling on a footpath and heading my way. As I fell—ninety-two, ninety-three, ninety-four—these questions went through my mind: Will I finish before they reach me? Will they, can they, stop me? Who called them? Why?

By ninety-six the ambulance pulled up in front of me and alongside my stand with its postcards and inscribed-upon flag. A paramedic rolled down his window—ninety-seven—looked at the cards and the flag—ninety-eight—looked at me—ninety-nine—rolled up his window and the ambulance drove on.

In the ambulance's wake I was struck by a sudden and raw surge of emotion. I wanted to cry out. To hurl myself to the ground. To weep, and scream: Emergency! Emergency! Emergency!

Replete with symbols of nationalism, Highway of Heroes memorials are part of what Howard Fremeth has called an expanding Canadian military-cultural memory project that is produced not through a simple top-down propaganda mechanism, but rather through a complex network of organizational and institutional stakeholders that have become adept at using popular media.[13] More than simply compilations of particular historical narratives, military memory projects have their own poetics constructed of signs, symbols, and gestures. At Highway of Heroes memorials, flags abound (Figure 5). They're draped over freeway overpasses, flown on fire-engine ladders, held aloft by veterans, waved, and held abreast by civilians. As the motorcade bearing the bodies of the dead, their families, and their military escort pass, uniformed personnel—military, police, fire and rescue workers—stand at attention and salute. Un-uniformed citizens mimic the militaristic gestures. Some salute. Others choose the more civilian but equally patriotic and nationalist display of placing hand over heart. While not all of these gestures are driven by a singular intention or performed as acts of compliance, taken together, military commemorations construct a cohesive and codified nationalist choreography. Grief, as affective fuel, generates a communal and public pledge to nation, a pledge whose performance extends far beyond the temporal and corporeal boundaries of the memorial event through its representation and re-representation in both mainstream and grassroots social media.

Like many a Canadian identity tale, the Highway of Heroes is often framed as an example of Canadians' elevated morality compared to that of our less caring southern neighbours. Former prime minister Stephen Harper's failed 2006 attempt to emulate the Bush administration's prohibition only added to the story of difference by demonstrating Canadians' superior capacity to resist government censure. Pete Fisher, a photojournalist from Cobourg, Ontario, who spearheaded the drive to rename a section of Highway 401 as the Highway of Heroes, writes: "It's been called a 'grassroots phenomenon,' and it truly is. No organization started it; certainly no town or city started it. It's something distinctly Canadian, something we as a large family from coast to coast do, to show our collective grief. It's about patriotism, and about honouring the great sacrifice made on our behalf by the fallen soldiers and their families."[14]

Lest his celebration of the Highway of Heroes be seen as reflecting a purely Canadian bias, Fisher includes in his book *Highway of Heroes: True Patriot Love* a number of U.S. voices praising Canada's roadside memorials. Of an interview with a *Los Angeles Times* journalist, Fisher writes: "I'll never forget his words to me that day: 'You guys do it right up there.' My answer: 'It's not that we do it right, it's just the right thing to do.'"[15] In keeping with the becoming spin of Canadian nationalism, the message is clear: Canadians know the "right" way to honour their military dead, and it is a way that is morally superior to that of the United States.[16]

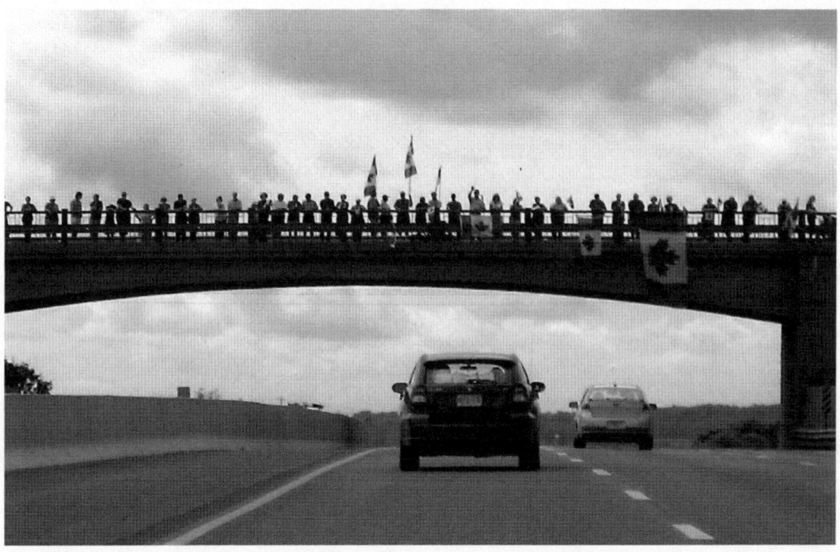

Figure 5. Highway of Heroes. People waiting on a freeway overpass on Highway 401 for repatriation motorcade on its route from Trenton, Ontario, to the Toronto coroner's office.

Within Canadian popular discourse, the absence of Highway of Heroes–like rituals in the United States is often reductively associated with the "Bush ban" and accompanied by the assumption that unlike Canadians, U.S. citizens either do not know how to honour their military dead or do not care enough to do so.[17] It is certainly true that whereas the return of each of Canada's 158 Afghan war casualties was commemorated through highly visible Highway of

Heroes memorials, only a select few of the over 2,000 U.S. Afghan war military casualties were allotted public memorials. But formal censure does not fully account for the contrast between Canada's and the United States' responses to their Afghan war causalities, as became evident when President Obama's 2009 lifting of the ban generated no significant increase in public displays of mourning for the nation's repatriated soldiers.

An alternative explanation for the lack of public repatriation ceremonies in the United States can be linked to how the public awareness of the rising numbers of U.S. military casualties during the Vietnam War—in concert with the U.S. military's reporting of "enemy" body counts—helped fuel the country's growing anti-war movement. The United States' media ban during the wars in Afghanistan and Iraq and its no body count policy both have their roots in the response of the U.S. government and Pentagon to perceived failures in managing domestic attitudes regarding the Vietnam War. As former U.S. defense secretary Donald Rumsfeld explained in 2006, the no body count policy was a reversal of U.S. practices during the Vietnam War: "If you'll recall the Vietnam War, they had body counts that went on day after day after day. . . . The implication of that was that you were winning if the body count went up and losing if the body count went down."[18] In contrast to Canada, where the channelling of grief through military commemoration shores up patriotic sentiment, in the United States, the high visibility given to the war dead during the Vietnam War continues to undermine the value of military commemoration as a pro-nationalist, pro-military strategy for the state.

In his comparative analysis of how war is remembered on both sides of the U.S.–Canadian divide, historian Robert Teigrob notes that in the United States, "alongside an admitted enthusiasm for employing warfare as an instrument of foreign policy," dissent and public debate in relation to the nation's past, present, and pending military exploits is significantly more robust than in Canada.[19] Of (English) Canada's legacy of wartime experience, Teigrob writes: "It is best characterized by a blend of celebration (particularly where deeds of heroism can be mustered as evidence) and silence (particularly where experiences and actions do not ennoble the nation's image)."[20] With their focus on heroism, Canada's elegiac performances of military commemoration de-realize not only the inconvenient "others" who are cast outside of the frame, but also the inconvenient experiences and narratives of the very soldiers who occupy a privileged position within the nation's frame of grievability.

It is not my intention here to question either the motives of individuals who attended Highway of Heroes memorials or the value the memorials might have for friends and families of the fallen. My interest in the Highway of Heroes—and in Canadian military commemoration more broadly—is in the overarching narrative it produces and in how that narrative is politically deployed. As critical race and anti-colonial scholar Sherene Razack suggests of popular media stories about traumatized Canadian peacekeepers, individual narratives are assembled to produce an overarching codified narrative about Canada as a (white) nation guided by the logics of rationality and compassion.[21] Like the memorials themselves, the narrative surrounding the Highway of Heroes acts as a frame. The Highway of Heroes tells a story not only of just warriorship but also of a pluralistic assemblage—or as Fisher writes, "a large family"—of citizens who, without outside (state) direction, know how and when to set aside differences in the performance of patriotic commemoration.

Remembrance Day 2010
Queen's Park, Toronto
falls 13,300–13,400
As I fell in Queen's Park today a soldier stood at attention about fifty metres in front of me. After each fall, I rose and we stood facing one another.

One hundred times.

He was too far away for me to make out his face, but he looked young.

Young and fragile.

After I completed my falls I stayed to witness the twenty-one-gun salute: The soldiers at attention. The order to fire passed down a chain of command. The cannon's explosive roar. The smoke.

Twenty-one times.

The Canadian government's sustained commitment to public Remembrance Day ceremonies began in response to the First World War, a conflict in which Canada suffered especially heavy losses: Out of a population of 7.5 million, close to 70,000 died on the battlefield and another 140,000 were wounded—losses so high that few Canadians were left unscathed by grief and by the war's ongoing material effects.[22] Within the Canadian imaginary, however, glorified narratives of national pride have over the past several decades overshadowed outrage over the First World War's devastating effects. As Ian McKay and Jamie Swift argue, today the First World War is largely remembered as the war "in which individual soldiers proved their mettle and Canada somehow became a nation."[23] The reiterated performance of Remembrance Day ceremonies has been instrumental in the ongoing production and dissemination of Canada's foundational mythology of national "self-sacrificial chivalry," a mythology that relies on the denial of Canada's decidedly unchivalrous colonial history with its ongoing violent effects.[24]

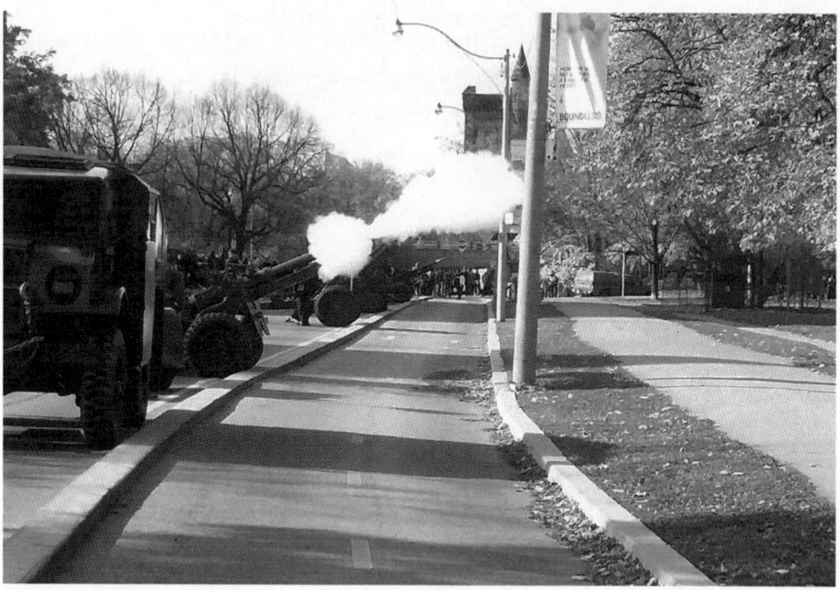

Figure 6. Remembrance Day cannons, Queen's Park, Toronto, 2018.

Both in spite and because of its origins as a non-governmentally sanctioned memorial ritual, the Highway of Heroes, with its militarized gestures of commemoration, is evidence of the degree to which Canadians have internalized the lesson of channelling the grief associated with war losses into pro-nationalist narratives. In addition to telling us who and what to remember—and through omission, who and what to forget—Canadian military commemoration trains civilians in the protocols of remembrance. Generations of Canadian schoolchildren have been instructed in how to perform the obligatory reverentiality that military commemoration demands. They have been taught to stand silently at attention, to wave the Canadian flag, and to don a poppy during what, in Canada, has become an extended season of remembrance. The memorization and recitation of Canadian First World War medical officer John McCrae's "In Flanders Fields" has been standard fare for generations of children in Canadian schools. Today, curriculum about Canadian military history, the meaning of the poppy, and other aspects of military commemoration ceremonies is widely disseminated through teaching guides produced by both the Royal Canadian Legion and Veterans Affairs Canada.

Even if one chooses not to actively participate in Canada's seasonal rite of remembrance, its symbols signal remembrance's protocol of silent reverentiality. With Highway of Heroes memorials, these symbols are no longer constrained by season or ceremony. They have become part of the Canadian landscape. Highway 401—the nation's busiest traffic corridor—has become a permanent site of commemoration. Lest freeway travellers forget, the renamed sections of Highway 401 are lined with signs bearing the highway's new title together with images of the familiar poppy—a reminder of not only who, what, and how to remember, but also of military commemoration's expanding territorial claims. In similar fashion, less travelled highways and roads across Canada have also been designated as routes of remembrance: an Autoroute du Souvenir (Remembrance Highway) in Quebec in 2007; a Highway of Heroes in British Columbia and Saskatchewan in 2011; in Manitoba and New Brunswick in 2012; in Alberta, Nova Scotia, Newfoundland, and the Northwest Territories in 2013; and in Prince Edward Island in 2014. The ongoing—post–Afghan war—nationalist value of Highway of Heroes–designated roads was dramatically illustrated when thousands gathered along these routes to honour Corporal Nathan Cirillo, who was shot and killed on 22 October 2014 while he stood sentry at Ottawa's National War Memorial.

The story of the Highway(s) of Heroes' "spontaneous" emergence masks the degree to which Canada's almost century-long institutionalized practices of military commemoration have become naturalized and their silencing rules of patriotic engagement internalized by many Canadian civilians. As a national story, the Highway of Heroes is particularly enticing because it casts Canadians in such a becoming light. As has become a norm with Canadian identity tales, the story of Canada's moral superiority is enhanced through comparisons with the United States. Under the menacing shadow of the United States' more callous imperial nationalism—and despite being allies with the United States in the war in Afghanistan—the light of Canada's constructed sense of national innocence glows ever more bravely and brightly.

In media, government, and military representations, civilian participation in displays of collective mourning for Canada's military dead is framed as an indication of the country's national goodness. By default, public dissent is deemed unbecoming and dishonouring of the dead. Channelled through elegiac military commemoration, mourning is reduced to a binary—either you respect and honour those who have sacrificed their lives for "the greater good," or you do not. This binary frame silences inconvenient debates over foreign policy, removes war's inconvenient dead from view, and either absorbs or absolves the inconvenient experiences of those who are granted a space within the national military memorial frame.[25]

The unnamed dead situated beyond the boundaries of our national commemorative frame are not *ours* to mourn, not *ours* to remember. *Our* military dead are just warriors who, having sacrificed their lives in selfless acts of benevolent militarism (on *our* behalf), have in death been reborn as homogenized heroes. The stories of those who were disillusioned, those who took their own lives, those who died in military training accidents, those who had abuse perpetrated on them by their peers, those who perpetrated abuse on their peers, their spouses, and the nameless others they were sent to "rescue"—all are absorbed into this larger narrative. The complexities of war and grief have no place within military commemoration's elegiac frame.

REFRAME 2:
The State's Management of Grief in Times of War

30 October 2010
Dufferin Grove Park, Toronto
falls 12,100–12,200
On the website of the Revolutionary Association of the Women of Afghanistan (RAWA) there is this warning: "CAUTION. CAUTION. CAUTION. This page contains links to photos which some viewers may find disturbing" (RAWA Photo Gallery).

What are the consequences of not disturbing? Images or reminders of death are, in large measure, contained within media genres ranging from news to an ever-expanding "entertainment" industry. In his study of post–First World War mourning practices in Britain, anthropologist Geoffrey Gorer argues that by the mid-twentieth century death had become, paradoxically, increasingly absent and increasingly present in the day-to-day lives of most Westerners. Gorer links the near disappearance of public mourning rituals to a mid-twentieth-century emergence of what he dubs the "pornography of death" (as evidence he points to a proliferation of violent horror movies, comics, and magazines as well as books on the horrors of war and concentration camps).[26]

If anything, Gorer's "death pornography" analogy is more valid today than when he published his study in 1965. Though few of us are required to rub shoulders with death and grief prior to its intimate intrusion into our personal lives—and the women from RAWA feel it necessary to attach warnings to images of wounded and killed Afghans—a quick perusal of television programming reveals an overwhelming prevalence of forensic crime shows as just one of a plethora of popular-culture genres through which death's gory and cellular details permeate our collective imaginations via an entertainment medium.

Grief, intimately experienced, just happens. It rages in our bellies. It breaks open our hearts. Our dead visit our dreams. They haunt our thoughts. But mourning—the outward expression of the powerful range of emotions associated with grief—is another matter. We are taught *how* to mourn. Our families and communities, our religious, educational, and public institutions train us in the rituals and protocols of mourning. Over time these mourning practices become so naturalized that we cease to recognize their social construction or question their social effects.

Though many of the gestures and protocols of mourning performed in Canadian military commemoration ceremonies have become naturalized and go largely unquestioned, evidence of some of the overarching factors that influence their construction nevertheless remain visible. The most obvious piece of evidence is the flag. Canadian military commemoration rituals—official and unofficial—take place under the Maple Leaf banner, thereby signalling the state's hand in the construction of the memorial frame. Without such signifying flags, however, the historical and geopolitical influences that have contributed to our contemporary protocols of mourning are—like war's inconvenient dead—less apprehensible.

During times of war, nation-states tend to exert increased control over the mediation of grief. As Gorer notes, with hundreds of thousands of military casualties a year during the First World War, Britain's established public mourning rituals became untenable. Not only would a visibly grieving nation have been a threat to the war effort, the war also produced pragmatic considerations that affected conventional mourning rituals and protocols: often there was either no body to mourn or the body was so violently fragmented and abject that its disavowal became necessary. And with the deaths of so many young men, an "army of widows" dressed in black would be bad for morale, while established periods of social or romantic withdrawal could not be followed if the nation was to reproduce itself in the post-war period.[27]

Like Britain, Canada managed war-related grief on the home front during both the First and Second World Wars. The overarching mandate of Canada's news media in reporting the war was to minimize home-front knowledge of the violent effects of war while maximizing heroic and patriotic narratives. As Canadian military studies scholar Robert Bergen writes of First World War journalism: "Most of the news reports received were not of the 15,600 Canadians dying horribly in less than a month in the mud of Passchendaele, but of ridiculously upbeat versions of battle."[28] Though there has been no "official" censorship of war reporting in Canada since the Second World War, Bergen's comparative analysis of news media coverage of Canada's military engagements in the First and Second World Wars, the Korean War, the Gulf War, Kosovo, and Afghanistan, leads him to observe that "journalists and the military alike have been involved in censorship at different times and to varying degrees throughout these conflicts."[29]

In some ways, the highly visible Highway of Heroes memorials complicate Gorer's observation of the decline in public rituals of mourning and the overall disavowal of mourning during times of war. But the Highway of Heroes is more than a public mourning ritual. It is also a spectacle of military pageantry that is influenced by Canadian Armed Forces public-relations narratives. As with combat zones, military commemoration ceremonies are not designed as spaces of critical reflection or public discourse. Both are arenas in which the gestures and actions of participants—combatants and mourners—are rigorously and ritualistically prescribed and proscribed.

As author and activist Yves Engler notes, the Canadian military is one of Canada's largest public-relations organizations: in 2010 the Canadian Armed Forces spent $354 million on and devoted 661 staff members to public relations and war commemorations.[30] One method of regulating the voices of the bereaved that is practised within the Armed Forces is to have military family members write eulogizing statements before their loved ones are deployed to combat zones.[31] These pre-written statements are kept on file, to be released to the press in the case of a soldier's death. The rationale for this practice is to alleviate the burden of making a statement while in a state of grief. These pre-written (and pre-vetted) statements do more than cleanse the family's words of the messy emotions associated with grief, they also ensure that any change of heart or increase of critical analysis that a soldier may have communicated with family members during their deployment does not become part of the commemorative process.

If remembering our nation's "fallen heroes" who died in acts of benevolent militarism is the primary message of Canadian rituals of military commemoration, a key subtext is silence. Performances and sites of commemoration demarcate spaces in which debate is construed first as disrespectful of the dead, and second as anti-nationalist. In our era of prolific media reiteration, these sites of social censure multiply as they are transported across temporal, corporeal, digital, and spatial geographies. One of the powerful effects of contemporary Canadian military commemoration is that its silencing demands can be issued through such varied venues—official and unofficial public rituals, mainstream and social media, military and government ad campaigns, monuments, and road signs. Whether delivered literally through prescribed "moments of silence" at one of Canada's proliferating array of public military commemoration ceremonies—or signalled more subtly through the presence of a poppy, a flag, a uniform, a monument, a commemorative sign, or any of the growing genre of televised military commemoration–themed public relation and commercial advertisements—the call to silence rings resoundingly clear.

Like the upbeat battle stories from the trenches of Passchendaele, the Highway of Heroes memorials for Canada's repatriated Afghan war casualties convey an elegiac celebration of heroism wherein the violently fragmented bodies of the dead are shrouded beneath symbols of Canadian nationalism and narratives of military humanitarianism. But unlike the First World War, in which almost 70,000 Canadians died, during the ten years Canada was officially at war in Afghanistan there were 158 Canadian military casualties. In contrast, tens of thousands of Afghans died as a result of the war in their country. Since this kind of geopolitically disproportionate distribution of death has become characteristic of contemporary warfare, in which far more civilians than soldiers die in the faraway conflict zones where Canada, the United States, and other Western militaries engage, I suggest that Canada's spectacularized roadside ritual of military commemoration may be less about mourning and more about the disavowal of loss. Less about feeling grief and more about masking violence's real effects.

REFRAME 3:
The Gendered Bifurcation of Grief

2 October 2010
Laura Secord School, Winnipeg
falls 9,300–9,400

I've been feeling a kind of bittersweet heartbreak lately. Though at times I feel on the verge of tears, it's nothing like depression. It lacks depression's relentless nihilism and self-criticism. I'm not exactly sure how it relates to Impact, *but it seems that the more I fall, the more tender I become.*

The tenderness is also connected to visiting my family. It's Dad's eightieth birthday tomorrow, Mom came home from the hospital where she's been recuperating from another kind of fall, my sister and her partner arrive from the west coast tonight, and tomorrow the whole family will gather for a birthday celebration. Last night, Cassie and I joined two of my nieces and my sister-in-law on Winnipeg's "Take Back the Night" march (my first Take Back march was here in Winnipeg thirty years ago)—it was sweet to walk with my nieces, the newest generation of feminists in the family. I've also been extremely touched by my brother's help with documenting my falls. I'm not sure what this all has to do with Impact *except to say that the more I fall, the more in touch I become with the fragility and vulnerability of life—with how precious it is.*

Just as the military has its own internal set of rituals and practices designed to transform recruits into battle-ready warriors, public military commemorations transform participating civilians into reverential patriots. We stand at attention. We adhere to the rules of engagement—even if only temporarily. Through participation in the Highway of Heroes popular repatriation memorials or Remembrance Day ceremonies, through the wearing of poppies (or our silence in the face of their prolific seasonal blossoming on jacket and coat lapels) we are temporarily "interpellated"[32] as what sociologist Jackie Orr calls "civilian soldiers."[33] Writing about the United States, Orr traces the history of that government's manipulation of insecurity and terror as a means of militarizing civilian psychology and calling into being the "civilian soldier." Likewise, Canadian social theorist Brian Massumi argues that the modulation of fear through its production as an "affective fact" has become an increasingly pervasive and instrumentalized political tactic in post-9/11 United States.[34]

In Canada, with its greater state investment in military commemoration projects, it is grief rather than fear that becomes the primary affective vehicle through which the country's more "reluctant militarists"—to borrow a term from Sara Ruddick—are conscripted into war:[35]

> Reluctant militarists must keep their eyes fixed on justice despite the absence of moral or political connections between the capacity to out-injure and the cause in which one fights. Whatever the cause, "our boys" must be seen as defenders and victims, not killers. Accordingly, military thinking provides indentifiable [*sic*] techniques of redescription and evasion that focus the mind on strategy rather than on suffering; on sacrifice rather than on killing; and on the cause rather than the bodies torn apart in its name. Primary among these conceptual strategies is the creation of the "just warrior" using interlocking myths of masculinity, sacrifice, and heroic death.[36]

Massumi explains that the effective modulation of affect is achieved through bifurcation—splitting off the emotional and phenomenal experience from cognitive or critical interpretation. By rendering "affective experience" subjective (or private), it becomes bracketed off from the political (or public) process of producing rationalized narratives of nationalism with their accompanying military and foreign policy agendas. Whereas in Massumi's example of the U.S. Department of Homeland Security's colour-coded terror alert system, fear is the "affective fact" through which the narrative for the necessity of a "war on terror" is produced, in the case of Canada's military memory projects, grief becomes the affective fact through which narratives of humanitarian militarism and heroic sacrifice are manufactured and maintained.

This is not to suggest that Canada has not also used fear as an affective mechanism through which to rally civilian support for military agendas. For example, during his tenure as prime minister, Stephen Harper emphasized security over peacekeeping as a rationale to justify participation in non-NATO or UN-supported military engagements and the "anti-terror" Bill C-51. As the popular appeal of the Highway of Heroes illustrates, however, grief continued to play a primary role in the interpellation of Canada's civilian soldiers. Canada's long and institutionalized practice of public military commemoration serves not only as a mechanism whereby dissent is managed (and silenced), but also as a means whereby Canada's reluctant warriors can maintain a sense of national identity rooted in the intersecting narratives of heroic sacrifice and Canadian humanitarian militarism.

The bifurcation of the performance of mourning functions through the gendering of grief into a cognitive/rational (masculinized) and embodied/emotional (feminized) binary, and through grief's spatial organization into public (formally and politically modulated) and private (familial and psychologically interiorized) realms. The emotions associated with grief are also split off into anger (gendered male) and sorrow (gendered female). In addition to becoming the just warriors' justified response to violent deaths, military retribution provides a distancing antidote to grief's feminized attributes—a mechanism by which masculinity is shored up and sorrow warded off with the guarantee that one's death will be forever memorialized as heroic. Through the gendered bifurcation of the emotions associated with loss and the accompanying allocation of separate arenas in which the expression of different emotions are deemed appropriate, the emotions themselves are taken out of dialogue with one another.

In both official and popular public military memorials, the powerful emotions connected to mourning are simultaneously evoked and contained. In concert with the containment of emotions there is an imposed reverentiality that results in the silencing of public discourse. In this way, the bifurcation of experience into affective (emotional) and cognitive (rational) arenas performs a crucial managerial function in the ideological processes of engendering military and nationalist rationalities. Military commemoration's bifurcated—but deeply interconnected—meaning-making components produce a regulatory and disciplinary ideological effect that reaches far beyond its reverential participants. Purged of war's brutality and the anger associated with loss, commemoration's elegiac pronouncements have proved well-suited to the production of Canada-the-good nationalism.

While civilian participants in the Highway of Heroes, Remembrance Day ceremonies, and other acts of military commemoration perform their ritualized enactment of patriotic silence, it is military and state officials who shape the overarching narratives that attribute meaning to the deaths. The reiterated news reports following the death of each Canadian Afghan war casualty—affectively buoyed by images from the Highway of Heroes memorials, of military personnel performing their regimented displays of mourning, of grieving family members, and of civilians silently performing their ritualized gestures of remembrance—are punctuated by meaning-making narratives delivered by those in positions of national and/or military authority:

> Our Canadian Forces members . . . face an enemy that will go to any length to try to undermine any progress made. The courage demonstrated by Pte. Todd speaks volumes to his dedication to our country and to this mission. (Defence Minister Peter MacKay on the death of Private Tyler William Todd)[37]

> The bravery and remarkable commitment of Canadians like Sapper Collier are bringing safety and stability to the people of Afghanistan. . . . Every day, their dedication and work protect our interests and values here at home and around the world. Sapper Collier's sacrifice will not be forgotten. (Prime Minister Stephen Harper on the death of Sapper Brian Collier)[38]

In her analysis of cultural representations of women and grief, Jenny Hockey notes that while contemporary cultural representations of grief (images and narratives) commonly associate grief's emotional expression with women, it is men who are more closely associated with the event of death through its narration and professional mediation.[39] As the public relations quotations by Canadian politicians and military representatives cited above demonstrate, the bifurcated gendering of the cognitive (rational) and phenomenal (emotional) aspects of mourning's affect is evident in media reports of Canadian military casualties in Afghanistan. While it is predominantly male (military and state) spokespeople who shape the cognitive meaning-making narrative surrounding the deceased and the circumstances of their deaths, the media images signifying the emotional expression of loss that affectively bolster these narratives are more often those of women—the wives, mothers, or "girlfriends" of deceased soldiers.

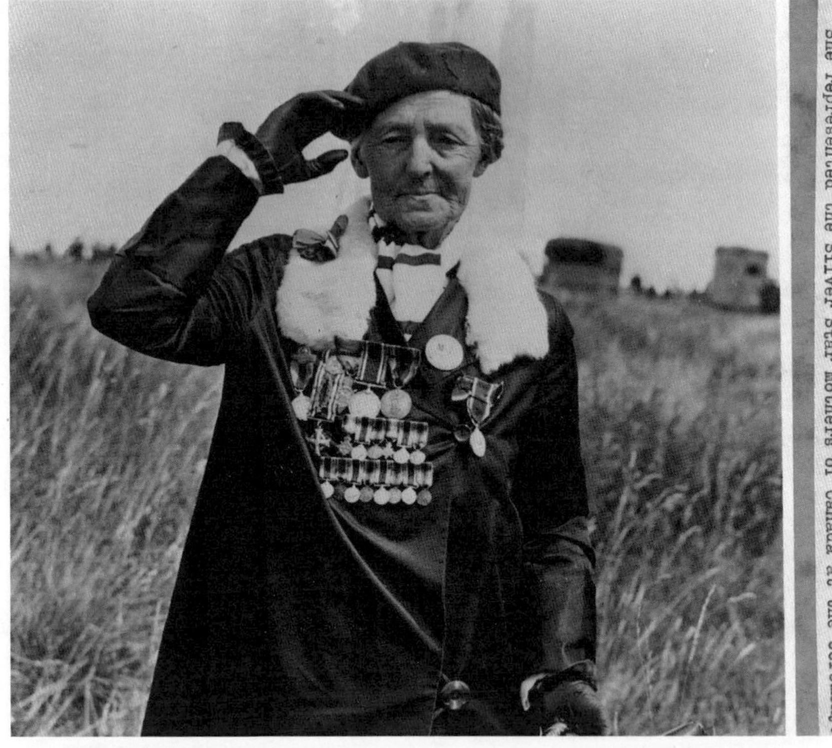

Figure 7. In 1936, Mrs. Charlotte Susan Wood from Winnipeg, Manitoba, became the first National Memorial (Silver) Cross Mother.

In Canada, mothers in particular have long played an iconic role as the emblematic bearers of the nation's grief in military commemoration ceremonies. The Silver Cross is a Canadian invention and institution (Figure 7). The Canadian government began awarding the medal to mothers and widows of soldiers who had died during the war in 1919, and every year since 1950 the Royal Canadian Legion has named a national representative for all Silver Cross Mothers. It is she who lays the Remembrance Day wreath at the foot of the National War Memorial in Ottawa on the eleventh minute past the eleventh hour of the eleventh month. As Graham Carr notes, the role of Silver Cross Mothers in Remembrance Day imagery makes a crucial symbolic connection between "war as the guarantor of national security" and the nuclear family as "society's [and the nation's] most cherished institution."[40] The message is clear: war and the nation-state are both family affairs. The protocols of belonging to this caring national family during times of war are also clear: at best—participation in reverential acts of military commemoration; at a minimum—silence.

REFRAME 4:
From Peripheral Poetics of Lament to the Structural Forgetfulness of Commemoration

10 August 2010
Cedarvale Park, Toronto
falls 4,000–4,100

Just returned from vacation. For most of the trip I've been afraid. Afraid to talk about Impact. *Afraid to be seen falling. Afraid of disturbing the status quo. In the midst of all this fear, I feel a profound, almost overwhelming, sense of alienation and isolation.*

Feminist scholar Nadia C. Seremetakis argues that historically, women's lament in Greece's southern Peloponnese operated as an "empowering poetics of the periphery."[41] *Similarly, Angela Bourke writes: "The Irish lamenter had license to behave and speak disruptively, but her craziness was not the isolating kind that makes people unable to communicate. If lament poets were crazy, it was surely only in the way a quilt may be crazy—in an articulate and structured way and as a creative response to containment."*[42]

Deep down, I think Impact *is my attempt to awaken my courage. The courage to break free of the alienating containment of grief. The courage to act disruptively, to refuse conscription into the univocal elegiac poetics of Canadian military commemoration. The courage to dissent.*

Whereas in Canadian military commemoration ceremonies the emotions associated with war-related grief are used to shore up nationalist and militarist narratives, historically throughout the West, women have used their role as the primary mediators of lament not to maintain the status quo but to channel the complex emotions related to death to comment on, critique, and influence their social world. Writing about ancient Greece, Gail Holst-Warhaft notes that through the use of counterpoint—a central compositional component of lament in most pre-industrial societies—skilled lamenters performed and conducted structured and collectivized improvisations that incorporated elements of sound, poetry, and affective performance to convey the myriad of emotions associated with death, and to assist the bereaved in communicating their overwhelming and often "inarticulate grief."[43] Similarly, Angela Bourke argues that Irish lament poets took full advantage of the central position they occupied during the time of death and of their licence to speak and behave disruptively to communicate their concerns and negotiate conditions of their social marginality.[44] Just as a death disrupts the emotional, physical, and economic lives of those closest to the deceased, in many cultures its accompanying rituals of mourning have been, and in some cases still are, understood as a kind of liminal space in which accepted social norms are turned upside down.

I want to acknowledge that the notion of "the West" is problematic in many ways, including its historical (and biased) function as the signifier of "culture" and "Western civilization" as positioned against the "Orient" and the "uncivilized other," as well as its homogenization of the plurality of identity within and throughout the West. My use of the term here is not intended to deny these problematics. Rather, by focusing on how the dominant and dominating culture has constructed public mourning practices, my intent is to examine how and why some practices of public mourning have come to be normalized while "others" have become marginalized or altogether disappeared. Moreover, following performance studies scholar Joseph Roach and critical race scholar Paul Gilroy, I use the concept of the West not as a fixed and essentialized geographic location bounded by a set of national boundaries but rather to convey the larger fluid and mobile processes of western geopolitical expansionism.

For many Westerners it is difficult to imagine mourning as a public practice—except in cases where it is practised under the umbrella of state-sponsored commemoration—let alone an activity that disrupts social norms and challenges the status quo. In part this is because of the immense influence that Sigmund Freud's 1917 publication of *Mourning and Melancholia* had and continues to have, not only on theoretical, psychiatric, and popular *conceptions* of grief and mourning but also on individual, social, and institutional bereavement practices. In *Mourning*, Freud argues that the bereaved individual, having invested their ego in the deceased, must "work through" a process of mourning to let go of the lost "love object" in order to liberate their ego. If unsuccessful, the individual will remain in a (pathological) state of melancholia or despair in which they are unable to fully love or to embrace life.

Freud's theories—as Gorer and Holst-Warhaft (among others) argue—have contributed significantly to the redefinition of mourning as a private and internal process, as opposed to a public and social one. Critical memory scholar Allen Feldman argues that the large-scale popularization of Freud's psychoanalytic notions of mourning, melancholia, and trauma has had insidious geopolitical consequences. In his analysis of South Africa's Truth and Reconciliation Commission, Feldman asserts that grief's internalization and individualization serves to dehistoricize historical trauma and decontextualize the present by facilitating national and transnational processes of "structural forgetfulness."[45] This social forgetfulness is structural on two counts—in its manufacture, as well as in the way it obscures the larger geopolitical forces that produced the historical trauma in the first place. As many critics of the Truth and Reconciliation Commission (TRC) of Canada have noted, the commission's focus on Canada's residential school abuses has a potentially de-historicizing effect because it contributes to the institutional bracketing off of "land, treaty, and sovereignty issues from historical consciousness."[46] While I agree with those who argue that the shortcomings of the TRC and the Canadian government's deployment of a reconciliatory technology of apology are immense, I also believe that that the TRC has been highly successful in producing a living counter-memorial that is skillfully and creatively exceeding the de-historicizing and reconciliatory mandates of the Canadian government.

Unlike Freud's interiorization of grief as a process to be worked through by the individual, women's lament in many pre-industrial cultures neither contained nor tamed mourning's complex array of affective, social, and political expression. Lament was a community-based practice that took place in the public arena, where its uncensored and affective expression challenged dominant social orders. One does not have to know much about Greek theatre to be familiar with two of its most notoriously tragic heroines—Medea and

Electra—whose rage-filled grief drove them to bloody acts of vengeance with monumentally devastating consequences. But beneath these epic and cautionary tales about the capacity of women's grief to "incite revenge" lies the lesser known role of lament in ancient Greece.[47] Like the laments of our tragic heroines (and their accompanying choruses) the real-life laments that were a common part of early Greek mourning rituals were artful performances. Unlike those written for the stage, however, real-life laments were constructed and performed by women.

As a social practice, lament threatened the authority of the increasingly centralized emergent city-states of ancient Greece in several ways. Leaving control over lament and other rituals and rites related to death in the hands of women challenged the increasingly rigid and hierarchical patriarchal order of the emergent city-states. At times, lament was also used as a tool in inciting reciprocal violence or revenge killings. And most significant to the discussion at hand, lament's focus on grief and loss interfered with the state's ability to control attitudes about the "value of death for the community or state [thus] making it difficult for authorities to recruit an obedient army."[48]

In response to the challenge lament posed to the gendered and racialized hierarchical order in ancient Greece, interdicts against women-led community mourning rituals began as early as the sixth century BCE, when Solon introduced laws restricting the practice of "lamenting the dead" to those directly related to the deceased.[49] Solon's interdiction effectively contained lament by taking it out of the social arena and situating it in the privatized spheres of home and family. Religious authorities throughout Europe issued similar prohibitions against lament from the beginning of the Christian era through the twentieth century. As Holst-Warhaft notes, England's extensive efforts (often exercised through the authority of the Church of Ireland) to silence Ireland's lamenting women corresponded to its lengthy reign of terror over the Irish peasantry and its subsequent need to "quell the potential for violent revenge."[50]

Looking beyond the boundaries of the British Isles, postcolonial feminist scholar Parita Mukta asserts that restriction of women's lament was part of England's "civilizing mission" throughout its colonies.[51] Control over women's mourning practices, Mukta argues, was an important ingredient of a larger recipe of Western colonization and an example of one of the ways the West functions as a mobile geopolitical and ideological force: "In different societies, over varied times, and under very different political economies, when state powers have been consolidating their authority, this has necessitated (with varying degrees of success) both the displacement of mourning, the harnessing of the force of lament in their own aggrandizement and, in extreme cases, the erasure in social memory of the dead."[52]

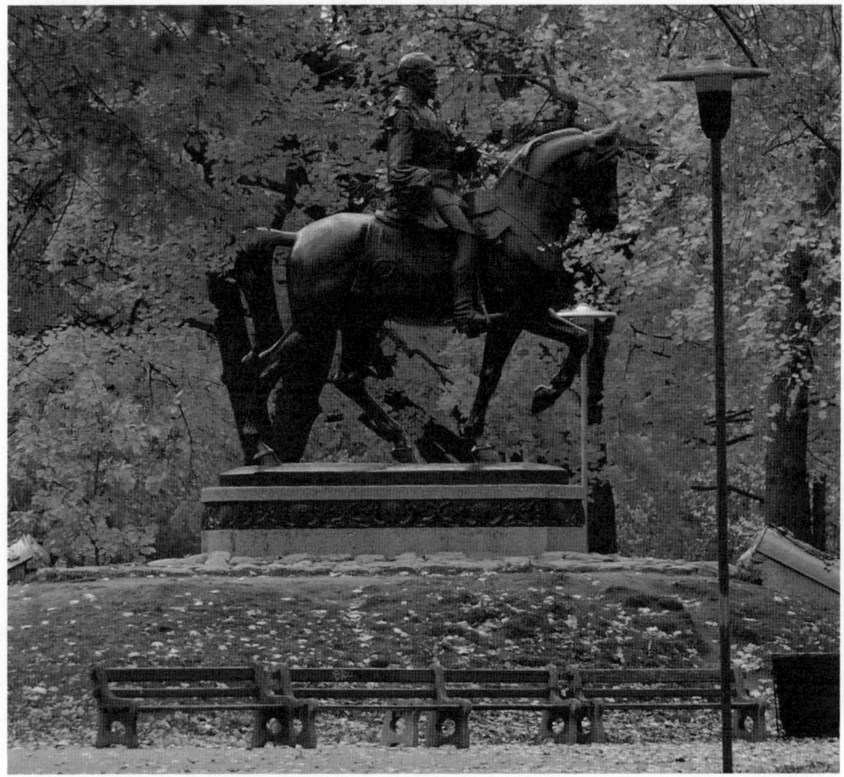

Figure 8. King Edward VII monument.

In concert with interdictions against women's lament, practices of public mourning moved away from polyvocal expressions of the complex emotions and narratives associated with grief and toward univocal and homogenizing narratives of praise. The foregrounding of praise for the dead conveniently rids commemoration of both complexity and critique. Those subjects whose presence would interfere with nationalism's elegiac narratives are necessarily disavowed, war's blood-soaked bodies are shrouded beneath the flag, and the nation's mourners are hailed as silent civilian soldiers. Purged of war's brutality and the anger associated with the violent loss of loved ones, commemoration's elegiac pronouncements have proved well-suited to the production of Canada's particular brand of nationalism. After all, in Canada it is not so much the drumbeat of war that enlists the necessary support for the nation's military actions—Canada's "reluctant militarists" are more effectively rallied through narratives of peacekeeping and benevolent militarism.

July 2011, Canada Day
Queen's Park, Toronto
falls 36,500–36,600

Queen's Park had the eerie atmosphere of a military occupation as Kim and I approached it for the gathering of Impact*'s year-end group fall. There were roadblocks through which only military vehicles were allowed passage. Brad was waiting for us inside the park and the three of us watched as uniformed personnel secured the area surrounding a line of cannons.*

As it became increasingly clear that a twenty-one-gun salute was going to take place we discussed whether we should fall in conjunction with the firing of the cannons but decided instead to continue as planned and wait for the rest of those who had signed on to fall to arrive. The cannons were ear-splittingly loud. Laura arrived carrying her young son, Jackson. He was frightened and she was trying to explain to him that we were friends and everything was okay.

I couldn't help but wonder how it was for others who, like us, were caught off guard by the cannon's roar but who, unlike us, were also survivors of wars. A sad irony of the juxtaposition between Impact*'s poetics of vulnerability and the militaristic poetics of the twenty-one-gun salute is that each of the military personnel taking part in the ritual—those who stand at attention, those who issue the repeated orders to fire the cannons, and those who unflinchingly respond—have far more intimate relationships with the very real and embodied vulnerability associated with war than do we.*

While I hadn't anticipated that Canada Day in Queen's Park would be celebrated with such militaristic zeal, it somehow seemed disturbingly fitting to fall with the cannon's reverberations echoing through our bones; with the backdrop of military personnel and vehicles; and at the foot of one of the multitude of monuments (this one to King Edward VII) to imperialism that occupy our public landscapes (Figure 8). *With each rise and fall I imagined us as a living and ephemeral monument to the Afghan dead and to all those whose lives remain unmemorialized and unmonumentalized.*

When I began *Impact* I felt distressed at the notion that my intentions might be misconstrued. For eight months during the year that I performed *Impact*, I was doing coursework for my PhD and working as a teaching assistant at York University, which meant that I did my daily falls on campus three to four times a week. At one point during my year of falling I happened upon a York University Facebook group page that had phone-recorded video footage of me falling to the accompaniment of the laughter of the video's maker and their friends. The video post was followed by a series of comments. In concert with the dismissive laughter was some name-calling. By internet standards, these comments were relatively innocuous and consisted mostly of suggestions that I was "crazy," drunk, or both. What most fascinated me, however, was how quickly a polyvocal meaning-making chorus emerged. People who had witnessed *Impact* during the months that I had been falling on campus began to share with others what they understood about the project. When one person explained that each fall was in honour of a Canadian soldier who had been killed in Afghanistan, someone else chimed in to say that actually, the falls were dedicated to the Afghan dead whose deaths go unacknowledged in Canada. Colleagues at York have shared similar stories of their experience overhearing conversations about *Impact* while travelling on public transit or sitting in campus cafes.

Over time, I've come to realize how integral ambiguity was to *Impact*'s dialogue with the Highway of Heroes and other popular and state-sponsored Canadian military commemoration ceremonies. *Impact*'s intent was never to hail a chorus of mourners who would echo a singular refrain. It was to draw attention to the foreclosing frame of Canadian military commemoration and to engage witnesses in a polyvocal process of collective reckoning with what lies beyond the frame's forgetful parameters. If the regimented gestures of the soldiers assigned to command the Remembrance Day and Canada Day cannons—*the order to fire passed down a chain of command, the cannon's explosive roar*—can be seen as an unflinching disavowal of vulnerability, with *Impact* I endeavoured instead to privilege a gesture of vulnerability. Through its repeated performance of falling, *Impact* sought to make strange the normalized gestures of militarism and nationalism and the elegiac performance of commemoration.

The day before *Impact*'s culminating Canada Day falls in Queen's Park, I fell in Toronto's Trinity Bellwoods Park. As had been the case throughout the year, most of *Impact*'s witnesses were accidental and watched in passing, on their way to or from somewhere, from bicycle seats and car and bus windows, from café patios, apartment balconies, and park lawns. Only a very small percentage of those who encountered *Impact* actually stopped to read the flag's inscribed message or to take a postcard. Even fewer stayed to witness more than a couple of falls. But on this day, a man was playing nearby with his two kids when his daughter, who was about five or six years old, walked over and began to watch me fall. Untrained in the protocols of silence or in the silencing of curiosity, she asked her father what I was doing. "Dad" took a postcard and read it to her. They had a short conversation and then the girl sat on the path in front of me and watched. Following in his big sister's footsteps, her brother also asked their dad what I was doing. Looking to his young daughter, Dad said, "You explain it to your brother." For the remainder of my falls, the two of them sat and watched while Dad packed up their belongings. I will never know the effects that witnessing *Impact* had on this girl, her brother, her father, the multitude of accidental witnesses who caught a glimpse, or the few who lingered to watch. My hope is that in some small way *Impact* disrupted the silencing effects of Canadian military commemoration's elegiac poetics and raised questions about the forgetful peripheries of national memory.

With this brief tracing of the Western historical routes of women's lament, my intention has been twofold: first, to denaturalize military commemoration's elegiac and silencing poetics; and second, like Mukta, to turn attention toward the interface between state-issued interdictions against women's public mourning practices, the rise of military commemoration, and the spread of nationalism through Western expansionism, colonization, and imperialism.[53] Where Holst-Warhaft troubles the relationship between the censure of women's lament (as well as that of women's participation in the larger public realm) and the emergence of democracy in ancient Greece, with her postcolonial analysis Mukta adds a critical intersectional layer to the feminist project of re-historicizing women's lament. Through her insistence that control over women's mourning practices was essential for the manufacture and maintenance of an "increasingly important (and privatized) domestic realm" as well as for "the security of the emerging colonial state," Mukta asserts that there is a crucial link between the need to control and contain affective expressions that were historically performed by women—like lament—and the colonial (and capitalist) state's need to control and contain populations, land, and resources.

Following Mukta, I propose that these are also the larger stakes of Canadian military commemoration—control of populations, land, and resources. In enlisting generations of Canada's civilian soldiers in the censorial protocols of obligatory reverentiality, parameters are established around who we do and do not mourn; who are and are not considered war's fallen; what our military is and is not fighting for; even what is and is not considered war or state violence. Alongside Canada's iconically grievable soldiers, inside the Highway of Heroes' frame is the story of a becoming nation dedicated to acts of humanitarian militarism. Outside the Highway of Heroes frame are not only the de-realized Afghan dead but also the less altruistic, political, and economic motives of the Canadian nation.

Within popular discourse in Canada (which is heavily influenced by the Canadian Armed Forces public relations machine) our nation's engagement in Afghanistan is framed as a humanitarian mission against the Taliban and a fight for the rights of Afghan women and girls. In keeping with this dominant Canadian war narrative, Paul Gross's award-winning Afghan war epic *Hyena Road* (2015) depicts a multicultural peacekeeping force—though the film's lead Canadian Forces characters are white—heroically attempting to do good while caught in an intractable war not of their making. Notably, *Hyena Road* ends its tale of a deeply troubled humanitarian mission to build a road into the heart of Taliban territory with the cathartic rescue of kidnapped Afghan girls locked in animal cages.

In contrast to the often troubled but always benevolent military framework proffered by Canadian Forces public relations and spectacularly rendered on the big screen by Gross, the authors of the collection *Empire's Ally: Canada and the War in Afghanistan* frame Canada's role in Afghanistan within the context of the intersecting interests of Canadian foreign policy and Canadian political economy.[54] As development studies scholar Adam Hanieh points out, the very fact that there was no significant public debate among Canadians about Canada's role in Afghanistan until early in 2008 is an indication of how successfully the war was framed within Canadian public discourse as a "morally necessary step to protect human rights and ensure peace in the region."[55] Missing from this purified depiction of Canadian military motivations is an analysis of salient geopolitical and economic factors.

Nations do not send armies to defend roads that are being built to rescue little girls. They send armies to defend roads and other infrastructure built to facilitate access to resources. But resource exploitation and economic expansionism make for a decidedly non-compelling story for Canada's reluctant militarists, or for those who serve, or have loved ones serving, in the Canadian Forces. Though it may not play well on the big screen or in the dominant Canadian imaginary, gaining access to resources—in other words, development—is a key component of Canadian foreign policy. In 2003, Paul Martin's Liberal government initiated a new "whole-of-government" Canadian foreign policy strategy. Also known as "3D" (development, diplomacy, and defence), the military approach combined under one umbrella the agendas of the Department of National Defence and the Department of Foreign Affairs and International Trade with that of the Canadian International Development Agency.[56] "Afghanistan," writes political studies scholar Angela Joya, "became a laboratory for [this] new international policy agenda, centred around the [Department of National Defence] and a war-making strategy for failed or failing states, in alliance with US foreign policy objectives."[57]

The relationship between Afghanistan's estimated $1 trillion in mineral resources and Canadian mining interests are nowhere to be found in the popularized narrative of the humanitarian militarism that *Hyena Road* so dramatically stages.[58] The road is not framed as a route of foreign incursion; it is a necessary path into Taliban territory, one that through the magic of cinema becomes affectively linked to the rescue of innocent girls from an amoral enemy. There is no suggestion that the fictionalized road may be essential infrastructure needed to pave the way for foreign capital. Nor is there mention of the fact that, as Michael Skinner of Global Research writes, "On 24 November 2011, the Government of Afghanistan awarded a Canadian mining company, Kilo Goldmines, approximately 25 percent of the stake to develop the massive Hajigak iron deposit in Bamiyan Afghanistan."[59] Lest the Kilo Goldmine's contract be perceived as a resource grab, Ed Fast, Canada's then minister for international trade, framed it thus: "Canada is strongly committed to helping Afghans rebuild their country, and this investment by Kilo Goldmines will create jobs for Afghans and Canadians alike."[60]

But is the Canadian government's 3D formulation really so new? Or is it simply a new name for an old devil? We need not look as geographically afar as Afghanistan for an example of Canada's whole-government approach or of the role of roads in facilitating economic expansion. The Canadian state's dispossession of Indigenous populations from their lands and resources is and has always been at the heart of settler colonialism. And, as Indigenous director Michelle St. John details in her 2016 documentary, *Colonization Road*, roads have long played a critical role in Canadian settler colonialism by providing routes to enable settlers to occupy the land and access resources. In the film, St. John follows Anishinaabe comedian and activist Ryan McMahon as he takes the viewer down the main drag—Colonization Road—of his hometown of Fort Frances. As the film continues, we visit a plethora of similarly named streets and roads throughout the province of Ontario.

The biggest difference between the Hyena Road of Gross's film and the Colonization Roads of St. John's film is not that the former is a fictive moniker and the latter the "real" name of multiple roads. It is in how Hyena Road, and the movie that takes its name, masks the geopolitical and economic motives that underpin the "hundreds of kilometres of roads [that] have been built or repaired" under the protection of the Canadian Armed Forces in Afghanistan, while the name Colonization Road unabashedly reveals the purpose of the roads that are so named.[61]

While "Colonization Road" blatantly signifies the colonial mission of these roads as mechanisms for the dispossession of Indigenous populations and the appropriation of lands and resources, Canadian settler colonialism remains nevertheless conveniently situated outside of Canadian military memorialization's definition of "war." I will return to this in my analysis of the Canadian War Museum in the following chapter, where I discuss in greater depth the relationship between the denial of the settler colonialism on which Canada is founded and the neo-colonialism of its contemporary military missions. For now, I propose that this placing of settler colonialism outside of the frame of Canadian military history and Canadian military aggression needs to be considered one of the larger stakes of Canadian military commemoration. Canadian military commemoration contributes to the manufacture and maintenance of a frame of structural forgetfulness that dehistoricizes the violent and material effects of Canadian settler colonialism. In concert with popularized Canadian peacekeeping narratives, Canadian military commemoration conveniently situates violence and human rights violations in faraway places.

Places to which "we," as a self-acclaimed peacekeeping nation and leader in the defence of global human rights, are compelled to send not only our military personnel but also our mining companies to pave the way for peace, stability, and prosperity. While Canadian Armed Forces were busy defending women's rights and roads in Afghanistan, here at "home" Indigenous women and girls were going missing and being murdered along Canadian highways.

REFRAME 5:
Lament as a Labour of Critical Engagement

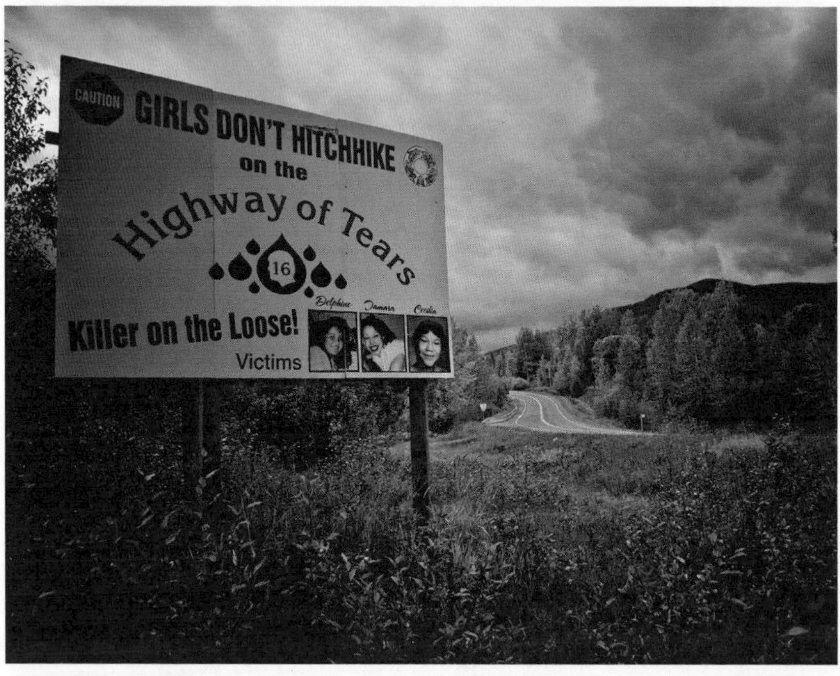

Figure 9. Warning sign on the British Columbia Highway 16 section known as "Highway of Tears," located 31.4 km north of Smithers.

It was during my year of falling that I first learned of the Highway of Tears—an 800-kilometre stretch of Highway 16 in northern British Columbia, where an estimated forty (mostly Indigenous) women and girls have gone missing or been found murdered. Like the Highway of Heroes, the Highway of Tears is a space of commemoration. Like the Highway of Heroes, the Highway of Tears is lined with signs informing those who pass through that they are traversing a memorial landscape (Figure 9). The similarities end there.

The Highway of Heroes is a site of celebrated public grieving for those elevated to the top of the Canadian nation's hierarchy of grievability. It is a space where grief spins loss into a national tale of elegiac heroism. Like Remembrance Day and other institutional and cultural performances of military Canadian commemoration, the Highway of Heroes constructs a narrative of the Canadian nation as an exemplar of humanitarian militarism and enlightened multicultural inclusivity, a narrative that relies on the erasure of Canada's history of colonial violence in order to sustain the popular settler-colonial myth of Canada as a nation born in innocence.

In contrast, when the bodies of Indigenous women and girls are found, sometimes decades after having gone missing, there are no state-supported processions along the Highway of Tears. The roadside is not lined with citizens gathered to honour those who died in the ongoing war against Indigenous women and girls that takes place at the intersection of settler colonialism's racialized and gendered violence. Their families and communities do not know the condolences of a nation that stands with them in their grief. And whereas at the Highway of Heroes military personnel, police, and other uniformed representatives of national authority stand at attention as the bodies of repatriated soldiers pass, along the Highway of Tears there is a long and notorious history of disregard on the part of law authorities for the missing women and girls and their families.

The Highway of Tears exposes the violence of national forgetfulness and reveals the unbecoming underbelly of white settler Canadian nationalism. With the name Highway of Tears, Indigenous community activists invoke the Trail of Tears, the name given to the death marches of the Cherokee, Muscogee, Seminole, Chickasaw, and Choctaw nations. Just as the forced removal of Indigenous peoples throughout the United States was institutionally legitimated by the passage of the U.S. Indian Removal Act of 1830, the Canadian Indian Act mandated the forced removal of Indigenous children in Canada from their families and communities. As a tool of settler-colonial patriarchy, the Indian Act also introduced and institutionalized racialized forms of gender discrimination against (and within) Indigenous communities that resulted in a loss of status for many Indigenous women, and the subsequent loss of land and property rights. As Yellowknives Dene political scientist Glen Sean Coulthard writes:

> In the specific context of Canadian settler-colonialism, although the *means* by which the colonial state has sought to eliminate Indigenous peoples in order to gain access to our lands and resources have modified over the last two centuries—ranging from violent dispossession to the legislative elimination of First Nations legal status under sexist and racist provisions of the Indian Act to the "negotiation" of what are still essentially land surrenders under the present comprehensive land claims policy—the *ends* have always remained the same: to shore up continued access to Indigenous people's territories for the purpose of state formation, settlement, and capitalist development.[62]

As a result of the governmentally instituted diminished legal status within their communities, a disproportionate number of Indigenous women have been placed in precarious economic and social circumstances. Combined with the ongoing legacies of colonialism's use of sexualized violence, this precarity has proved to be lethal for many Indigenous women, girls, and two-spirit peoples in Canada (and throughout the Americas), and needs to be recognized as part of the ongoing violent effects of settler colonialism.

"The 'phenomenon' of the disappeared women," as Mohawk anthropologist Audra Simpson asserts, "is not a mystery, is not without explanation." Simpson points out that a host of Indigenous and critical race scholars, community activists, and families of the disappeared "have all documented, theorized, and written about this disappearance, which is explained by Canada's dispossession of Indian people from land."[63] Dispossession of Indigenous peoples from the land has taken many forms in Canada, from treaties to a host of development projects—mines, timber harvests, pipelines, hydroelectric dams. Similar to the development projects that come under the Canada's 3D foreign policy agenda, these projects are framed as benefiting the very communities they dispossess.

A century of Remembrance Day ceremonies—together with the multitude of cultural and educational productions that accompany them—preconditioned Canadian civilians for their "spontaneous" Highway of Heroes gatherings and their compassionate outpourings for Canada's military dead. In

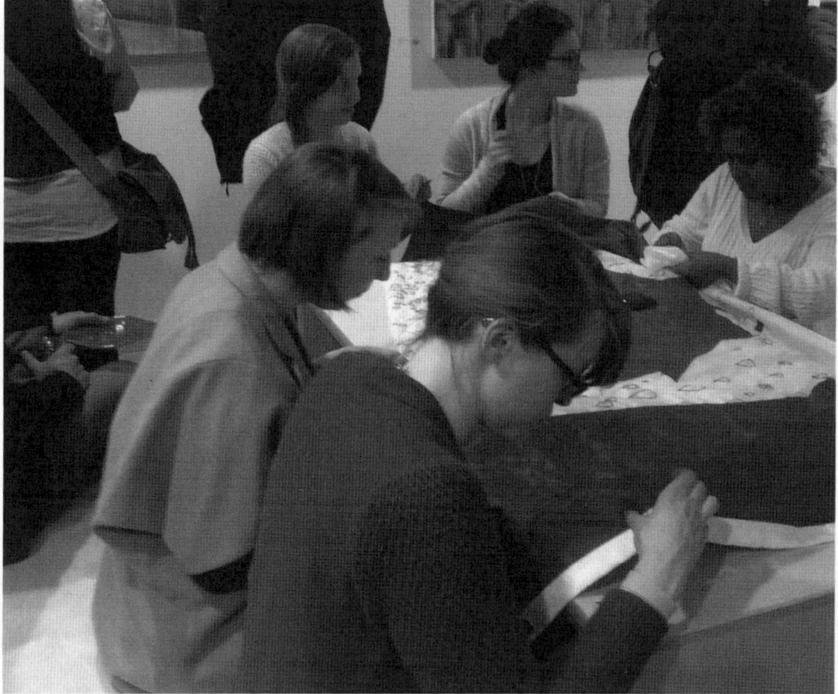

Figure 10. Sewing circle at *You're Not Here* exhibition launch, Daniels Spectrum.

contrast, centuries of institutional racism and structural forgetfulness dispose settler-Canadian populations to disavow the deaths and disappearances of missing and murdered Indigenous women, girls, and two-spirit people in Canada. It is only through decades of durational labour on the part of Indigenous activists, scholars, artists, community members, and settler allies that the issue of the disappeared made it to national consciousness. It was only after Amnesty International Canada released *Stolen Sisters* (2004) and *No More Stolen Sisters* (2009) that the media began reporting on the over 500 missing and murdered Indigenous women and girls across Canada that were documented in the Amnesty reports. And it was only after Maryanne Pearce completed her doctoral thesis, "An Awkward Silence: Missing and Murdered Vulnerable Women and the Canadian Justice System," that the Royal Canadian Mounted Police (RCMP) finally released their 2014 report that raised the number of missing and murdered Indigenous women and girls in Canada from 500 to an *official* 1,181.[64]

3 March 2015
You're Not Here exhibition launch, Daniels Spectrum, Toronto
The tear is a messy abomination amidst the drops of carefully embroidered tears. It's not the sewer's "fault." It's we who failed in our task as the embroidery circle's facilitators. We all stepped away from the table to watch some of the evening's performances. By the time I returned, it was too late to offer guidance. Too late to delicately lay down embroidery's rules of engagement. The sewer went rogue. Their offering is a sloppy eruption of red thread. I am too off-centre to inquire in earnest. Too consumed by the effort to maintain the inviting tenor of my embroidery circle hostess demeanour. All I can manage in the moment is an abrupt assurance to the sewer that their contribution is just as it should be. It's an offering I make despite my inner recoil and the obviousness of the globule-like tear's misalignment with the hundreds of other tears that have already been carefully stitched onto the flag.

At first, it took great will on my part not to "fix" the tear, not to restore the flag's aesthetic order. But perhaps the sewer has deliberately asserted this ruinous aesthetic. Perhaps they have set out to disrupt the notion that care is necessarily equated with order and precision. Over time my gratitude for the rogue tear grows. It is a reminder that grief demands a messy affective mix, far from the disciplined poetics of military commemoration, or the illusive innocence of Canadian nationalism. Tears—like blood—defy the containment of elegiac order. And like the lamenting women who tear at their hair, who bare and beat at their breasts, grief defies aesthetic constraint.

In the fall of 2014 I began *Flag of Tears: Lament for the Stains of a Nation*, a memorial project in which tears—each in recognition of one of Canada's missing and murdered Indigenous women, girls, or two-spirit individuals—are embroidered onto a large Canadian flag in a task-based act of lament and collective reckoning. In taking its name from the Highway of Tears, with *Flag of Tears* I too seek to draw connections between the murders of Indigenous women, girls, and two-spirit people and the long history of patriarchal settler-colonial violence and its institutionalization through the mechanisms of the Canadian nation. I am also gesturing back to the Highway of Heroes and endeavouring to counter white settler Canadian nationalism's hierarchy of grievability that provides its privileged national subjects with celebrated sites of commemoration, while casting the forgotten dead of its dominant constructions of history outside of the realm of grievability.

Though I had already embroidered several hundred red tears onto the flag, *Flag of Tears* did not really begin to make sense to me until I saw a call for proposals for an International Women's Day exhibit at Daniels Spectrum that was being curated by the Feminist Art Conference. The show's title—*You're Not Here*—was designed to address issues of displacement (and its disavowal) that are so palpable in the gentrification of Toronto's Regent Park area where Daniels Spectrum's fancy digs are both located and implicated. The theme also spoke to the historical and ongoing processes of dispossession of Indigenous populations across Canada that generations of settler Canadians are implicated in.

Flag of Tears had begun as a solo undertaking. From the start, I had a difficult time getting the project going. Despite my year of sustained engagement with *Impact* I now seemed unable to summon the self-discipline to sit down and embroider on a daily basis. Weeks, sometimes months, passed between embroidery sessions. I grew critical of my lack of commitment to the project and became increasingly unsettled by how my behaviour reflected the disregard of Canadian authorities and the settler Canadian general public to the disappearances of Indigenous women, girls, and two-spirit individuals, reflecting a return to the collective default mode of settler nationalism's forgetfulness.

I realized that unlike my approach to *Impact*, I had conceived of *Flag of Tears* more as a product than a process. I had a goal in mind—to produce a flag with 1,181 red embroidered tears. The Feminist Art Conference's call helped me remember how this goal was fundamentally at odds with the entire concept of a living memorial as a site of critical reflection and afforded me an opportunity to re-situate the project as a task-based community lament. I contacted several feminist colleagues—Thea Fitz-James, Paula John, and M.e. Lepp—who work with textiles as a performative medium and asked if they would help me host a series of embroidery circles as part of the *You're Not Here* exhibit (Figure 10). We came together to embroider several times prior to the exhibit and at the opening launch facilitated a porous embroidery circle where for hours participants and witnesses visited. Some embroidered. Some watched. Some ran their fingers over the flag's tears. Those who stitched did so with patience and expertise, with clumsy care, and awkward unknowing.

CHAPTER TWO

THE CANADIAN WAR MUSEUM

IMAGINING THE CANADIAN NATION THROUGH MILITARY COMMEMORATION

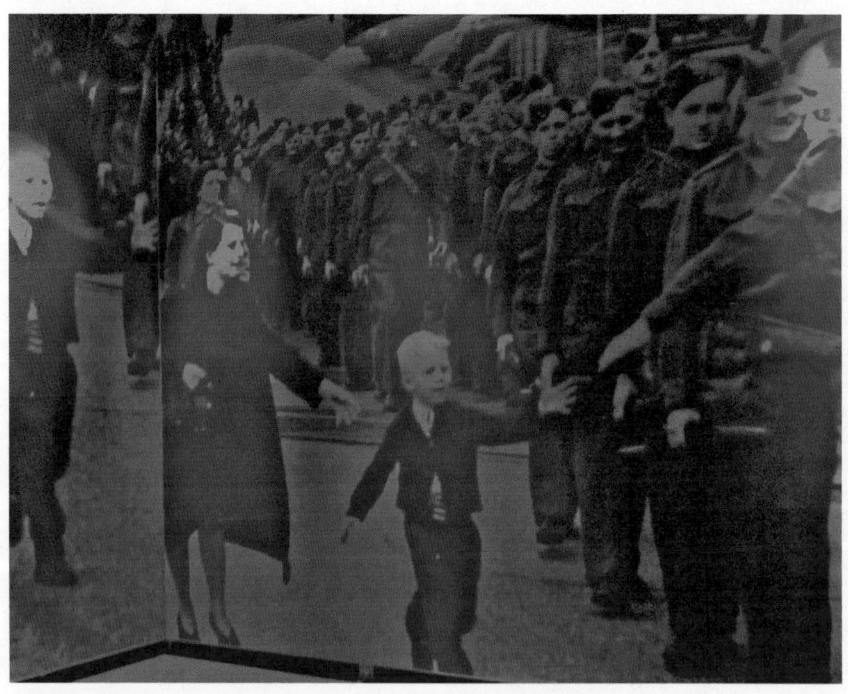

Figure 11. Mural of Claude P. Dettloff's 1940 photo *Wait for Me, Daddy*, entrance to the Canadian War Museum exhibits.

9 August 2013
Canadian War Museum, Ottawa: Entrance to exhibits
The boy runs. He's located his father among the hundreds of uniformed men marching off to war down this street that just yesterday had a more innocent choreography. Some of the men smile, but only "Dad" breaks rank as he looks back and reaches his hand out to meet his son's outstretched hand. Mom follows, also reaching toward the boy. To snatch him back? To intervene? Is she sorry she brought him to see his father off? Or is she proud? Maybe she isn't reaching to pull her young son back. Maybe she nudged him forward. Maybe she and the boy's father are impressed by his fearlessness, his precocious compulsion to enlist.

A larger-than-life version of the iconic Second World War photograph—*Wait for Me, Daddy*—graces the entrance to the main galleries of the Canadian War Museum in Ottawa. Taken by Claude P. Dettloff on 1 October 1940 in New Westminster, British Columbia, the image captures the moment when young Warren "Whitey" Bernard breaks away from his mother and runs toward his father—Private Jack Bernard—who is marching with the British Columbia Regiment on the way to war. Marching three abreast, the regiment is so large it disappears over a distant hill. Selected by *Life* magazine as their photo of the week, *Wait for Me, Daddy* was accompanied by the caption: "One little fair-haired boy had spotted his father and had broken away from his mother's hand. Without breaking step, the father holds out his hand. The other men smile and the column goes on."[1]

Not all the men are smiling though. In fact, few are. Many look resolute, perhaps even grim. Barely men at all, most are far younger than Private Bernard, somewhere between his age and that of five-year-old Warren. Will Private Bernard, who is leaving behind his own young son, reach out to some of these younger men in the weeks, months, and years to come? Will these stoic men marching off to war comfort one another when they cry out with fear or pain? Will they hold one another as they lie dying? Will it be their grim task to gather the fragmented remains of their dead comrades?

But the focus of the image is not the men. It is Warren, one foot off the ground, hand stretched open, as he enthusiastically propels himself toward his father, his mother lagging behind unable (or unwilling) to halt his momentum. In the museum, the photo's focus on Warren is further accentuated both through the image's enlargement—Warren, still a child, is now the size of a man—and with the placement of a second image, a ghostly echo, in the wake of the first. The second image is cropped. We no longer see Warren's mother, father, or the column of marching men. All we see is Warren running, hand outstretched, into the museum itself. Nationalism's fundamental constellation of the heteronormative family—with mother standing for the domesticated home front and father for the militarized battlefront—has receded from view. In casting Warren's mother and father outside the image's frame, the museum relegates the nuclear family to its unmarked and naturalized role in the (re) production of the nation-state and its armies of emerging soldiers.

Between 2012 and 2014, I made three trips to Ottawa to visit the Canadian War Museum. During each trip I spent three to four hours a day for three days (a mix of weekdays and the weekend) and one Thursday evening exploring the various spaces and exhibits throughout the museum and observing other museum goers. What became immediately evident was that the Canadian War Museum's primary constituency is children. On weekdays, children arrive by the busload, sporadically transforming the museum's otherwise cavernous and conspicuously uninhabited environment—or as one museum visitor put it, "Oh wow, the museum of empty!"—into one that is cacophonously enlivened. On weekends, the museum's population wanes considerably and is reduced to a mere spattering of family groups taking advantage of the two-museum ("War" and "Civilization") family package. During my visits, the one exception to this pattern was a weekend in August 2012, when Ottawa's Ceremonial Guard hosted the sixteenth annual Fortissimo celebration on Parliament Hill, which draws military bands from across Canada and around the world. This was the busiest I ever saw the museum galleries. On this weekend, busloads of cadets toured the museum, guided by legions of veteran docents. It was also the time with the greatest mix of adults and children/youth I ever witnessed at the museum, and one of the few times when the parking lot had more cars than buses, as tourists who had come to see the Fortissimo also came to see the War Museum and its highly promoted *War of 1812* exhibit.

With the exception of the weekend of the Fortissimo celebration, attendance at the Canadian War Museum was sparse. Even the museum's free Thursday evening attracted only a smattering of visitors. In fact, aside from the August 2012 weekend and during the sporadic deliveries of busloads of school children, the only time I saw the museum truly abustle was after hours, when the museum's LeBreton Gallery is abuzz with gala goers. During one of my trips to Ottawa I happened to be staying near the museum and chanced upon these galas when I returned "home" each evening. Dressed in evening finery, gala attendees mixed and mingled amidst the LeBreton Gallery's collection of artillery, aircraft, and armoured vehicles. Artfully lit for these occasions, these weapons of wars past become part of the evening's ambiance, while to the north, a large expanse of windows provides those inside with a skyline view of Ottawa's Parliamentary precinct and downtown.

But while the LeBreton Gallery might serve as a spectacular backdrop for adults attending gala events, the museum proper is primarily designed for the edification of children and youth. Speaking in 1998 before a Senate committee about the need for the new Canadian War Museum, Daniel Glenney, the museum's former acting director general, argued that "young people" in Canada had become ignorant of Second World War history and that "only by education can we ensure that commemoration remains alive."[2] As Graham Carr notes in "War, History, and the Education of (Canadian) Memory," the concern that Canadians were out of touch with their military "history and evolution" began to be expressed by Canadian military historians, military organizations, and veterans groups in the early 1990s.[3] As I discussed in the Introduction, this "unease about the precarious future of social [military] memory"[4] was exacerbated by—or as Howard Fremeth suggests, triggered by—the film series *The Valour and the Horror* and its representation of the Royal Canadian Air Force's involvement in the Bomber Command mission that targeted and killed 600,000 German civilians. A repeated apprehension expressed by *Valour*'s critics, especially those belonging to military and veterans groups, was that the episodes, which aired on prime-time television and were to be made available to schools and public libraries, would have a negative effect on "impressionable Canadian children."[5] The Canadian War Museum is one of many media- and youth-savvy military memory projects that have emerged out of this concern and as a response on the part of military memory network stakeholders to what General Rick Hillier dubbed the Canadian military's "decade of darkness." More than simply a site for the commemoration of past battles and lives lost, the museum is an ideological battleground for the hearts and minds (and perhaps, in the not-so-distant future, the bodies as well) of Canada's children.

Just as young Warren has not magically transported himself across time and space in his enthusiastic dash to enter the Canadian War Museum, many of the children and youth who come to the museum do not come of their

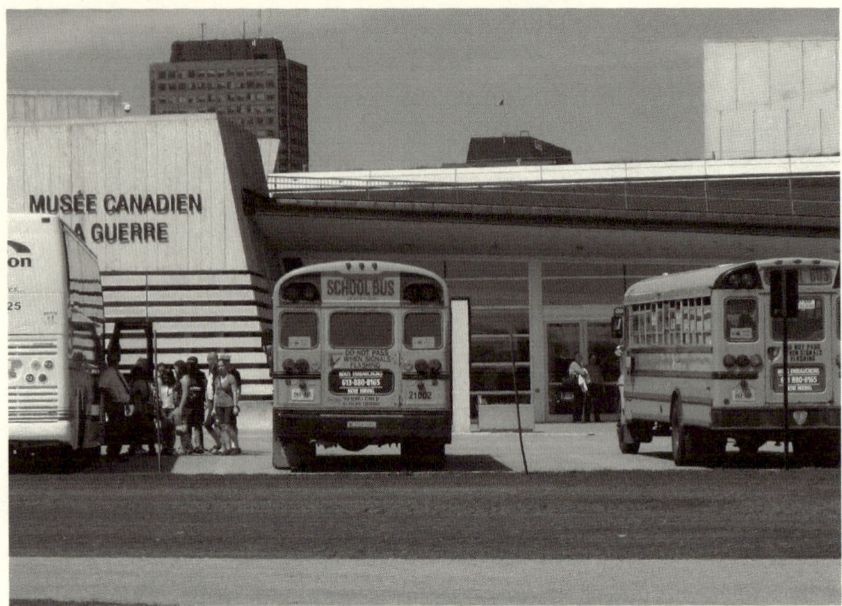

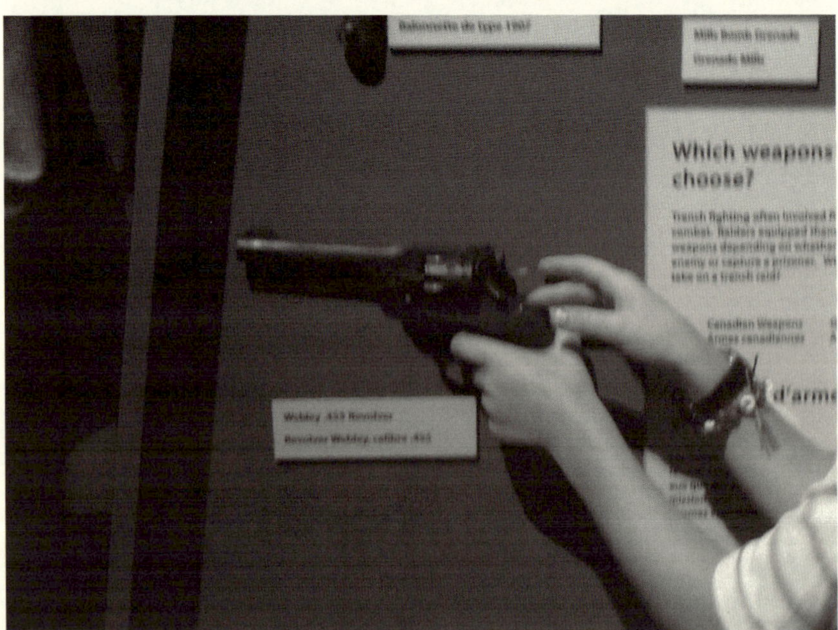

Figure 12. Buses outside of the Canadian War Museum.
Figure 13. Boy wrapping finger around trigger at First World War weapon display.

own volition. They are brought on school, cadet, community group, or family outings. Once there, however, most enthusiastically partake in the museum's exhibits, many of which invite hands-on exploration: there are buttons to press, games to play, quizzes to take, uniforms to don, trenches to traverse, and weapons to handle. During my visits, the latter were always a favourite with the boys. One First World War exhibit displays weapons that were used in the trenches. Mounted on one side of the display are Canadian weapons (1907 Patten bayonet, .455 Webley revolver) and on the other, German (dagger, Luger pistol). Each side has its own collection of truncheons. The one lone Mills bomb grenade seems to beg the question, Are grenades non-partisan? At the centre of the display a museum label asks visitors: "Which weapon would you choose?" To facilitate choosing, the weapons are made accessible. Unhindered by a glass panel, they are mounted so that the children can conveniently wrap their small hands around the weapon's handles and hook their fingers around triggers.

In *Between Hope and Despair*, Roger Simon, Sharon Rosenberg, and Claudia Eppert argue that the preservation and remembrance of historical violence is guided by two pedagogical imperatives: first, remembrance "constituted as a *strategic practice* in which memorial pedagogies are deployed for sociopolitical value and promise"; and second, "enacted as a *difficult return*, a psychic and social responsibility to bring the dead into presence."[6] Though these dual pedagogical imperatives can be productively deployed in unison to mobilize communities to advocate for human rights, they also have important differences. As a strategic practice, remembrance is a means through which "harmonious social relations" are achieved.[7] But when the memory of mass violence cannot be integrated into the limiting frames of contemporary social memory, remembrance as difficult return destabilizes strategic practices in order to keep alive in the present the psychic and social wounds of "what cannot be redeemed."[8] When positioned under the umbrella of nationalist and militarist agendas, strategic practice frequently overshadows difficult return, thereby enabling privileged subjects to bypass the sustained labour of critical engagement that is necessary before "harmonious social relations" or meaningful "conciliation"—to borrow a term from Métis curator-scholar David Garneau—can begin to take place.[9]

As the examples of Canadian military commemoration discussed in the previous chapter illustrate, when control over processes of commemorating loss come under the domain of the nation-state, both the strategic deployment and the accompanying sociopolitical value assigned to performances of remembrance are shaped by the interests of the state. Similarly, since they operate under the umbrella of the state, archival institutions of social memory like the Canadian War Museum must also be understood to be performing on behalf of the state. While the dead may well be rendered present through performances of national commemoration—be they repertorial or archival—in death they are strategically deployed by the state.

One way the tension between strategic practice and difficult return plays out in the Canadian War Museum is in the dissonance that exists between the museum's architectural design and the nationalistic pedagogical agenda conveyed through its exhibits. As sociologist Katarzyna Rukszto argues, the museum's architecture, designed by Raymond Moriyama "to facilitate a critical reflection engagement with history, war and nation," is in conflict with the museum's nation-building agenda, which calls for the construction of a unifying national narrative that works against the kind of critical engagement that a difficult return demands.[10]

What is it that the Canadian War Museum's memorial pedagogy endeavours to teach the hundreds of thousands of children and youth who arrive by the busload to trek the museum's two and a half kilometres of exhibits? Other than which weapons they would bring with them into a First World War trench, what are these children to learn from their encounter with the museum's history of Canadians at war? While the museum is full of the personal stories of past and present Canadian military personnel, following critical race scholar Sherene Razack, I differentiate "personal story" from "narrative."[11] Like Razack's, my interest lies in the cumulative effect of the museum's integration of personal voices and how they are assembled to construct a larger narrative about Canadian nationalism. What is the overarching narrative about war, militarism, and the nation-state that the Canadian War Museum communicates to the "impressionable Canadian children" who pass through its galleries, play its games, press its buttons, run through its trenches, and make pseudo life-and-death choices based on the museum's multiple abstracted and interactive scenarios? Conversely, what stories are omitted or subsumed under the larger narrative of Canadian military history and Canadian multicultural nationalism?

The Canadian War Museum, Part 1: Guarding History

The Canadian War Museum opened on 8 May 2005—the sixtieth anniversary of VE (Victory in Europe) Day. The expansive new museum, prominently located at Ottawa's LeBreton Flats, was born of controversy. In 1997, the museum's then director, Daniel Glenney, announced that one-third of a proposed expansion at the museum's existing Sussex Drive location was to be dedicated to a Holocaust exhibit. The idea for the permanent Holocaust exhibit originated after the museum hosted the well-attended *Anne Frank in the World, 1929–1945* exhibit in 1992 and an accompanying visitor poll showed strong support for the inclusion of a Holocaust exhibit within the museum.[12] In addition to these indicators of local public interest in a permanent Holocaust exhibit, the museum's directors were further influenced by the 1993 opening of the highly "successful" United States Holocaust Memorial Museum in Washington, DC, and the announced plan that the Imperial War Museum in London, UK, would dedicate two floors of its in-progress expansion to a permanent Holocaust exhibit.[13]

But when the plan to situate a permanent Holocaust exhibit within the Canadian War Museum was made public, Canadian war veterans cried foul. In part, their response was a well-founded critique of the lack of public and stakeholder consultations on which the museum's decision was based. It was also reflective, however, of the growing influence of Canada's network of military memory stakeholders. Despite the defeat of their class action lawsuit against *The Valour and the Horror*'s producers, in the mid-1990s Canadian veterans emerged from the highly publicized struggle over the control of the transmission of military memory as a mobilized, politically organized, and media-savvy group. As was the case with the *Valour* controversy, at the behest of veterans' organizations a Senate subcommittee was formed to discuss the future of Canada's new war museum. Veterans and their representatives testified that the museum should be solely devoted to Canada's military history and that designating a portion of the museum to a permanent Holocaust exhibit or to "any display, regardless of space, other than that of Canadian military heritage . . . would be an absolute insult to the Canadian soldiers who participated in the making of that very history."[14]

The veterans' appeal was successful on two fronts. First, they prevailed in vetoing the permanent Holocaust exhibit; and second, they planted the idea within the imaginations of both the museum leadership and the general public that the existing location and scale of the museum were not commensurate with the vision of a Canadian national war memorial museum. Of the Senate subcommittee's twelve recommendations, three read as follows: "That the Department of Veterans Affairs or the Department of National Defence assume the responsibility for the newly constituted and independent Canadian War Museum"—a point that signals a lack of critical reflection on the notion of what might constitute an *independent* body; "That a survey of alternative sites for the [museum] be conducted by the appropriate government department or agency"; and "That the Government undertake a meaningful and thorough study as to the feasibility of a national holocaust and/or other acts of genocide gallery."[15]

In May 2001, a new site—the LeBreton Flats—had been found, and by October 2001, the architectural firm Moriyama and Teshima were selected to design and oversee the construction of the museum. Far from its humble beginnings as a $12 million expansion project at 330 Sussex Drive, the new museum is a 440,000-square-foot structure built at a cost of $137 million and occupying 18.5 acres. As art historian Reesa Greenberg notes, the Canadian War Museum had "morphed from an addition to an existing building, to . . . a prominent addition to the capital's museal, ceremonial, and war memorial landscape."[16] Moreover, the public cost of the museum's original construction pales in comparison to the cumulative costs of its ongoing maintenance. According to the museum's 2014/15 to 2018/19 corporate plan, the Canadian War Museum only generates a little over $3 million a year in revenue, receiving the remainder of its $17 million yearly operating budget from government funding.[17]

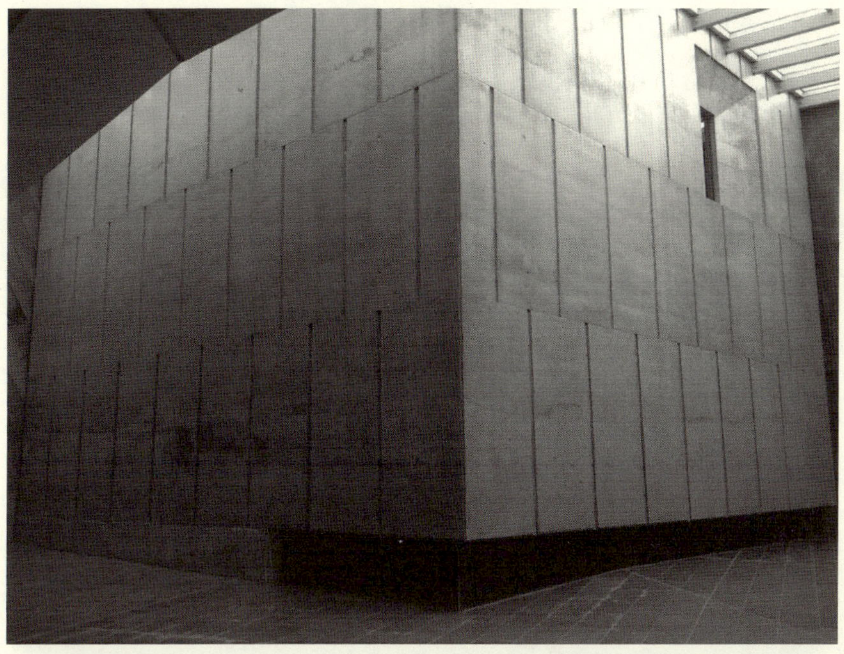

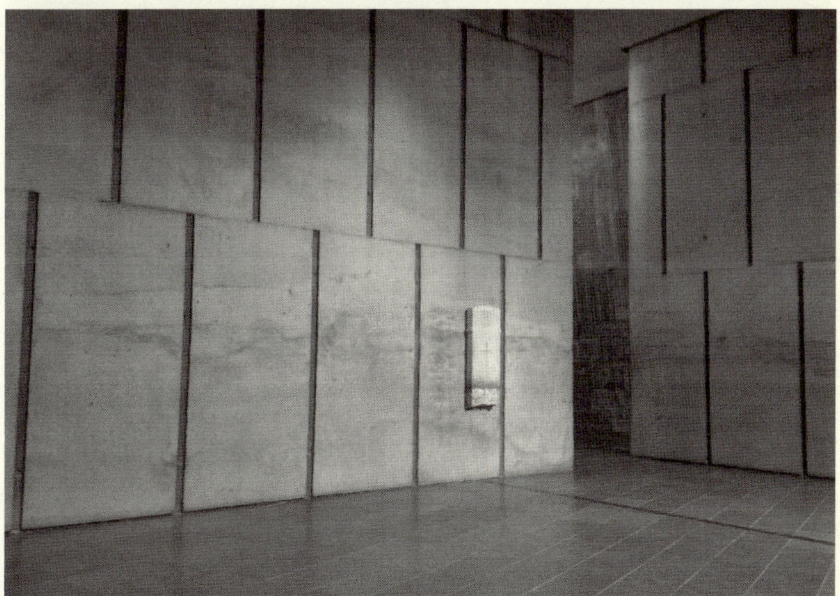

Figure 14. Outside Memorial Hall.
Figure 15. Headstone of the Unknown Soldier, inside Memorial Hall.

The Canadian War Museum, Part 2: An Architecture of Remembrance

10 April 2014
Canadian War Museum, Ottawa: Memorial Hall
Blocks of monumentalized order; rectangular hard order constructed of concrete, slate, marble, and glass; order bisected by a disorienting array of lines. Is this what the inside of a tomb feels like? Is this the weight of monumentalization? The only objects in the room (apart from its cold hard beautiful architecture) are (1) the headstone of the Unknown Soldier (Figure 15)*; (2) a smattering of coins at the bottom of the long shallow rectangular reflection pool; and (3) a surveillance camera.*

I like this room. In fact, I've come to like all the cavernous and tomb-like spaces of the museum. Spaces eerily well-suited for the contemplation of loss. I am growing increasingly proprietary and am resentful of the invasions of schoolchildren with their exuberant irreverence.

"A pirate gun!"

"Look, a grenade!"

For architect Raymond Moriyama, the stakes in designing a museum that could express "the contradictions and ambiguities of war and sacrifice" and compel visitors "to think hard about themselves, the nation, and the world" were high.[18] Moriyama and his family were among the 22,000 Canadian residents of Japanese descent—most of whom were born in Canada—who were labelled "enemy aliens," rounded up, and sent to internment camps in the aftermath of Japan's 1941 attack on Pearl Harbor. After refusing to abandon his pregnant wife and three children to go to an all-male work camp, Moriyama's father was arrested by RCMP officers and held as a prisoner of war. Moriyama, his mother, and sisters were interned for two years at a camp in Slocan, British Columbia, where Moriyama's mother miscarried. Moriyama was twelve when he entered the camp.

In Search of a Soul, Moriyama's personal account of conceiving, designing, and building the new Canadian War Museum, is a testament to the complexity of not only the museum's physical architecture but also Moriyama's ideological, pedagogical, and spiritual vision. The museum's design and

Moriyama's memoir both reflect his overarching focus on regeneration and reconciliation. The reconciliation Moriyama seeks to evoke through his animated architecture is not a simple one. "My objective," Moriyama writes, "is to make [visitors] think, to question, to go through an emotional and physical process and arrive, hopefully, at rebirth."[19] Through a "complex system of [jagged] tilting planes that collide with one another, some at dramatic angles, others with almost imperceptible subtlety," Moriyama intentionally sets out to provoke unease.[20] Unlike dominant elegiac tropes of military commemoration, through this architectural evocation of precarity Moriyama works to construct a memorial that stages an encounter, not with nationalistic heroism but with the disorienting ambiguity of our "half-guilt and half-innocence" as national subjects.[21]

Sociologist Avery Gordon suggests that we live in a world in which the presence of the past lingers and seethes—a world that is ghosted by the "lost subjects of history."[22] Haunting, Gordon explains, is "the way of the ghost," the means through which the "not there" of an "occluded and forgotten past" is collectively and cross-temporally animated.[23] From the first time I entered the museum, Moriyama's architecture had an unsettling effect on me. But my time spent in Memorial Hall (Figures 14 and 15) marked my first truly contemplative engagement with the museum's evocative architecture and the lost subjects of history it called forth.

I did not discover Memorial Hall until my third trip to Ottawa and my seventh visit to the museum.[24] This is likely because on prior visits I spent the bulk of my time shadowing (in what I hope was a not-too-creepy way) groupings of children as they made their way through the museum's galleries. Off the beaten track of the main galleries, Memorial Hall is hidden in plain sight in a corner of the museum's main foyer. A nine-by-nine-metre enclosed concrete cube (Figure 14) that can only be accessed through a dimly lit triangular antechamber, it is easily overlooked as part of Moriyama's war-torn architecture.

In his memoir, Moriyama asks, "Can architecture itself be an exhibit?"[25] While I believe it can, had it not been for my repeated visits to the War Museum, the performative power of Moriyama's architecture with its messages of precarity, ambiguity, and loss cemented into its lilting walls, its weighty sinking ceilings, and its jagged surfaces would have been lost on me. I attribute this to several factors. First, to a lack of architectural literacy on my part—a lack that I suspect is shared by many of the war museum's mostly young visitor population. This factor could easily be overcome in a number of ways: the museum could integrate explanatory panels that bring attention to some of Moriyama's architectural features; information about the museum's architecture could be included among the teacher and student resources that the museum makes available online; the museum could offer architectural tours; the museum's gift shop could stock Moriyama's book; and the museum's extensive research department (which produces many of the books that are carried in its gift shop) could produce a pamphlet about the museum's architecture. As I will discuss in Chapter 4, the Canadian War Museum's dearth of information about Moriyama and the symbolism of the building's architecture starkly contrasts the Canadian Museum for Human Rights' exalted celebration of its architect, Antoine Predock, and the iconography of its building.

A second factor that interferes with the potential of Moriyama's architectural vision can be illustrated through an example. Without consulting either Moriyama or any members of his architectural team, the War Museum's directors made the decision "to install a floor tile in the Foyer and other public areas to improve the [museum's] look.'"[26] Moriyama writes: "The floor was to have been finished in grey motley concrete patterned to point in the direction of the Peace Tower; large, black, elongated triangular concrete patterns at strategic locations would have intensified the sense of compression one experiences on entering the Foyer. The decision to add floor tiles had a seriously negative impact on the symbolic and visual strength of the Foyer and other public areas."[27]

This example suggests that one reason the Canadian War Museum's architecture does not function as an exhibit is because its decision-making (or influencing) stakeholders do not treat it as one. Moriyama did not design the museum to look good or "to be loved."[28] Nor did he design it as an inert white box to serve as a blank backdrop for the museum's narration of Canadian military history. Moriyama's dilapidated, weighty, and disorienting architecture was intended to evoke the trauma of war's impact both on the battlefield and in centres of civilian population. But as Rukszto argues, "the relationship between the [museum's] architecture and [its] exhibition[s are] ill-fitting, compromised by divergent pedagogical goals."[29] Whereas the symbolism Moriyama poured into his jagged war-torn concrete vision was in keeping with remembrance "enacted as a *difficult return*," the war museum's stakeholders were guided by a more strategic approach to educating children about Canada's military history. The museum's emphasis on a military history grounded in Canadian national mythologies of unified multiculturalism and benevolent militarism works against the kind of critical engagement that

Moriyama endeavoured to provoke through his architecture. Overshadowed by the Canadian War Museum's pedagogical mandate, Moriyama's affectively animating architecture is reduced to a spectacular backdrop and bunker-like warehouse for the museum's exhibits and a delivery system for the museum's more instrumentalist memorial pedagogy.

The Canadian War Museum, Part 3: Museum as "Contact Zone"

In addition to being a product of the increased influence of Canada's growing military-cultural memory network, the war museum's expansive new digs and its phenomenal architectural design also reflect a broader shift in museology that has taken place over the past three decades. Emblematic of what museum scholar Ruth Phillips calls the "second museum age," the Canadian War Museum is part of a global twenty-first-century museum renaissance that in Canada has seen the construction of museums that are "spectacles of architectural virtuosity" designed to "bring major economic benefits to Canadian cities."[30]

Characterized by a "new museology" approach "that promotes education over research, engagement over doctrine, and multivocality over connoisseurship," the second museum age is a move away from the museum as a temple of knowledge and toward the museum as an inclusionary and collaborative "contact zone."[31] Through its use of interactive methodologies, the new museum does more than engage its visitors in a collaborative process. Visitors are cast as actors in the process of what performance studies scholar Rebecca Schneider calls "making belief."[32] Through the process of trying on military uniforms, running through faux trenches, playing First and Second World War online "adventure" games, and proffering pre-scripted (multiple-choice) opinions, the museum's young charges are enlisted in the construction of an ideology of a pluralistic Canadian nationalism founded in benevolent militarism.

In "Neocolonial Collaboration: Museum as Contact Zone Revisited," Robin Boast critically examines the celebratory ways museum scholars, directors, and curators have taken up the concept of the museum as a "contact zone." In his influential 1997 essay, "Museums as Contact Zones," James Clifford reflected on a particular interaction with Tlingit Elders who were consulted by the Portland Museum of Art to provide information about artifacts in the museum's collection. He wrote: "What the museum thought was going on was an elucidation of additional context and information that would enrich the collection. What the people representing the Tlingit were doing was much broader. The objects represented, for them, 'ongoing stories of struggle,' an opportunity to remind the museum of its responsibilities over its stewardship of clan objects, and an appeal to the museum to be accountable in ways that went beyond 'mere preservation' and contextualization."[33]

Boast argues that post-Clifford descriptions of the museum as contact zone paint an overly rosy picture of the contemporary museum as a space of transcultural exchange and dialogue. What Clifford was describing was less an orchestrated and mutual exchange and more a performed "détournement" of the museum as a temple of Western knowledge. Coined by the French Situationists, *détournement* refers to a kind of hijacking—or detouring—of a dominant media representation. Through their use of oral history and storytelling, the Tlingit Elders gave the Portland Museum's curators more than they asked for when they requested "information" about archival objects in its collection. Refusing to adhere to the dominant and dominating logic of archival knowledge production, the Tlingit Elders used the objects to reveal how past and present "inter(in)animate" one another.[34] Theirs was not an exercise in archeological cataloguing strategically undertaken toward the securing of "harmonious social relations."[35] Rather, it was a modelling of remembrance as difficult return, wherein stories of the dead are brought into the here and now in order to unbecome dominant social memory.

While Clifford proposed that the contact zone could serve as a model for de-centring and democratizing museums, museum scholar Tony Bennett argues that in practice, the contact zone has become "an instrument of governmentality, expressed as multiculturalism."[36] Boast similarly asserts that the real lesson of the contact zone is that in the process of setting up a system of pluralistic exchange, it frequently masks the asymmetrical power relations that ensure that control remains in the hands of the museum and the museum's key political and economic stakeholders. I propose that the commanding roles played by the Canadian government, Veterans Affairs Canada, the Department of National Defence, and other military-cultural memory network stakeholders in the construction of the Canadian War Museum's overarching mandate reflect what Boast calls "the dark underbelly of the contact zone."[37] Some overt examples of the power of the war museum's military memory network stakeholders include the vetoing of plans for a permanent Holocaust exhibit within the museum, the overriding of Moriyama's foyer design plans, and the successful bid to change to the museum's representation of the Second World War Bomber Command display.

In some cases—like the aborted Holocaust exhibit and the Bomber Command display—the influence of this stakeholder network is made visible through its generation of public controversy. In other cases—such as the changes to the museum's foyer design—the role, if any, played by Canada's broader network of military-cultural memory stakeholders is less clear. As Fremeth suggests, this is in part the brilliance of how the network functions. Because it is not a simple top-down structure, its influence is not always traceable, and its activities often look like grassroots advocacy on the part of a particular group of citizen stakeholders. I will return to the slipperiness of this network's influence later in this chapter in my discussion of the museum's final exhibit—*The Savage Wars of Peace.* Like Boast, I am concerned not only with overt examples of control over museum content but also with how the contact zone can mask less observable but "far more fundamental asymmetries, appropriations, and biases."[38] In an instrumentalist celebration of unified multicultural nationalism, the Canadian War Museum strategically deploys the contact zone as an interactive, pluralistic meeting ground. Many voices, one nation—held together through the self-sacrifice of the nation's benevolent militarists.

The task of making the history of Canadian militarism palatable to a broad range of children and youth, whose attention spans have been shaped by interactive multimedia saturation, requires a range of techniques of engagement. In keeping with its new spectacularly expansive home, the Canadian War Museum dusted off its old-museology approach to imparting military history when it moved from the old location on Sussex Drive. While military historians are welcome to visit the museum's Military History Research Centre with its archive of 500,000 military-related objects, for the general public the museum serves its carefully constructed multicultural Canadian military education through an engaging range of interactive and media-savvy exhibits, accompanied by sound-bite explanatory display panels.

Just as the Royal Canadian Air Force veterans who so vehemently challenged the narrative of *The Valour and the Horror* also recognized the effectiveness of docudrama as a method "of populariz[ing] the past and mak[ing] it aesthetically pleasing for the public and, in particular, for youth who had trouble relating to military history," war museum stakeholders have integrated docudrama audio narratives and oral histories into many of their exhibits.[39] Similarly, many of the museum's on-site and online displays also use a form of interactive docudrama. For example, in the online First World War "adventure" game "Over the Top," actors perform readings of trench warfare scenarios that enlisted players must then respond to by selecting from the pre-scripted multiple-choice options. Wrong choices—like removing one's helmet to use as a stepstool to help retrieve a pack of cigarettes from no-man's-land—result in the email delivery (to the player) of an imitation telegraph death notice addressed to one's faux parents. Performance is used as both entertainment and an affective delivery system through which the museum conveys its message of Canadian multicultural nationalism that is born of, and reliant on, a strong military.

Interestingly, though the majority of the museum's exhibits engage new museology's interactive approaches, in the two exhibits I discuss in the following sections—the opening exhibit focused on "First Peoples," and the closing exhibit on Canada's "peacekeeping" missions to Rwanda and Somalia—there is no invitation to interact. The First Peoples exhibit adopts an old-museology natural history approach, with its use of diorama-like exhibits, and a spectacular video montage projected onto three massive screens and narrated by children dominates the museum's final "peacekeeping" exhibit.

If the Canadian War Museum has gleaned tactical approaches from new museology's handbook, in its layout it appears to have borrowed from IKEA's retail-marketing floor plan. The museum's four main galleries—Battleground: Wars on Our Soil: Earliest Times to 1885; For Crown and Country: South African and First World War, 1885–1931; Forged in Fire: Second World War, 1931–1945; and A Violent Peace: The Cold War, Peacekeeping and Recent Conflicts, 1945 to the Present—are devoid of easily accessed exits or straight aisles through which one can walk quickly. While visitors can choose to skip a gallery in its entirety, once they enter one, the only way out is through it. Each gallery is a serpentine maze designed to bring visitors into face-to-display-contact with the museum's myriad of exhibits. Throughout the journey, visitors are kept busy taking in displays, reading brief explanatory plaques, pressing buttons, answering quizzes, listening to dramatized audio docu-narratives, watching museum-produced mini docudramas, and playing games. So busy, in fact, that they may be unaware of the ghosts that abound.

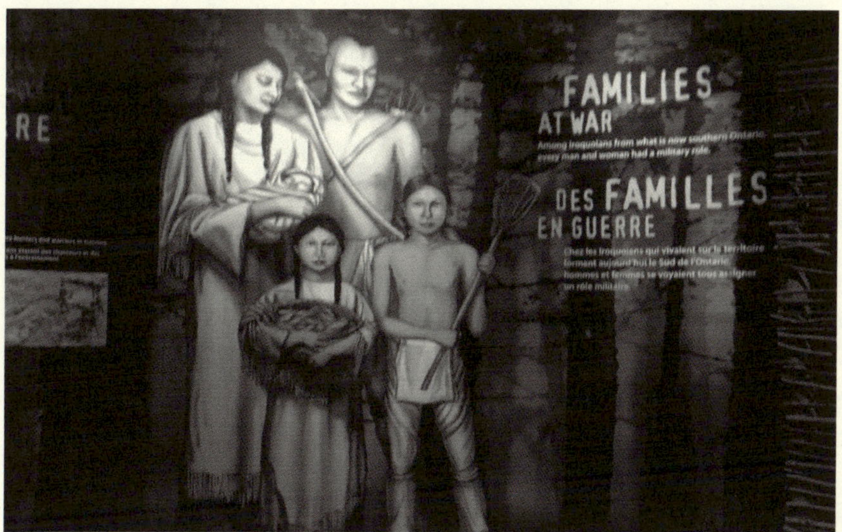

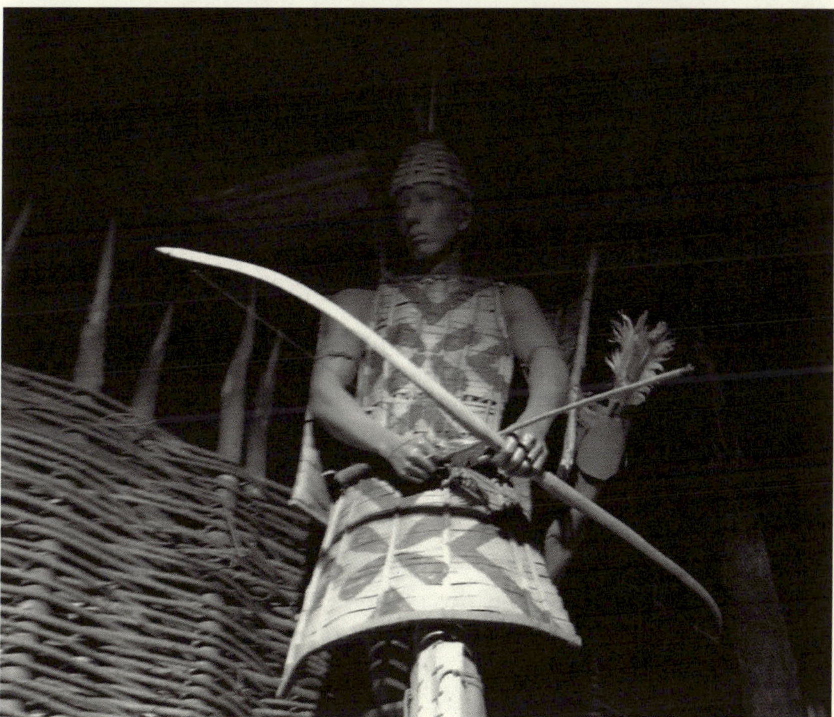

Figures 16 and 17. Images from the opening display in the Canadian War Museum exhibit *Wars on Our Soil: Earliest Times to 1885.*

GHOST STORY 1:
Colonialism in the "Contact Zone"

4 May 2013
Canadian War Museum, Ottawa: Battleground: Wars on Our Soil: Earliest Times to 1885 gallery
Entering the museum's first gallery I feel an uncanny disconnect. Have I taken a wrong turn, somehow crossed the river and landed in Gatineau's Museum of Civilization? In front of me is a mural. The scene is eerily bucolic. The backdrop is a forest of black trees silhouetted against a haze-green sky. In the foreground stands a family. Mom holds a swaddled infant. Dad, standing slightly behind, has a bow and a quiver of arrows slung over his shoulders. In front of Mom and Dad are a girl—holding a basket of corn—and a boy—wielding a lacrosse stick. Like Mom, the girl is covered shoulder to toe in a fringed deerhide dress. Like Dad, the boy is bare-chested and wears a breechclout draped over deerhide pants. Mom and Dad gaze lovingly at their children. It is the girl and boy who face the museum visitors. It is their eyes we look into.

Except for the props, clothing, and hair—a dark strip in the centre of Dad's otherwise-shaved head, and braids for Mom, daughter, and son—this could be the quintessential Hallmark image of a Canadian-nuclear-family-in-the-wilderness. Incongruously, then, next to this happy-family portrait is large oozy-yellow text that reads "Families at War" (Figure 16). And below, in smaller white font: "In Iroquoian communities in what is now southern Ontario, every man and woman had a military role."

Is this what the girl and boy are communicating with their stern, not-quite-happy gazes? That war is imminent and we all have no choice but to take part? These children have none of young Warren's plucky momentum. They are not the protagonists of military adventures in faraway places. The museum's display informs us that for Iroquoian communities in pre-contact Canada, war was a way life. Moreover, it suggests to visitors not only that the familiar Western nuclear family is at the heart of Iroquoian life, but also that the family is essential to war's re-production.

Above and to the left, on a ledge constructed of wooden stakes that extend over the gallery's entrance, stands a mannequin (Figure 17). His skin is an odd grey hue. He wears shin guards, a breastplate, a frontal skirt-like shield, and a cone-shaped hat—armour made of thick flat grass woven around wooden splints and painted with ochre dye. He holds a bow and arrow—not drawn, but with arrow notched at the ready. Like the two-dimensional adults in the mural, his gaze is averted—signalling that he is not part of our world; he is of another time and place. Explanation for his hovering presence is communicated through a display panel with a quote attributed to the eighteenth-century Kahnawà:ke Mohawk chief, Tecaughretanego: "The art of war consists in ambushing and surprising our enemies, and in preventing them from ambushing and surprising us."

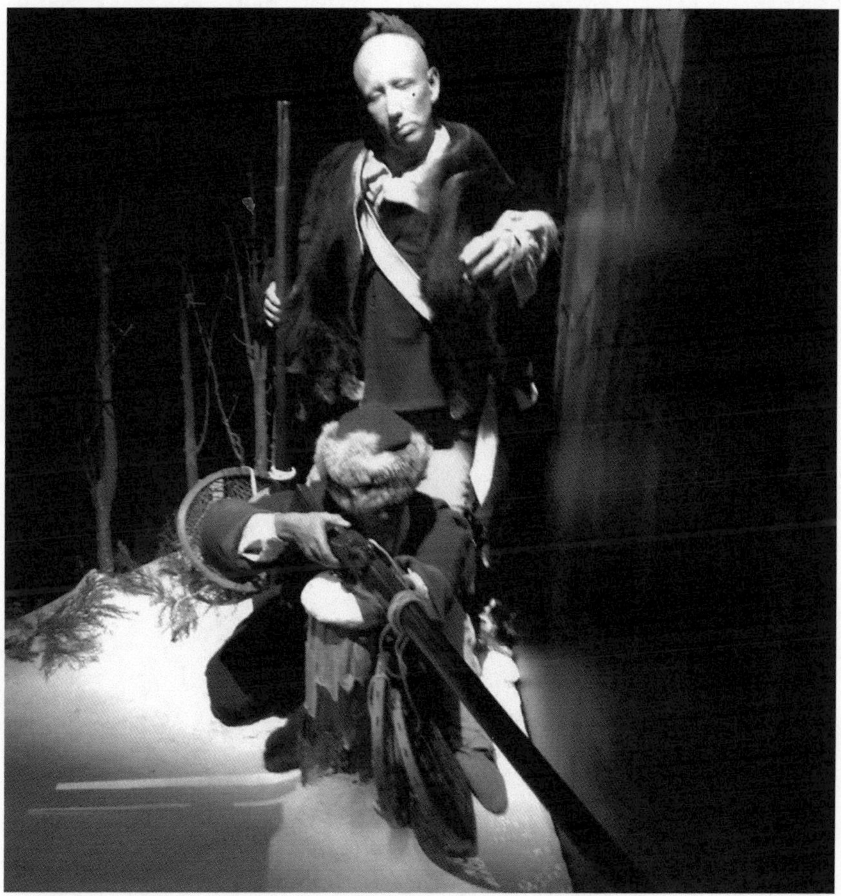

Figure 18. *Comrades in Arms.*

Two small images are also part of the display. One is of an Iroquoian village with rows of longhouses ringed by protective palisades set in front of a field of crops, and a second of warriors approaching through the woods. The exhibit's supplementary text explains that the two sections of the exhibit illustrate an "Iroquoian community in peacetime and under attack" and that the two best-known of the Iroquoian groups—the Huron League and the Iroquoian Confederacy—"fought a long war over control of hunting grounds north of the St. Lawrence."

Having established that the Iroquois were a warring people who had fought among themselves long before the arrival of the French and the British, and that the family is foundational to the workings of war, the exhibit's narrative moves on. A new diorama has two more grey-hued mannequins. One is an Ojibwa warrior, the other, a French militiaman (Figure 18). The Frenchman crouches in the snowy landscape. He rests his matchlock musket on a tree stump and takes aim along its long wooden barrel. The Ojibwa warrior stands behind and above him, his musket at rest in one hand while the other points yonder. The display tells us that the two are allies in the war against the Iroquois League. It also tells us that the Ojibwa warrior is "teaching" the Frenchman about warfare and that it is the Ojibwa warrior who "speaks," the Frenchman who "listens." We have entered the militarized world of men and masculine camaraderie.

I wonder if the museum's positioning of the Ojibwa warrior standing above the squatting Frenchman is an unacknowledged reference to historical debates and struggles that played out over the Samuel de Champlain monument that stands just kilometres away on Nepean Point, where the "Father of New France" overlooks Parliament Hill. Installed in 1915 to commemorate the 300th anniversary of Champlain's second voyage on the Ottawa River, the original monument depicted a larger-than-life Champlain atop a pedestal. Two years later its creator, Hamilton MacCarthy, was commissioned to amend the monument by adding a life-size bronze of an anonymous Anishinaabe scout onto a plinth at its the base.

Like the museum's Ojibwa warrior mannequin, MacCarthy's bronze scout is pointing. Unlike the museum's comrades in arms, however, the positioning of Champlain and the Anishinaabe scout do not convey a relationship of equitable camaraderie. "It is clear that the scout was executed on a much smaller scale," writes Cherokee Nation art historian Lara Evans, "and is in fact physically dwarfed by Champlain in addition to being placed quite near to ground level in comparison to the approximately sixteen feet of pedestal which elevates Champlain's bronze figure."[40] In 1997, then chief of the Assembly of First Nations Ovide Mercredi led a bid to remove the scout from his subservient position at Champlain's feet. The "Indian scout" was relocated to Ottawa's Major's Hill Park in 1999 leaving Champlain to reign solo atop his pedestal overlooking the Ottawa River.

Both prior to and since the scout's relocation, the Champlain monument has been a site of critical creative intervention into Canada's settler-colonial iconography. In the early 1990s urban-Iroquois artist-curator Jeff Thomas began using photography to interrogate the monument and Canada's romanticized representations of "Indians" as a people forever located in a vanishing past. In a 1998 photograph taken before the scout was moved, Thomas's son Bear sits in front of the nameless kneeling Anishinaabe warrior (Figure 19). Bear and the scout occupy the foreground of the photograph's frame. All that remains of Champlain are the disembodied raised letters of his name on the monument's pedestal. With his framing, Thomas performs a reverse eviction, dispossessing Champlain of his privileged location while securing the territory for Bear and the scout.

Just as the bronze scout is iconically cast in a romanticized past that exists outside the frame of the present, his gaze is also directed to a horizon beyond the image's frame. Bear, on the other hand, looks unflinchingly at the viewer from behind his sunglasses. He is the image's mediator. In contrast with the scout's bare chest, Bear wears a sweatshirt with an altered image of three nineteenth-century Plains Indians printed onto it. Like him, they wear shades from behind which they direct their equally unflinching gazes. The acronym FBI is printed above the image, and beneath, the text "Full Blooded Indian."[41] With his composition Thomas defies the bronze fixedness of settler Canada's monumentalized first contact memory, instead creating a "jarringly urban and contemporary challenge to the image of the breechclothed scout."[42]

After the scout was no longer part of the Champlain monument, Thomas began using the vacated plinth as a site of critical intervention. In 2000, Thomas invited Kanyen'kehak and French artist Greg Hill to place a canoe Hill had constructed of cardboard cereal boxes onto the plinth and to then pose inside it wearing "the traditional Onkwehonwe *gustoweh* headdress" that he had also constructed of cereal boxes (Figure 20).[43] Also as part of his "Seize the Space" Champlain series (2000–11), Thomas continued to photograph friends posing with the monument and then inviting them to

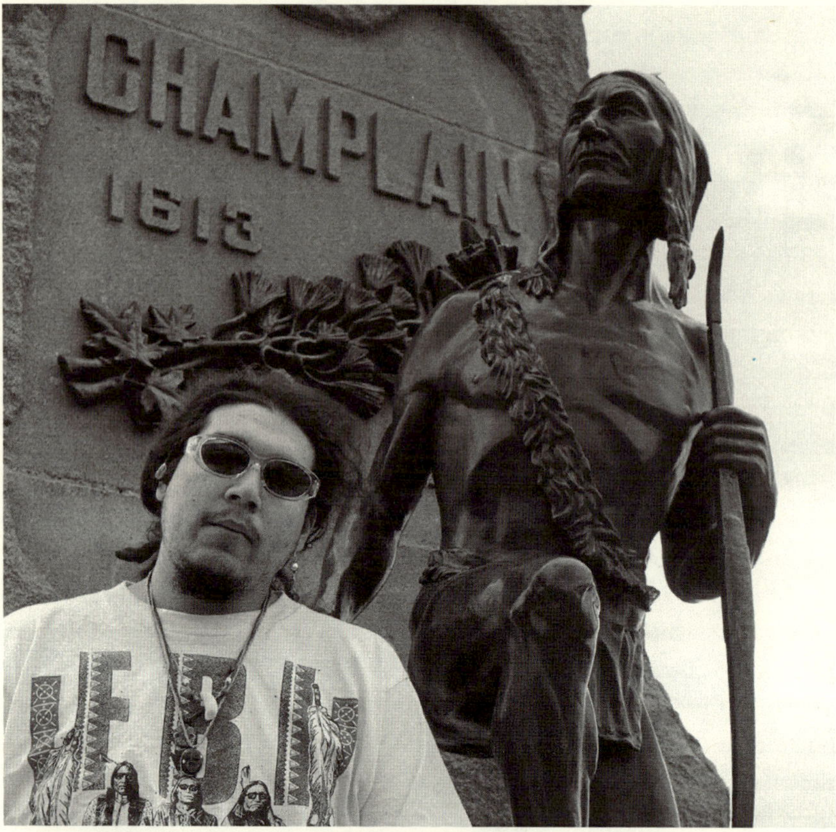

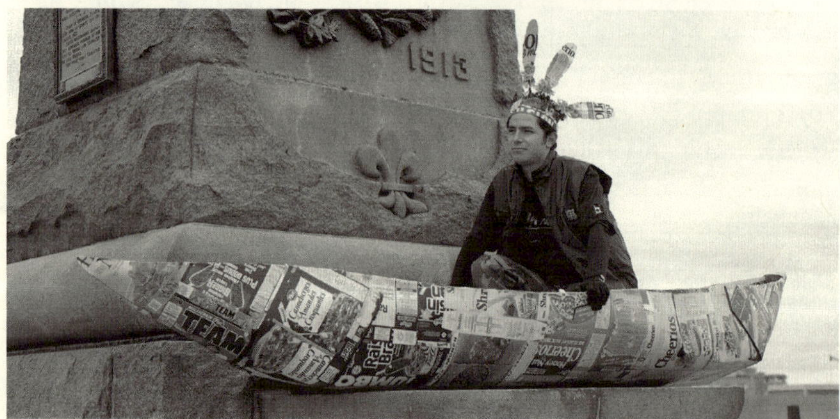

Figure 19. *F.B.I.* (1998), by Jeff Thomas.
Figure 20. *Seize the Space: Greg Hill in His Canoe, Nepean Point, Ottawa* (2000), by Jeff Thomas.

write about their experience.[44] Through his photographic engagement with settler Canada's monumental iconography, curator and art historian Richard William Hill (Cree) writes, "[Thomas] meets the narrow didacticism of the monument with a pedagogy of his own, turning the monument into a vehicle for a process of critically engaged thinking about power and representation."[45]

While the Canadian War Museum may be commended for its decision not to replicate the imperial power dynamics of the original Champlain monument, it fails to make visible the critical role of Indigenous communities in challenging those representations. Instead, the museum uses more equitably positioned mannequins to paint a reductively uncomplicated picture of a respectful and reciprocal relationship between the French and their First Peoples allies; a relationship of two peoples united through shared interests and shared enemies. It is through their trading of "tactics and technology," the display tells us, that the First Peoples and the French survived the "post-contact wars."

Somehow, in the course of a few short steps on the museum's meandering path, we are transported from the pre-contact wars of Iroquoian communities to post-contact wars fought by a French–First Peoples alliance. In the contact zone of the Canadian War Museum there is little mention of contact wars. Here, there is only the early "long war" of the Huron League and the Iroquoian Confederacy, and the post-contact wars in which the "Algonkians, Iroquois from Kahnawake and Kanesatake, Hurons, and the French formed a powerful alliance that fought the Iroquois League until 1701 and the British until 1760." Here, displays celebrate a transcultural exchange between the First Peoples and the French of all manner of expertise, equipment, and other accoutrements—tomahawks, muskets, snowshoes, moccasins, canoes, beads, furs, European textiles.

Though throughout most of its galleries the war museum embraces new museology approaches—like interactive displays—these opening dioramas and diorama-like exhibits are an old-museology throwback. Most often associated with natural history museums, dioramas have historically been used, as Ho-Chunk anthropologist Amy Lonetree argues in *Decolonizing Museums: Representing Native America in National and Tribal Museums*, to "fix [Indigenous] cultures in a romanticized, static past."[46] By presenting Canada's First Peoples in this kind of "evolution-oriented" model, the museum reinforces the "vanishing Indian" stereotype.[47] Together with representations that show the land as a vast and relatively uninhabited wilderness, the portrayal of Indigenous populations as a dying race helped to legitimate European encroachment and to mask the brutality of the colonization of the Americas. In the national mythology of white settler societies, as Razack asserts, "Aboriginal peoples are presumed mostly dead or assimilated. European settlers thus *become* the original inhabitants and the group most entitled to the fruits of citizenship."[48] The denial of European conquest and colonization supports Canada's unbecoming national mythology that "ours" was a nation that was "peacefully settled and not colonized."[49]

With its dioramic allusions to the vanishing Indian, the museum's portrayal of a reciprocal relationship between the First Peoples and the French takes on new meaning. If Canada's First Peoples are cast as part of a dying culture, then the French—with their sharing of modernity's miraculous bounty of metals, guns, beads, and cloth—become benevolent rescuers who help usher their allies into a new age. While the museum glosses over the colonial violence of the British–First Peoples relationship, their portrayal of the early contact between Canada's French and Indigenous populations is almost celebratory. As one display unequivocally sums up the French–First Peoples encounter: "Neither side dominated the other; both First Peoples and the French remained *entirely* independent."[50] To confirm that this feeling of mutuality was a shared perspective, the museum offers these words from an unnamed seventeenth-century Abenaki chief: "Know that the Frenchman is my brother . . . we dwell in the same cabin at two fires, he is at one fire and I am at the other fire." The one exception that the museum makes to its discourse of harmonious exchange is to note that in addition to their alliance, the French also brought with them "epidemics and new technologies that disrupted the balance of power among First Peoples groups."

While a central tenet of new museology's contact zone is the production of multi-vocal exhibits curated in collaboration with community representatives, the Indigenous voices that are included in Canadian War Museum are largely those of the dead. As in other forms of military commemoration, these dead are not called on to speak on their own behalf or on behalf of their communities. Rather, they are enlisted by, and put in service to, the nation. Unlike Jeff Thomas's photographic interventions into settler Canada's monumental iconography, or the narrative interventions performed by the Tlingit Elders in their consultations with curators at the Portland Museum of Art, neither Tecaughretanego's words nor those of the unnamed Abenaki chief are used as a means of inter(in)animating past and present in such a way as to remind the museum and its visitors of their responsibilities in regards to the ongoing struggles of Indigenous Peoples in Canada. Nor does the museum provide any context for how the words of these Indigenous leaders from centuries past became part of its Canadian military archive. Instead, the inclusion of their words is used to support the museum's narrative of a long-standing multicultural nationalism that has been, and continues to be, made possible through militarism.

Having been brought into modernity's fold by the French, the First Peoples' military history need no longer languish in the dioramas of a vanished culture. Across the snaking aisle from our Ojibwa and French comrades, on a flat-screen monitor, a video montage shows us images of "First Peoples warriors, soldiers, sailors, and air force personnel" who have "from the beginnings of war in Canada up to the twenty-first century . . . shaped Canada and the world." In the course of a few twists and turns of the gallery, Canada's First Peoples have time-travelled 5,000 years and are now fully integrated into Canada's contemporary military and the museum's modern display technologies.

Later in the exhibit, a small series of display panels accompanied by maps briefly addresses Britain's colonizing of Vancouver Island (1849) and British Columbia (1858). (Interestingly, this is the only time the museum uses the term colonization in relation to either Canada's First Peoples or to the founding of Canada as a nation-state.) "The Prairies" also have their moment with a panel titled "Settlement and Accommodation" that explains: "In 1870, First Peoples controlled the Prairies. By 1880, Canadian settlers dominate the region." While the display makes no mention of the role of the emergent Canadian state in dispossessing Indigenous communities of their land or of Indigenous Peoples' resistance to the incursion of these settlers, it does acknowledge that "many First Peoples resented the Canadian settlers." Despite these resentments, however, the museum assures us that the First Peoples of the Prairies "worked to convert their economies from hunting to farming [and] relied upon negotiations to resolve their differences with Ottawa." Manitoba is allotted its own panels. After crediting Louis Riel and the Métis with securing Manitoba (from the Hudson's Bay Company) for Canada, the next panel explains that Métis and Native grievances led to an insurrection in the Northwest to which Ottawa dispatched 8,000 regular and militia troops. Over 100 died in the battle and Riel was hung for treason, "an act," the museum informs its visitors, "which severely damaged *linguistic* relations in Canada."[51]

In addition to the regression to an old-museology approach, two things stand out about the museum's First Peoples exhibits: first, the limited space allotted to the colonial encounters the French and the British had with Canada's First Peoples; and second, the haunting absences within the narrative the museum constructs of this encounter. The gallery Battleground: Wars on Our Soil: Earliest Times to 1885 purports to cover "First Peoples Pre-Contact Conflicts (over 5,000 years ago)"; "First Peoples' Contact with the French and the British"; the "Seven Years War"; and the "War of 1812." Yet in its entirety, it is less than one-third the size of each of the other three main galleries. And to the extent "contact" is addressed, it is predominantly in the context of alliance, reciprocity, and negotiation—not in terms of colonial aggression, land and resource appropriation, the dispossession of Indigenous Peoples from their lands, or Indigenous resistance.

Given the exalted narrative of French–First Peoples alliances, I found the absence anywhere in the museum of an exhibit addressing the 1990 Oka Crisis to be a glaring and simultaneously understandable omission. The "seventy-eight-day armed Indigenous resistance to land expropriation" was, in Mohawk anthropologist Audra Simpson's words, "the most recent act of 'domestic warfare' in [Canada's] Indian-settler relations to date."[52] The Oka Crisis tells a very different story of the French and First Peoples, or in a broader sense, of colonial-Indigenous relationships than the one the museum puts forth. The historical roots of the Oka confrontation took place 150 years before Confederation, when the French aristocracy appropriated land west of Montreal that was part the Kanehsatà:ke and Kahnawà:ke Mohawk territory and gave it to a group of Catholic priests. In 1990, months after a land claim filed by the Kanehsatà:ke was rejected for failing to meet legal requirements, the mayor of Oka announced that a golf course and resort expansion would extend onto Kanehsatà:ke territory and Mohawk burial grounds. A blockade was set up that became a twentieth-century rallying point for Indigenous sovereignty struggles in Canada. It also became a highly militarized site when "2,650 regular and reserve troops from the Thirty-Fourth and Thirty-Fifth Brigade Groups and the Fifth Canadian Mechanized Brigade Group" were brought in to put an end to the protests.[53] As Razack notes, "without a trace of irony" Canadian military historians J.L. Granatstein and David J. Bercuson argue that the "unique skills possessed by Canadian peacekeepers [were] honed while subduing Canada's native populations, most recently at the siege of Oka."[54]

When Raymond Moriyama travelled across Canada to seek input for his architectural design, he had this to say of his meetings with Indigenous communities: "Many of them were very interested in the museum, though many also feared their stories would be ignored. I assured them that would not be the case. Some were cynical, and for a few, the idea of inclusion was a distant fantasy. Some may have considered me an Uncle Tom."[55] Based on the museum's limited real-estate allotment to Canada's First Peoples, the absence of any discussion of colonial violence, and the near absence of Indigenous voices in the museum, it appears the cynicism Moriyama encountered was well placed. Perhaps the reason Moriyama fears that he may have been seen as an "Uncle Tom" by some Indigenous community members was because although he was passionately committed to an architectural design that spoke the hard truths of war, the hard truths of Canadian colonialism were nowhere on his or the museum's agenda.

While it is a common Canadian truism that the country's identity as a nation on the global stage was forged in the First and the Second World Wars, it was the War of 1812 that was pitched under Stephen Harper's administration as Canada's new military multicultural origin story. This previously under-recognized origin story was roused through a $28 million Department of Canadian Heritage investment that funded a plethora of War of 1812 Bicentennial Commemoration events. Elements of the Canadian War Museum's celebrated special *War of 1812* exhibit, which ran from June 2012 through January 2013, have since been integrated into the museum's permanent galleries.[56] The number of War of 1812 aesthetic productions—operas, plays, festivals, exhibits, and re-enactments—and the funnelling of arts and culture funding dollars into "branches of the Department of Canadian Heritage" confirm the reality of what Canadian theatre studies scholar Alan Filewod asserts is a thin line between Canadian cultural nationalism and Canadian military nationalism.[57] The museum itself as well as its war art program and many of the video presentations that feature prominently in its exhibits are likewise supported through this kind of blurred line between arts and military funding categories.

Conspicuously absent from these battlefield-birth-of-the-nation narratives is the violence of settler colonialism. For example, though for many settler Canadians the Oka Crisis may have appeared as "an exceptional 'event,'" it was, Simpson argues, "deeply structural." All we need to do, she writes, is "recall that settler colonialism requires an Indigenous elimination for territory."[58]

Not simply a denial of the historical encounter between uninvited European colonial occupiers and the Indigenous peoples for whom that encounter bore catastrophic effects, the erasure of Canada's violent colonial origins from dominant social memory and from Canadian military memory is integral to the continuing dispossession of Indigenous populations within Canada.

Though the Canadian War Museum is correct in its use of "First Peoples" as an umbrella term that includes First Nations, Métis, and Inuit, I propose that there is a correspondence between the absenting of Canada's violent colonial history and the absence of the terms First Nations and Indigenous from the museum's displays. Since the state is the governing body by which sovereignty is bestowed or legitimated, for the Canadian War Museum to include a First Nations perspective in Canadian military history would have necessitated including questions of sovereignty, treaty rights, and land claims. Likewise, since wars are understood as conflicts between nations, the refusal to recognize Indigenous peoples as having their own forms of nationhood enables the museum to frame European invasion of First Peoples' lands solely in terms of reciprocal trade and alliance.

Despite the generally accepted principle of "temporal priority"—or first come, first served—political science scholar Tom Flanagan asserts there should be an exception in relation to settler-European and Indigenous relationships in Canada.[59] While Flanagan concedes that it is undeniable that Indigenous populations occupied the land now known as Canada prior to the arrival of the French, the British, and subsequent waves of European settler populations, he nonetheless asserts that temporal priority only applies to "that form of political community we call 'the state.'"[60] If there were no states, France and Britain were not invading nations. In replacing French and British colonial violence with a tale of first contact as reciprocal alliance, the museum lays the foundation for its birth-of-the-multicultural-nation meta-narrative.

Similarly, though the term "Indigenous" is "embedded conceptually in a geographic alterity and a radical past as the Other in the history of the West,"[61] it also works to connect Canada's First Nations, Métis, and Inuit to a larger global movement engaged in legal and activist strategies of resistance to colonialism. In contemporary Canada, for example, unlike "First Peoples," "Indigenous" invokes the United Nations Declaration on the Rights of Indigenous Peoples (UNDRIP), the Truth and Reconciliation Commission of Canada's Call that the Government of Canada "fully adopt and implement" UNDRIP (Call 43), and Cree Member of Parliament Roméo Saganash's introduction of Bill C-262 calling on Canada to ensure that its laws are in full alignment with UNDRIP.

Performance studies scholar Diana Taylor argues that one of the mechanisms through which the archive produces, legitimates, and stores knowledge is through systems of classification or naming.[62] Within archival structures, how and what can be known depends on its being named. As a rhetorical act of exclusion, the decision by the Canadian War Museum not to use the terms First Nations or Indigenous in its exhibits conveniently disappears the historical and contemporary struggles for sovereignty of Indigenous peoples in Canada. The museum's absenting of language that rhetorically links Indigenous peoples to contemporary struggles for sovereignty and resistance to settler colonialism, together with its dioramic representations of the First Peoples' family, casts Canada's Indigenous into a past that predates contemporary notions of the nation-state before propelling them into a one-nation, many-voices, multicultural present.

By failing to bring its—mostly young—visitors face to face with the colonial violence on which Canadian settler nationalism is founded, the museum rejects the path of critical engagement and difficult return. Instead, it adopts an instrumentalist pedagogical approach that uses a multiculturalist discourse of national identity toward the production of a unifying Canadian identity grounded in national innocence. Moreover, in absenting colonial violence from its opening exhibit, the Canadian War Museum also sets the stage for an unfolding narrative of Canadian benevolent militarism and moral exceptionalism that crescendos to a climax in the museum's final exhibit, *The Savage Wars of Peace*, where Canada's celebrated role as a peacekeeping middle power is delivered with spectacular allure.

GHOST STORY 2: Rwanda and Somalia, the "Devils" and Martyrs of Canadian "Peacekeeping"

11 August 2012
Canadian War Museum, Ottawa:
The Savage Wars of Peace exhibit
The machete and the wooden club—with a crude metal dagger jutting from its end at a ninety-degree angle—appear to float of

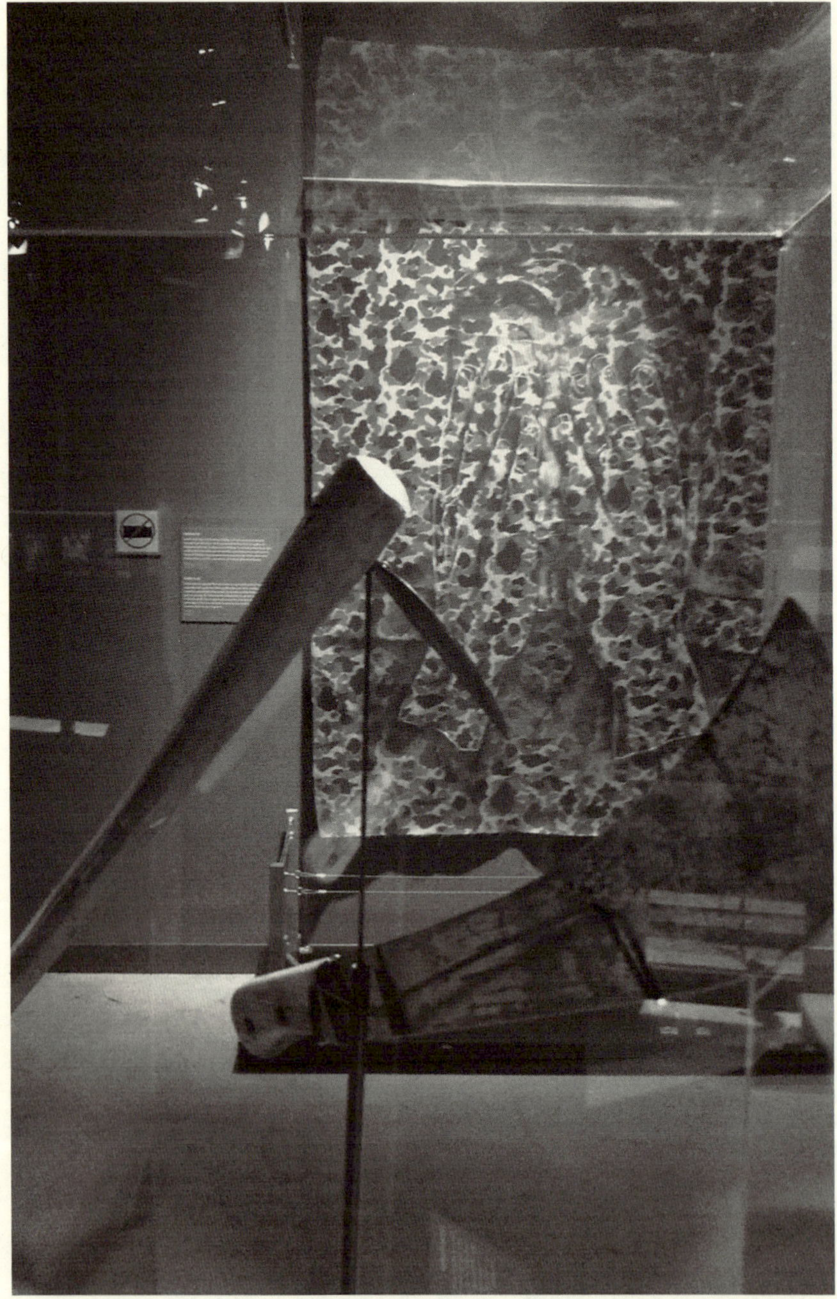

Figure 21. Weapons from the Rwandan genocide in front of *Dallaire #6*.

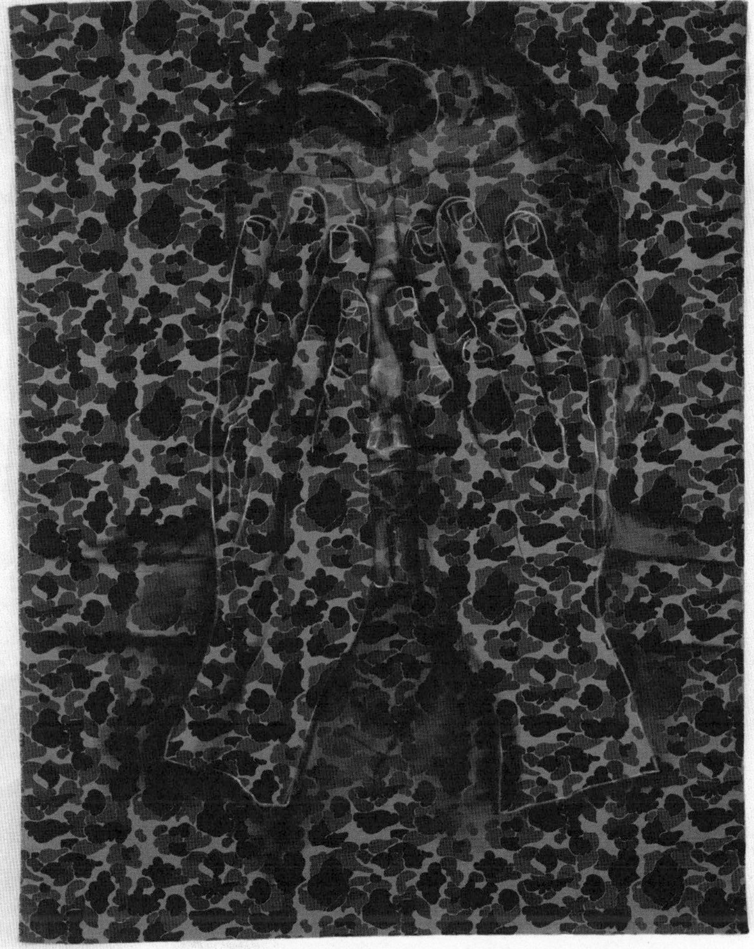

Figure 22. *Dallaire #6*, from the series Undone, by Gertrude Kearns.

their own accord (Figure 21). *Past these weapons of the Rwandan genocide, on the other side of their see-through enclosure, a painting acts as a backdrop* (Figure 22). *Thinking at first that it is a canvas completely covered in camouflage, I'm confused. But then, I make out the white painted outline of a man's face buried behind his camouflaged hands. A thin red cross etched into the lines of his forehead.*

Nearing the end of my two-and-a-half-kilometre trek of the Canadian War Museum's circuitous trail, I arrive at *The Savage Wars of Peace*, the final exhibit in the last (and largest) of the museum's four main galleries—A Violent Peace: The Cold War, Peacekeeping and Recent Conflicts, 1945 to the Present. Ahead, strung across the passageway leading to the gallery's exit, are three massive video screens with rows of empty benches in front of them. *The Savage Wars of Peace* occupies one large round room and comes with a trigger "WARNING," informing visitors that the video that dominates room—*My World: Hope and Peace*—"contains images of cruelty, violence, human suffering, and death, and may not be appropriate for all viewers."

The disappearance of the snaking trail, the WARNING, the dimmed lighting, the incessantly chaotic activation of the room by the video, and the absence of interactive displays—all signal a shift. We have left behind the war museum's new museology contact zones where children are invited to learn about Canada's pluralistic military history by listening to dramatized personal stories, playing "adventure" games, testing their knowledge through computer-generated multiple-choice quizzes, and touching weapons. As with the tomahawk and bow and arrow in the opening First Peoples exhibit, the weapons on display here—machete and club—are untouchable. These are not weapons deemed appropriate for children's hands or LeBreton banquet ambiance. These are not the weapons of contemporary nation-states. These are "other"-worldly weapons. Weapons of "tribal" conflicts, past and present.

If in the First Peoples exhibit the museum retreated to old museology's natural history methodology of static dioramic-like display, here in *The Savage Wars of Peace* the museum has adopted the spectacular approach of what James Der Derian has dubbed the "military-industrial-media-entertainment-network."[63] The video's cacophonous soundscape is an orchestrated mix of affect-generating cinematic scores juxtaposed with a news media mash-up that includes sound bites from politicians and newscasters, gunshots, explosions, sirens, shouts, screams, wailing. The only voices that speak directly to us are those of the video's child narrators. Just as we were ushered into the museum by the echoing image of ethereal young Warren and met in the opening exhibit by the unflinching gaze of Iroquoian brother and sister, now, prior to leaving, we are detained by the haunting and disembodied appeal of a chorus of children who speak the following refrains throughout *My World*:

My world started with hope, hope for peace, hope for life.
But my world was not free from war.
My world was filled with violence and death. My family was safe but my world was not.
My world is filled with heroes, they make choices too.
It's your world now, how does it start.

Each line is repeated three times in English, three times in French, each spoken by a child of a different age. Because the video's soundscape can be heard in neighbouring galleries, their ghostly appeal is unsettlingly familiar. The children's repeated phrases act as an affecting accent to the video's narrative arc as it progresses from the celebratory but fleeting "hope" of the fall of the Berlin Wall—*My world started with hope, hope for peace, hope for life*—to an increasingly frenetic audio and visual display of sites of global violence (most from the global south, some from Eastern Europe)—*But my world was not free from war*—that peaks with dramatically enlarged black-and-white photographs of ash-covered New Yorkers fleeing the World Trade Center—*My world was filled with violence and death. My family was safe but my world was not.* The video's final montage—*My world is filled with heroes, they make choices too*—is of Canadian "peacekeepers" patrolling war-damaged streets, carrying children, tending to the wounded, distributing food, and grieving fallen comrades. The video closes with the children's final interpellating appeal—*It's your world now, how does it start?*—then back to the beginning as the twelve-minute video loops throughout the day.

The video's erratic illuminations animate the machete, the dagger-club, and the man's face shrouded in camouflage. The painting—*Dallaire #6* by Gertrude Kearns (Figure 22)—is of Lieutenant-General Roméo Dallaire, commander of the failed United Nations (UN) mission to Rwanda in 1994. "Traumatized by the event, and by the international community's unwillingness to prevent it," the display explains, "General Dallaire became a passionate advocate of humanitarian intervention and the protection of children affected by war." *Dallaire #6* was part of Kearns's series *UNdone: Dallaire/Rwanda*, which exhibited at Toronto's Propeller Centre for the Visual Arts in 2002 and featured ten large-scale works painted onto camouflage fabric: four paintings depicting scenes of the Rwandan massacre and UN helplessness, and six portraits of Dallaire. Of the exhibit's reception, Razack writes: "Viewers of the exhibition congratulated Kearns in the gallery's book of comments for her depiction of what it is to be 'powerless in the face of colossal evil.'"[64]

While it is unlikely that most of the Canadian War Museum's visitors have seen *UNdone*, they are undoubtedly familiar with the story of Dallaire's traumatic encounter with his powerlessness in the face the "colossal evil" of the Rwandan genocide. Dallaire's story has been disseminated through a range of Canadian popular cultural productions, foremost among them being Dallaire's best-selling and award-winning memoir, *Shake Hands with the Devil: The Failure of Humanity in Rwanda* (2003), available in the museum's gift shop. There are also documentaries: *Witness the Evil* (1998), directed by Denise Withers and produced by the Department of National Defence; *The Unseen Scars: Post Traumatic Stress Disorder*, produced by CBC in 1998 and rebroadcast on numerous occasions since; *The Last Just Man* (2001), by Steven Silver; *Shake Hands with the Devil: The Journey of Roméo Dallaire* (2004), by Peter Raymont; and the 2007 Canadian feature film *Shake Hands with the Devil.* These are just a sampling of the multitude of popular media productions that feature Dallaire's story and are, at least in part, a product of what Fremeth calls the Canadian military-cultural memory network. Like Paul Gross's Canadian war epics *Passchendaele* (2008) and *Hyena Road* (2015), the multiple iterations of Dallaire's story by Canadian cultural producers reflect Canada's unique approach to "military entertainment" in conveying Canada's popularized national identity trademark as a nation of humanitarian militarists.

Through these and other popular media sources, Canadians have learned how Dallaire was called upon to lead the UN peacekeeping mission in Rwanda. How he desperately tried, but failed, to halt the unfolding genocide. How his hands were tied by "an inflexible UN Security Council mandate" and an indifferent world.[65] How he returned a broken man. How, suffering from PTSD, he attempted suicide. And how he emerged a "passionate advocate of humanitarian intervention." In her analysis of Canadian peacekeeper trauma narratives, Razack interrogates the way the suffering of "others" is transformed into spectacles for our national consumption and into opportunities "to contemplate our humanity."[66] This process of "stealing the pain of others," she argues, is "supported by a racial logic and a material system of white privilege" that, despite our much-celebrated multiculturalism, is deeply ensconced in Canada's white settler nationalism.[67] Put another way, whereas the "we" of Canadian identity and values—democracy, compassion, civility, humanitarianism—is, as Razack points out, understood as a "white category," the "they" who are in need of Canadian peacekeepers' compassionate and civilizing interventions are understood to be racialized "others."[68]

Just as the museum's material and institutionalized system of white privilege is demonstrated through its narrative of the European settlement of Canada existing almost entirely outside of the frame of European colonialism, it is similarly evident in the museum's construction of the Rwandan genocide as an "event" without context. The exhibit foregrounds Dallaire's suffering while simultaneously absenting any information about the long colonial history that produced the "Hutu and Tutsi as political identities of native and settler respectively."[69] By Dallaire's own admission, when he was appointed to command the UN peacekeeping mission in Rwanda he neither knew "where Rwanda was [nor] exactly what kind of trouble the country was in."[70] The fact that the UN Security Council would put someone who had no prior knowledge of Rwanda's geopolitical context—born of a history of colonialism—in charge of a peacekeeping mission reflects an institutionalized and structurally supported disavowal of the significance of the role of Western colonialism and imperialism in producing the conditions whereby contemporary global violence is made manifest. This disavowal is further amplified and disseminated through Dallaire's book and the documentaries and feature films that situate Dallaire as the martyred hero and portray the Rwandan genocide as a dramatic, bloody, and irrational descent into the barbaric realms of hell.

Whereas in the documentaries and films about Dallaire, the suffering of Rwandans is reduced to a spectacular backdrop for the story of Dallaire's heroic and selfless martyrdom, in the assemblage of artifacts that the museum has brought together for its final cathartic exhibit, all that remains of the Rwandans' suffering are their nightmarish weapons and a haunted Dallaire. There are no Rwandan voices in *The Savage Wars of Peace*. The Rwandan genocide is a story conveyed entirely from the perspective of Dallaire, the traumatized Canadian peacekeeper and courageous humanitarian. The video's chaotic soundscape and violent images serve to amplify a sense of the apocalyptic worlds into which Canadian peacekeepers heroically enter. In keeping with Dallaire's association of Rwanda as the place where he shook hands with the devil, the museum reproduces "a biblical narrative of a First World overwhelmed by the evil of the Third World."[71]

If the absenting of Canada's colonial history in the museum's First Peoples exhibit contributes to a narrative of multicultural nationalism that came about as the result of peaceful European settlement, here in *The Savage Wars of Peace*, the erasure of colonialism from its Canadian peacekeeping narratives serves several intersecting purposes. First, it helps produce a narrative of Canada as a morally superior humanitarian military middle power. Second, it reproduces colonial narratives of Africa as a barbaric "heart of darkness," in need of the civilizing intervention of benevolent Western nations like Canada.

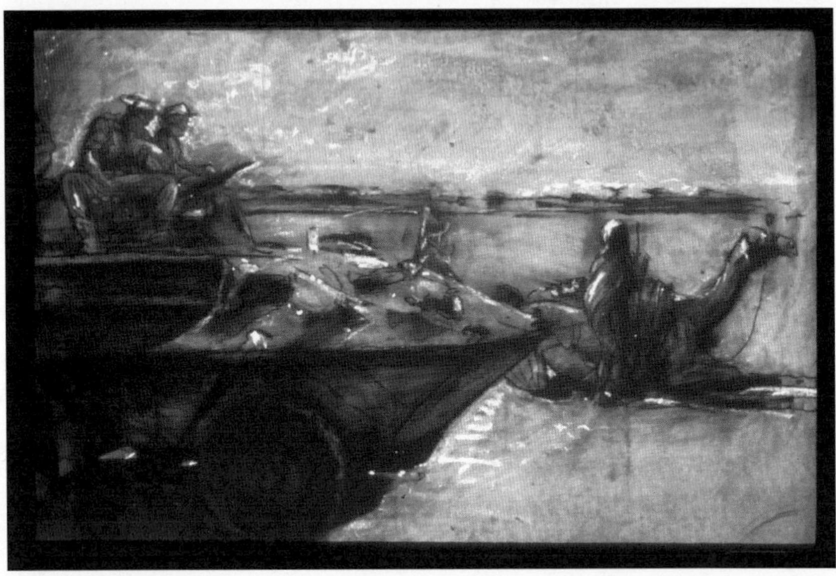

Figure 23. *Canadian (UN) Armoured Personnel Carrier, Somalia,* sketch by Allan Harding MacKay.

Written by Joseph Conrad in 1899, *Heart of Darkness* tells the tale of ivory exporter Charles Marlow's travels by steamship down the "snaking" Congo River into the dark heart of Africa, where he discovers the Ivory Export Company's accountant has gone mad and is worshipped by a group of "savage" natives. Despite criticism of the novel—in the 1970s, Nigerian postcolonial writer Chinua Achebe denounced it as a racist and dehumanizing representation of Africans—in 1979 Francis Ford Coppola adapted it for his film *Apocalypse Now*, setting the story in Vietnam. Like Conrad's character

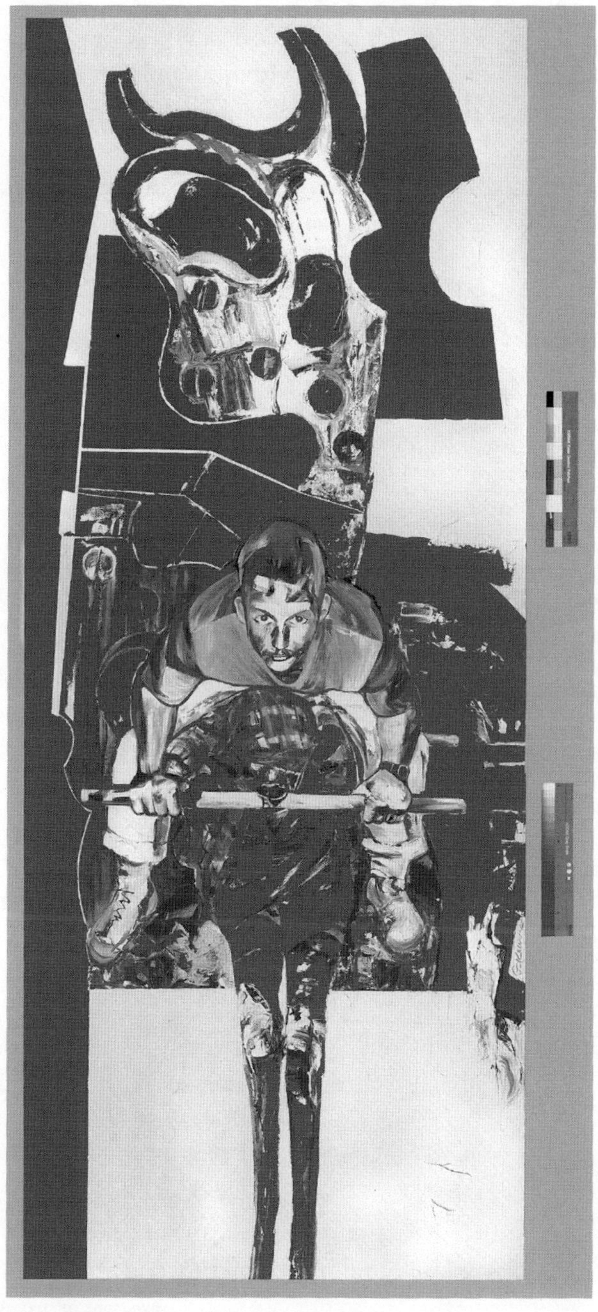

Figure 24. *Somalia #2, Without Conscience*, painting by Gertrude Kearns.

Marlow, Dallaire is shown as encountering a savage devil yet managing to emerge from hell, not unscathed but with his humanity intact.

As Razack writes of Canadian peacekeeping narratives: "In evacuating the specificities of the Rwandan genocide, the Rwandans themselves simply come to stand in for the worst that is human, while we in Canada, stand in for the best.... Genocide, far from depressing us, uplifts us. It uplifts us because the hero in the story is us."[72] The Canadian War Museum, having established in its opening exhibit that Canada—as a peacefully settled settler nation—is not implicated in the geopolitical histories of colonization, now extends this narrative in its closing exhibit to support the Canadian military's branding of itself as the exalted bearer of the contemporized "white man's burden," of humanitarian intervention.[73]

If Rwanda is Dallaire's dark heart of Africa, it is one he returned from as a martyr hero. Somalia is another story. Hanging beside Kearns's portrait of a traumatized Dallaire is a framed charcoal sketch by Allan Harding MacKay titled *Canadian (UN) Armoured Personnel Carrier, Somalia* (1993) (Figure 23). It is accompanied by a display panel that reads "From 1991 to 1993, Canada contributed 1,200 service personnel to a United Nations military intervention to relieve the suffering caused by famine and civil war in Somalia. Canadian soldiers escorted relief convoys to villages affected by famine, disarmed the population in the region surrounding their camp, and searched for bandits in patrols.... The torture and death of a Somali teenager at the hands of Canadian troops marred the otherwise successful deployment and led the government to commission a public inquiry into the mission."

MacKay drew his sketch while he was under contract as a Canadian civilian war artist and embedded with the Canadian Peacekeepers on their Somalia mission—Operation Deliverance. It is a strangely innocuous image for a mission that garnered much (albeit fleeting) public notoriety. While MacKay was immortalizing Canadian soldiers patrolling for Somali "bandits," some of Operation Deliverance's peacekeepers were busy creating their own mementos in the form of "trophy photos." One such image graces the cover of Razack's book *Dark Threats and White Knights* (not available in the museum's gift shop). In it, Captain Mark Sargent, a Canadian military chaplain, stands guard over four blindfolded and hog-tied Somali children. Their heads are drooping in the hot midday sun and hanging around their necks are signs (handwritten in Somali) that identify them as thieves. Lest anyone hastily assume this image demonstrates an abuse of power on the part of the chaplain, the "truth" of the image, according to the spin of Canadian peacekeeping nationalism and revealed by the military ombudsman by whom Captain Sargent was later employed as an investigator, is that Sargent was "protecting" the children from greater harm at the hands of local elders.[74] The military ombudsman's "percepticidal" spin shifts the public's gaze away from the violence (in plain sight) perpetrated by Canadian peacekeepers and onto a discursively produced "imagined Africa" that is seething with an ever-present threat of violence.[75] In Somalia, we are told, it is not only bandits who are to be feared. It is community elders as well.

The surfacing of trophy photos documenting the perpetration of additional atrocities against Somali civilians, of videos documenting the violent racism of the peacekeepers' hazing rituals, and of evidence of Canadian military cover-up led to an inquiry into the Somalia Affair and the eventual disbanding of the Canadian Airborne Regiment. One of the most disturbing photos to surface is reproduced in a painting by Kearns (Figure 24). The painting is large—nine by four feet. The background is a black-and-white abstraction, some kind of hybrid of dilapidated machinery and a large animal skull. In the foreground is a soldier. Between his legs sits a smallish blindfolded figure whose head hangs forward and is covered by a checkered hoodie. The figure's arms disappear behind his back and his slight legs are outstretched, limp and covered in an oozing mix of bruises and blood. The soldier wears an army-green T-shirt that shows off his bare buffed arms. In his hands he holds a stick that he has pressed up against the neck of the limp figure between his legs. The soldier's eyes look up and out, into those of the viewer.

Kearns's painting—*Somalia #2, Without Conscience* (1996) (Figure 24)—once occupied the place where MacKay's inoffensive sketch now hangs. The photo on which it is based is one of sixteen taken by Private Kyle Brown throughout the night of 16 March 1993, when sixteen-year-old Shidane Arone was brutally beaten and murdered by Canada's Operation Deliverance peacekeepers. It shows Master Corporal Clayton Matchee posed in the act of torturing Arone, the Somali teenager whose murder "at the hands of Canadian troops marred the otherwise successful deployment." But as the photograph of Captain Sargent standing over four blindfolded and hog-tied Somali children illustrates, the atrocities perpetrated by Canadian peacekeepers were not limited to the "torture and death of [one] Somali teenager." Just two weeks prior to Arone's murder, Canadian peacekeepers had shot two unarmed Somali men—Abdi Hamdare and Ahmad Aruush—for what the military called a "perimeter" breach.[76] Both men were shot in the back while fleeing and "Aruush was finished off at close range."[77]

While it is beyond the scope of this project to fully explore what came to be called the Somalia Affair, my interest here is in the museum's reductive representation of Arone's torture and murder as an isolated incident barely worthy of mention, and of Arone as invisible and nameless. Roméo Dallaire is a name recognized by most Canadians, but Shidane Arone remains a mostly anonymous anomaly in our national collective memory. What might Kearns's painting—once present, now absent—reveal about the politics that underpin the War Museum's construction of our collective memory of Canadian peacekeeping?

In "War, Unvarnished," a news article published in the *Ottawa Citizen* in 2005 seven days before the Canadian War Museum opened its doors to the general public, the author points to the museum's inclusion of Kearns's *Somalia #2, Without Conscience* within its exhibits as an illustration of how the new museum "will present a bleaker, more brutal and complex picture of war."[78] The author celebrates the commitment on the part of the War Museum's directors to "shy away from heroism" and the glamorization of war. Then museum director Joe Geurts is quoted as saying that the Canadian War Museum is committed to "including elements we may not be really happy about exposing." In addition to commending the museum for its inclusion of Kearns's painting of Arone's torture and murder at the hands of Canadian peacekeepers, the article also applauds the museum for including other controversial aspects of Canada's military history, like the "Allied bombing campaign during the Second World War, the conscription debate during the First World War and the execution of Louis Riel."

But the *Ottawa Citizen*'s celebration of the museum's representation of controversial aspects of the Second World War bombings of German civilian populations proved premature. A Senate committee report that acknowledged the veracity of the museum's representation nevertheless advised the museum to change the Bomber Command display to reflect the wishes and concerns of veterans groups, leading to Geurts's resignation from his position the War Museum's director after a two-year battle. And as noted previously in this chapter, while the museum credits Riel with his role in securing Manitoba for Canada, the consequences of his execution at the hands of the state are reduced to "damag[ing] linguistic relations in Canada."

The *Ottawa Citizen* article also cites the museum's war art curator, Laura Brandon, who points out that prior to the opening of the museum there was no controversy over the inclusion of Kearns's paintings in the museum's art collection—that in fact, *Somalia #2, Without Conscience* was donated by Friends of the Canadian War Museum, a group made up predominantly of veterans. As it turned out, controversy was waiting in the wings. Two days after the *Ottawa Citizen* published its article celebrating the museum's unvarnished approach to military memorialization, the newspaper received a letter to the editor from Second World War veteran Cliff Chadderton, then head of the National Council of Veterans Associations and the War Amps of Canada. Chadderton wrote that Kearns's Somalia paintings were "trashy" and an "insulting tribute," that they had no place in a museum dedicated to honouring Canada's military history, and that unless they were removed he would boycott the museum's opening ceremonies. It is important to note that not all stakeholders in Canada's military-cultural memory network concurred with Chadderton. For example, in their response to Chadderton's letter, the Canadian Legion expressed their dislike of one of the representations but nevertheless supported the museum in its "responsibility to tell the full and accurate story of our military history" and pointed out that the paintings that Chadderton objected to were among a "war art collection of 13,000 other pieces of art that help emphasize our magnificent history of courage and commitment."[79]

Chadderton's public stance against the inclusion of Kearns's Somalia paintings was not the first battle he had fought over representations of Canada's military memory, nor would it be the last. Chadderton was instrumental in both the 1992 fight to keep the CBC from rebroadcasting *The Valour and the Horror*, and in the bitter battle that forced the museum to change the wording of its Bomber Command panel and led to Geurts's resignation. While Chadderton did not succeed in his bid to have Kearns's paintings removed from the exhibit, both Kearns and Brandon "received abusive email directly stemming from the Internet debate that waged on the site www.army.ca for over five months."[80]

In 2010, the museum removed *Somalia #2* from *The Savage Wars of Peace* exhibit so that it could be included in the travelling exhibit *A Brush with War: Military Art from Korea to Afghanistan*. Curated by Brandon, *Brush with War* toured Canada from December 2010 through March 2011. When I inquired by email whether the controversy surrounding the painting had any bearing on the museum's decision not to return *Somalia #2* to its original place beside Kearns's *Dallaire #6*, I received this response from Andrew Burtch, the museum's acting director of research: "The decision not to return the painting was not related to the controversy that surrounded the painting in 2005. It was in response to the long duration of *Brush with War*'s run, and the need to revisit the exhibition space/content from time to time.... That said, we are looking at a full renovation of the concluding sections of Gallery 4, which would entail new exhibitions about Somalia, Rwanda, Former Yugoslavia, and Afghanistan, and may include *Somalia #2* and other works in the new space."[81]

The controversy over Kearns's paintings makes visible the tensions between stakeholders who embrace "difficult return" and critical engagement in the museum's approach to Canada's military history, and those for whom military history demands elegiac commemoration. Military memorial strategies that require praise as their central organizing trope necessitate both the omission of narratives that threaten to mar the image of Canadian military personnel as "just warriors" and the instrumentalist deployment of a pseudo-polyvocality toward the manufacture and maintenance of Canada's national identity as a multicultural nation dedicated to humanitarian militarism abroad.

The controversy also exposes some of the "deep politics" that shape the Canadian War Museum's exhibits over time and that, in a broader context, shape Canada's collective military and national memory. Coined by Peter Dale Scott, "deep politics" is a term that explains, first, the way societies collectively suppress facts when the costs of their exposure may be considered detrimental to the social order; and second, the way political decision making takes place hidden from the public sphere.[82] Just as Fremeth cautions that Canada's military-cultural memory network cannot be reduced to a simple top-down propaganda mechanism but rather is a porous system made up of a complex assemblage of stakeholders with divergent interests and goals, Scott differentiates deep politics from conspiracy, a term that suggests a centrally agreed-upon plan.

Both Fremeth and Scott assert that it would be a mistake to consider this lack of a centralized or top-down organizing structure as an indication of weakness. The absence of clearly defined power structures produces an accountability vacuum. Further, in the case of Canada's military-cultural memory network, the diversity of the range of stakeholders can generate an illusion of democratic pluralism. Canadian artists and other cultural producers occupy a perilous position in this network. As the power of

Canada's military-cultural memory network has grown exponentially since the Canadian Forces' "decade of darkness" and more arts funding has been funnelled into "heritage" commemoration projects, the line between cultural nationalism and military nationalism has become increasingly blurry. The very existence of both MacKay's and Kearns's artwork within the Canadian War Museum's collection, for example, is a result of the Department of National Defence's funding of the Canadian Armed Forces Civilian Artists Programme.[83]

A Pedagogy of Interpellation: I Fear (for) Those Who Fear Nothing

As anthropologist Talal Asad argues in his 2007 study of suicide bombing, the legitimacy or illegitimacy of an act of geopolitical violence is determined not by the act itself, but by the location of the actor.[84] Whereas suicide bombings are deemed illegitimate acts of aggression against "innocent" civilians by virtue of the fact that they are conducted by "terrorists," in the case of Bomber Command, the deaths of German civilians—however "regrettable"—are deemed the result of legitimate acts of war because the deaths were perpetrated by state-sanctioned "just warriors" and waged against a population whose innocence was eclipsed by nationality.

Dallaire's much-exalted personal story of being driven to the brink of madness by his encounter with the "devil" contributes to the production of a larger meta-narrative of traumatized Canadian peacekeepers struggling to do good, while maintaining their sanity in the face of the "other's" barbarism. If Africa is indeed home to the devil, it stands to reason that when Canadian peacekeepers become perpetrators of torture and murder, their acts, however unacceptable, are nevertheless understood as a consequence of their encounter with the "colossal evil" of African nation-states who have descended into (or returned to) stateless tribalism. This narrative is evident in the museum's minimization of Canadian peacekeeper crimes, which is disturbingly similar to the strategies of denial, minimization, and justification used by the Canadian military in its efforts to gloss over the Somalia Affair.

The equation of state-sanctioned acts of violence as just, and acts of violence by non-state actors as barbaric, is constructed through a variety of discursive framing mechanisms—from popular culture productions that include novels, films, plays, and news media, to more overtly pedagogical approaches like those delivered through educational curricula and museums. Since veterans groups and other military memory stakeholders develop much of the military history curricula that is used in Canadian schools, it privileges elegiac reverence over critical engagement.[85] These framing mechanisms also require upkeep to ensure that delivery systems can effectively address contemporary circumstances and target specific audiences.

The Canadian War Museum's integration of a range of new interactive museology approaches has been instrumental in making the museum a place that does more than engage children and youth. It also interpellates them as citizens in a nation whose military actions are understood as legitimized and just. Through their participation in war games, through the pseudo choices they are asked to make, through the questions that are put to them on the plaques that cover the museum's walls, the children are called upon. They are asked to identify through a process that facilitates the assimilation of some differences under the category of a unified Canadian multicultural nationalism while casting "other" differences to the realm of barbarism. The museum's use of an instrumentalist memorial pedagogy, with its emphasis on remembrance as a strategic practice toward the construction of a unified national identity, comes at the expense of the kind of critical engagement that would invite the museum's young charges to question the justness of all acts of violence—not only those of enemy "others" but also those perpetrated at the behest of the Canadian state.

Just as the museum was born of controversy, its stakeholders have continued to battle over the museum's pedagogical approach since its opening. Moriyama, Geurts, and Brandon (among others) have advocated for a museum that stages remembrance not only as a strategic practice but also as a difficult return. Chadderton and other military stakeholder representatives, on the other hand, have (with significant success) pushed for a more conventional approach in the production of elegiac narratives of remembrance and nationalist praise. But however diverse the stakeholders in this struggle over the museum's increasingly performative representation of Canada's military memory may be, the stage on which the battle is waged is not neutral.

As a governmental institution, the Canadian War Museum has a primary mandate—evident throughout its exhibits—to promote a unified Canadian nationalism. The War Museum's twofold agenda—military commemoration and nation building—is disseminated through a narrative of unified Canadian multicultural nationalism at home and humanitarian militarism abroad. To the extent that multiple voices are present within the museum they are in instrumental service to a becoming nationalist ideology, in which statehood is a signifier of civility and Canada's military state actors are cast as "just warriors." When states go to war, however horrific the effects, their actions are not framed as "savage." Military commemoration in this context becomes both a celebration of the Canadian multicultural nation and a justification for its ongoing and necessary military defence.

Just as the rough edges of Moriyama's foyer were paved over to improve the museum's "look," in the "contact zones" of the Canadian War Museum, Canada's military encounters, past and present, are given a feel-good shine. The two exhibits discussed in this chapter—*Battleground: Wars on Our Soil: Earliest Times to 1885* and *The Savage Wars of Peace*—act as colonial and neo-colonial bookends for the museum's main galleries. As a framing device, the opening gallery sets the stage with its depiction of Canada as a pluralistic nation that came into being through mutually beneficial encounters between Canada's (already warring) First Peoples and its (civilizing) European settlers. Having established Canada as a nation born in innocence, in its closing gallery the museum extends the narrative of national innocence to serve its contemporary geopolitical military interests. Through its spectacular display of a world that is threatened by the chaos of non- or failed-state violence, the last exhibit's video builds a case for the necessity of Canada's ongoing engagement in acts of "benevolent" military intervention. This message is most directly communicated by the video's narration—*My world is filled with heroes, they make choices too.* It is *My World*'s child narrators who—like dashing young Warren and the intently gazing Iroquois siblings—deliver the museum's final cathartic peer-to-peer address to the museum's young visitors.

Though *The Savage Wars of Peace* is not a space where children tend to linger, this does not mean they escape *My World*'s interpellating appeal. There is a small chamber on the other side of the large screens onto which *My World* is projected and before the main galleries' final exit. The space has two round tables surrounded by chairs and a metal board with rectangular black-on-orange word magnets. Shelves on either side of the room are stocked with postcards and pencils—one side of the card is blank, the other addressed to the Prime Minister, members of parliament, world leaders, veterans groups, and museum curators. As the children and youth gather in this space to compose their reflections they do so enveloped by the chaotic din of *My World*'s soundscape, which vacillates between apocalyptic foreboding and heroic fervour. The beseeching plea of the disembodied children who narrate the video—*It's your world now, how does it start?*—is echoed on the signs that line the walls enlisting visitors to share their reflections: "What will you do? Is there something you would like to say to the museum or others? The postcards here are pre-addressed for your convenience to public figures in Canada and around the world. There is no time like the present. . . . Sufficient postage can be purchased from the boutique in the museum's lobby."

On each of my visits to the museum, I sit on one of benches to watch *My World* and to watch the activity in the small room beyond. I'm not sure whether teachers and group leaders have instructed the kids to leave a message here or whether they choose to participate of their own accord, but it is definitely a place where youth linger. When school groups pass through, the kids tend to distribute themselves according to gender. The girls cluster around the tables, and the boys huddle together in front of the magnetic board. The position of the three large screens blocks my view of the two tables, so it is mostly the boys I watch as they jostle to collectively compose haikus from the Canadian-peacekeepers-at-war-themed magnets (Figure 25).

Before I leave, I always peruse the messages left by the youth. There is an array of hand-drawn and written postcards posted on display boards that line the two side walls. Despite the overwhelming presence within this room of *My World*'s soundscape, with its message of the urgent need for Canadian military humanitarian intervention, it is one of the few spaces within the museum where participant responses are not predetermined through pre-scripted computerized game and quiz selection processes. That said, most of the postcards reflect the museum's overarching message of national praise and elegiac reverence. There are pencilled poems of mourning; stories of great-grandparents and grandparents who fought in the First or Second World War, or of grandparents and relatives who were killed in concentration camps; sketches with Canadian flags, soldiers, poppies, and tombstones accompanied by the words "remember," "lest we forget," "for us," or "for freedom"; statements of nationalistic pride; and accolades for the museum. But on occasion, there are also traces of a more critical engagement with, and resistance to, the museum's dominant narrative of a unified Canadian multicultural nationalism in support of humanitarian militarism:

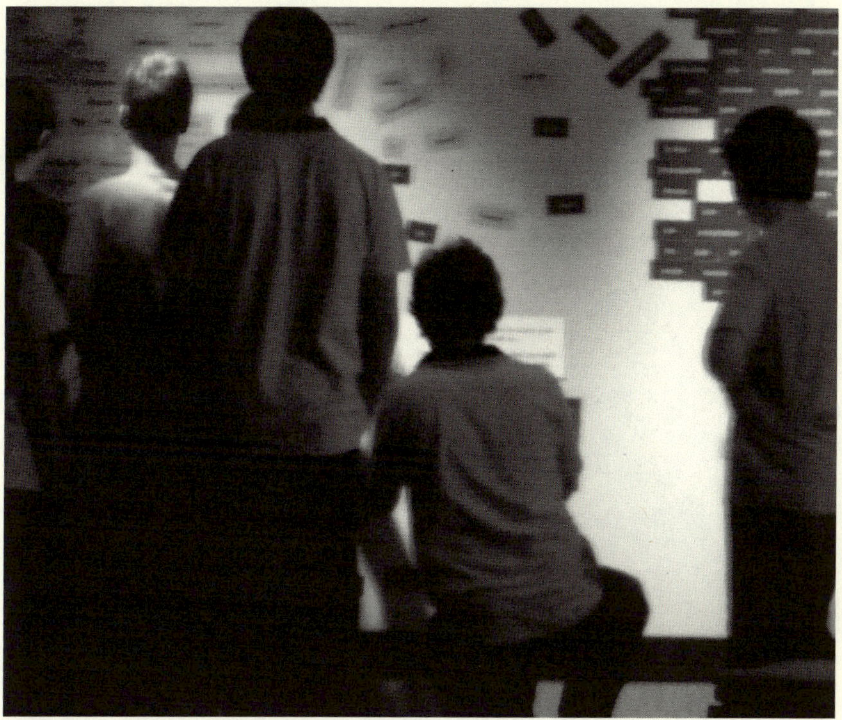

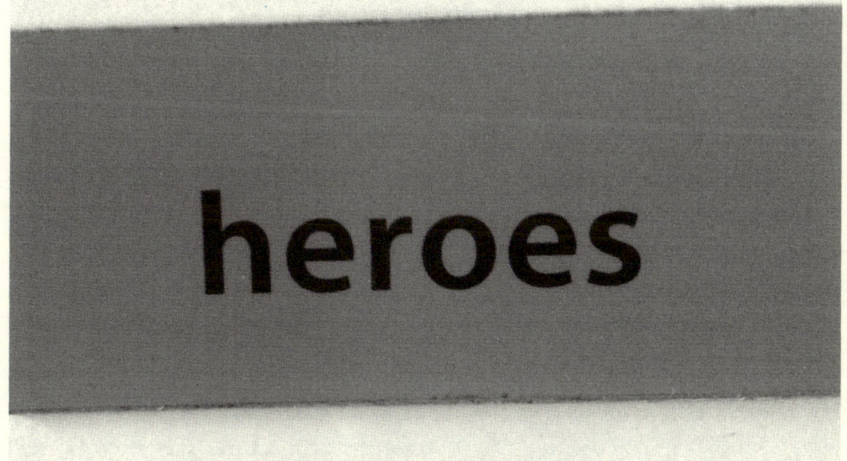

Figure 25. Boys gathered in front of magnet board.
Figure 26. "Heroes" magnet. In an effort to trouble the centrality of the notion of heroism within military memorialization, I removed the "heroes" tile from the exhibit's lexicon.

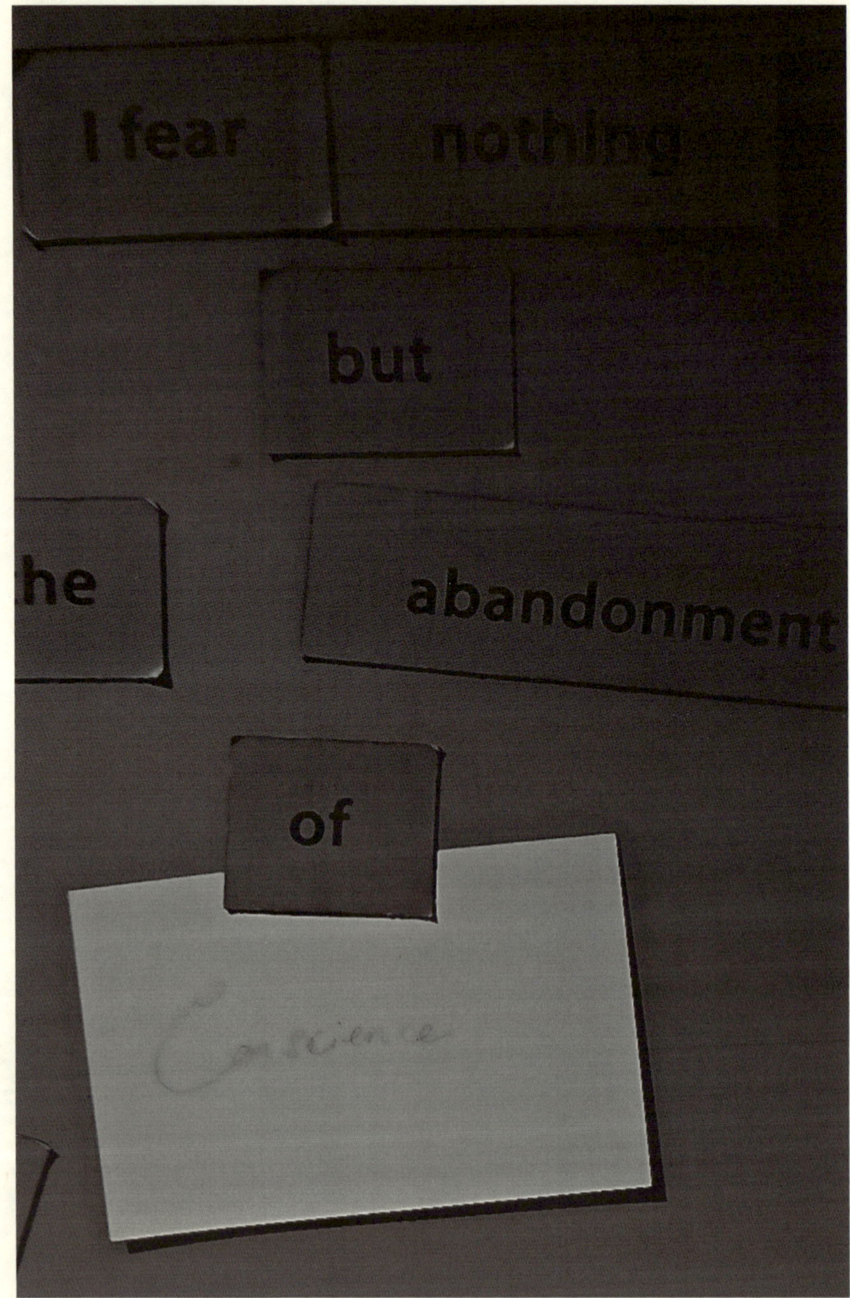

Figure 27. Expanding the limited lexicon of military commemoration.

> "I broke out, never returned." (Signed, "Trenton")
>
> "I am happy I am gone from Trenton and I won't let you make me." (Signed, "Stranger")
>
> "I'm not going to draw a happy soldier like some because nothing about war is happy. No one should have to go through it. Wether your [*sic*] attacking or being attacked. There is no good side or bad side. Our generation should stop it. Or, eventually there won't be anything to fight over." (Unsigned)
>
> "Louis Riel, hero for First Nations in regards to their fights." (Unsigned)

Because of my time spent watching the negotiated meaning-making process of youth at the metallic message board, I am most intrigued by the black-on-orange magnetic tile dispatches. Despite—or perhaps because of—the limited vocabulary provided by the museum, these magnet messages have a way of inviting dialogue as museum visitors add or subtract words and word phrases to alter a message's original meaning. When I'm at the museum I stop by several times a day to witness the fluctuating magnet-generated discourse. On my last visit to the museum, someone had put together the tiles "I fear" and "nothing." What does it mean when at the end of a visit to a war museum one walks away fearing nothing? Should war not frighten us? Surely for those who lived through a war or those who have loved ones either fighting or attempting to live in combat zones, fear must be ever-present. Fear born of the relentless knowledge of one's own precarity; fear of precarity as our shared condition. The message haunted me as I continued with my investigation of the museum's more peripheral galleries.

When I returned a few hours later, I found the message altered. To the original two-tile message—"I fear" "nothing"—someone had added the following four magnetic words—"but," "the," "abandonment," "of." Then, refusing to allow their contribution to the discourse to be limited by the words made available by the museum, they ad-libbed by writing "Conscience" on a postcard and tucking it under the final magnetic word, thereby constructing the phrase: "I fear nothing but the abandonment of Conscience."

CHAPTER THREE

UNBECOMING CANADIAN MILITARISM'S FORGETFUL NARRATIVES

UNRAVELLING THE UNIFORM'S AMBIGUOUS MEANINGS[1]

> The logical conclusion of the attitude that produces an isolated rape in England is the rape camps in Bosnia and the logical conclusion to the way society expects men to behave is war.
> — Sarah Kane, on her play *Blasted*[2]

19 October 2010[3]
Impact Afghanistan War blog post
I finally sat down to read one of the Toronto Star*'s daily reports on the trial of Canadian Forces' Colonel Russell Williams for the rape-murders of Marie-France Comeau and Jessica Lloyd. Like many, I'm deeply disturbed not only (and obviously) by Williams's acts of violation and murder, but also by the media's coverage of the trial. Williams's crimes—and by association all acts of sexualized*

violence—are treated as the anomalous actions of a "pervert." The Star*'s front-page image of Williams dressed in women's underwear functions as a code for his depravity—as though cross-dressing is a precursor to torture, rape, and murder.*[4] *Little attention is paid, on the other hand, to Williams's (until now) elevated status as a highly respected colonel in the Canadian military; or of his conditioning in a nationalistic and militarized hyper-masculinity; or of the well-documented historical relationship between war and rape.*[5]

By treating Williams's crimes as spectacular anomalies, Comeau's and Lloyd's rape-murders are framed as isolated events. But what of the multitude of acts of sexual violence routinely perpetrated in Canada and beyond? What of the 1,181 missing and murdered Indigenous women in Canada?[6] *And—given Williams's status as a colonel in the Canadian Forces—what of the hundreds and thousands of violent sexual assaults against civilians in conflict zones around the world, and against women in the military? While there has been a call to open up cold cases of women who have gone missing or been found murdered in Canadian locations where Williams was stationed, I've heard of no similar investigations being launched in conflict zones where Williams has served.*

Also disturbing is the juxtaposition of the Star*'s sensationalized reporting of the rape-murders of Comeau and Lloyd with its scathing review—by theatre critic Richard Ouzounian—of Buddies in Bad Times Theatre's presentation of British playwright Sarah Kane's play* Blasted *(2010). Ouzounian's main beef with* Blasted *is that it's "too much." He critiques Kane for her "maniacal excess" and argues that the play goes "too far" in its portrayal of violence. Moreover, Ouzounian also critiques Buddies for their decision to stage* Blasted, *arguing that it has nothing to do with "queer theatre" and that it doesn't offer "a special view of male sexuality [but rather] it's simply Sarah Kane's uniquely twisted view of the world."*

I couldn't disagree more. I applaud Buddies for their inclusion of Blasted *in its season and only wish they had gone further and hosted a community discussion of the larger question of what is/isn't a "queer" issue. Though watching* Blasted *was undeniably a jarring experience, as a lesbian/queer feminist, I found it queerly refreshing to see a play (on the stage of a queer theatre) that raises important questions about the relationship between society's production of attitudes of hyper-masculinity and their brutally logical conclusions.*

On 22 October 2010, Colonel Russell Williams was sentenced to two concurrent life terms for the rape-murders of Corporal Marie-France Comeau and Jessica Lloyd. At the time of his conviction, Williams had served twenty-three years with the Canadian Armed Forces, where he had climbed high in the military's ranks. Colonel Williams was an esteemed and decorated officer who flew Canadian Forces VIP aircraft carrying dignitaries like Canada's prime minister and governor general, and Queen Elizabeth II and Prince Philip. At the age of forty-six he was awarded command of Canada's largest military airbase—Canadian Forces Base Trenton—where he became a familiar figure at the base's repatriation ceremonies for Canadian Forces Afghanistan war dead.

Like Master Corporal Clayton Matchee (see Chapter 2)—who had "trophy" photos taken of him torturing Somali teenager Shidane Arone—Colonel Russell Williams documented his crimes in the form of hundreds of photos and videos. It is from this collection that the *Toronto Star* took its front-page image of Williams dressed in women's underwear.[7] But whereas Matchee's trophy photos—once they were publicly disclosed after an attempted cover-up by the military—launched a Senate inquiry and became part of the Canadian Forces' "decade of darkness," Williams's photos proved to be a public relations godsend for the Canadian Forces. One day prior to Williams's sentencing, while at a St. John's press conference announcing a $100 million military investment, then prime minister Stephen Harper did more than absolve the Canadian military of any accountability for Williams's crimes; he positioned the military—alongside Comeau and Lloyd—as another victim: "This is just a horrific event. . . . Our thoughts go out to all the members of the Canadian Forces who knew the commander and who have been very badly wounded and betrayed by all of this. Obviously, this in no way reflects on the Forces. . . . The Canadian Forces are the victim here, as of course are the direct victims of these terrible events."

The image of Williams dressed in ill-fitting women's undergarments became a cypher. The link made between his "queer" fetish and the violence of his crimes eclipsed the association of Comeau's and Lloyd's rape-murders with Williams's long and highly rewarded performance of military masculinity. To be clear, neither the media nor the Canadian Forces used the term "queer." However, the *Star*'s posting of images of Williams wearing women's underwear precipitated a deluge of derogatory adjectives: shocking, deplorable, disgusting, repulsive, depraved, deviant, perverse. Incongruously, the most abject of these adjectives were primarily associated with Williams's perverse "crime" of dressing in women's clothes (and the *Star*'s decision to publish them), not with his crimes of rape, torture, and murder.

In contrast to Kane's assertion that rape is not an isolated event but rather—like war—is the "logical conclusion" of attitudes of hyper-masculinity, the media colluded with the Canadian Forces in framing Comeau's and Lloyd's rape-murders as anomalous acts that were more a product of a deviantly feminized masculinity than of a nationalistic and militarized masculinity. Women's underwear became Williams's new uniform, conveniently replacing the Canadian Forces uniform that Williams wore for over two decades and that quite likely shielded him from suspicion during a three-year crime spree in which he burgled homes—some, two and three times—in the immediate neighbourhoods of his Cosy Cove Lane (Tweed, Ontario) and Ottawa residences. In fact, while male neighbours of Williams were questioned for the break-ins, sexual assaults, and murders, despite his proximity to the victims, police did not question Williams until they matched a tire tread imprint found at Lloyd's home to Williams's SUV.[8]

On the day of Williams's sentencing, the Canadian military officially disowned him. He was stripped of his commission, his senior military rank, and his awards. Three weeks later, on 18 November 2010, in a final gesture of purification, the Canadian Forces incinerated all of Williams's military uniforms (also shredding Williams's commission scroll, cutting his medals into pieces, and crushing and scrapping the Pathfinder SUV he had used to kidnap Jessica Lloyd). If, under the binary dictates of our dominant global gender order, masculinity is what femininity is not, Williams's trophy photos provided the Canadian Forces with the tactical rationale to cast him not only out of the realm of militarism, but also outside of masculinity itself. Similarly, by choosing to publish sensationalized images of Williams dressed in women's underwear on its front page, the *Toronto Star* helped to distance Williams and his crimes from both the military and masculinity. Rather than launching, as Kane might have proposed, an interrogation of the relationship between militarized masculinities, sexual violence, and war, Williams's crimes became associated in the public imaginary with the "crime" of gender-deviance.

As the most generic of military uniforms, camouflage fatigues are one of militarism's most recognizable objects. They are also highly ambiguous. On one hand, the uniform sits in intimate contact with the precarious flesh of its wearer and is tasked with safeguarding the vulnerable body in its charge. It protects by concealing, by rendering its wearers invisible, by allowing them to blend into the surrounding environment. On the other hand, the uniform performs a critical role in the production of a privileged national identity that grants its wearers the right to kill and to perpetrate other acts of violence in the name of the state, and—if killed—a guaranteed place at the top of nationalism's geopolitical hierarchy of grievability.

As performance studies scholar Laura Levin proposes, however, military camouflage functions as more than a protective cloaking device or a signifier of privileged national identity. It is also a "performance strategy" through which identities become located "within a larger environment or picture."[9] The proliferation of images of camouflage-clad soldiers in news and pop-culture media produces a bigger picture, one that supersedes both individual and national identities. Through its pervasiveness, the image of hegemonic global military masculinity becomes naturalized. The maintenance of this naturalized backdrop necessitates the purging of individual identities and acts that cannot be readily absorbed into militarism's larger (self-) image of just warriors fighting righteous wars.

It is not surprising, then, that within Canadian performances of military memorialization, there is little space for the uniform's ambiguity. The uniform that serves as the symbol of a soldier's remembrance does not bear the bloody traces of their annihilation. Dead soldiers are not remembered as vulnerable victims of violent acts but as exemplars of heroic masculinity. Nor is there space within commemorative performances of elegiac remembrance for militarism's inconvenient dead or its inconvenient killers. The inconvenient dead—those who take their own lives, those killed by comrades, those who have openly criticized a military mission, or those who die in "unfortunate incidents"—are all assimilated into heroism's homogenizing discourse.[10] And the military's inconvenient killers are deemed either lone bad apples or, as in Williams's case, deviantly depraved "others." The incineration of Colonel Williams's uniforms was an exorcism of ambiguity. It was an act of annulment, not only of the colonel's affiliation with the Canadian Forces but also of the entangled relationships of militarism, hyper-masculinity, and violent nationalisms and their role in the production and maintenance of a hegemonic global gender order.

Troubling the Gendered Lexicons of War, Peace, and Sexual Violence

18 September 2011
Visualeyez 2011, Edmonton
When I began Unravel *I was especially daunted at the thought of the thread-by-thread deconstruction of the fatigues. I anticipated boredom, backaches, and frustration. I assumed that the repetitive labour of the task would generate impatience in me. The pinching of each individual thread between finger and thumb. The pulling—slowly so as not to break the thread—through the fabric's weave. Retrieving those threads that do break, sometimes with a violent snap, other times with a disintegrating poof. Tasks my thick fingers are ill-suited for* (Figure 28). *Paradoxically, I've found that the visceral engagement with such an aggravating, yet necessarily care-filled task, simultaneously triggers and de-fuses my frustration. Through the doing—or undoing—I discover a kind of peace. Not a simple or static peace. Not a guaranteed peace. Not a peace innate to the affectively feminized lexicon of cradling cloth in lap, holding thread in hand. Not a romantic or nostalgic peace. A peace born and reborn—thread by thread—of the struggle with the ambiguity and ambivalence of the task. A peace requiring the constant negotiation and renegotiation of frustration, empathy, boredom, anger, resignation, hope, and despair.*

Unravel: A Meditation on the Warp and Weft of Militarism began as a week-long performance installation at Edmonton's Visualeyez Performance Art Festival in September 2011. During the festival's first three days I took a set of camouflage fatigues apart at the seams and laid the fragmented pieces out on the gallery floor (Figure 29). Visitors were then invited to join a porous (un)sewing circle in which they could participate in the thread-by-thread

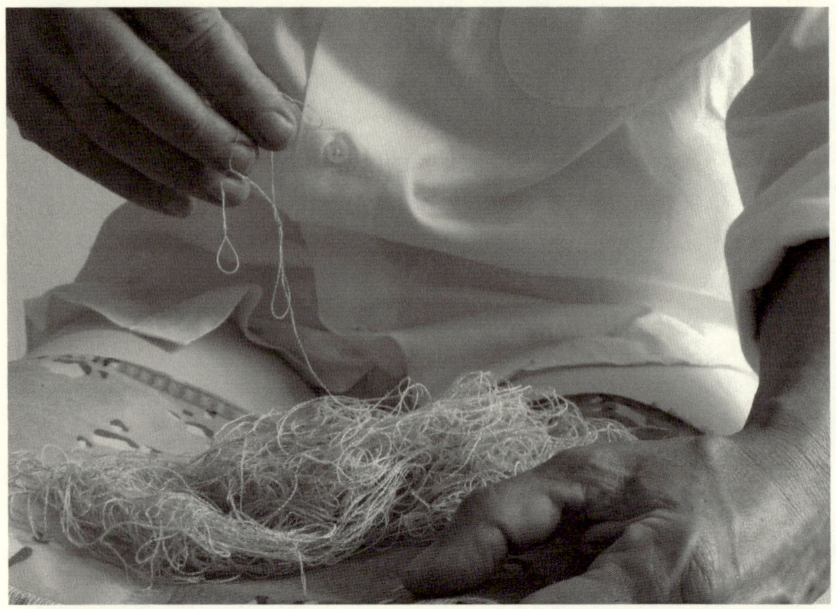

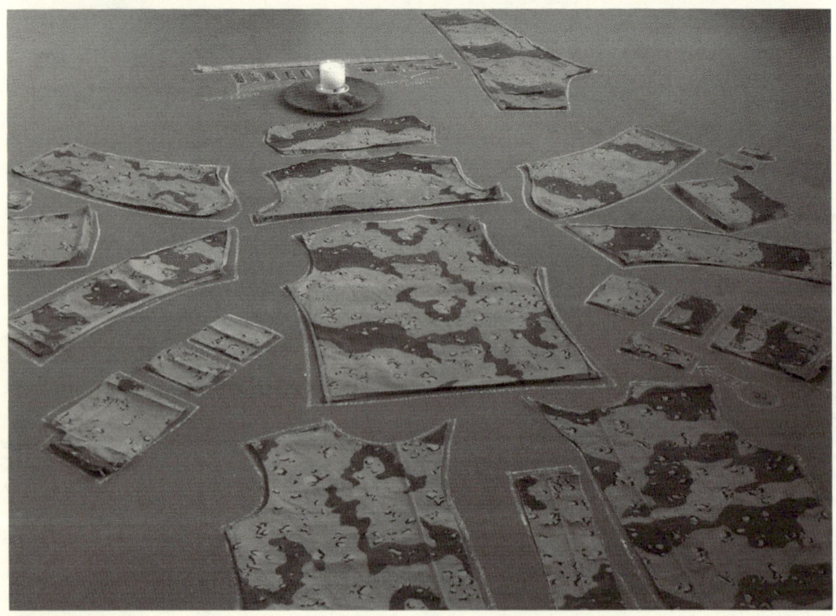

Figure 28. Thick fingers, fine threads.
Figure 29. Apart at the seams. September 2011, Latitude 53 Contemporary Visual Culture, Visualeyez 2011.

deconstruction of the uniform. Following the festival's completion I continued *Unravel* as a daily meditation practice and, on occasion, hosted (un)sewing circles at festivals and conferences throughout Canada and in the United Kingdom.

As with *Impact Afghanistan War*, *Unravel* began as a task-based performance meditation designed to focus attention on the differential grievability that is produced through nationalism, militarism, and war. Curiously, however, though my work is grounded in theoretical and historical investigations of the gendered (and raced) dynamics of militarism, war, and military commemoration, I did not intentionally devise either *Impact* or *Unravel* as gender-based inquiries. Nor did I anticipate how my focus during these meditations, rather than being contained by the performance of set tasks, would become unloosed through their daily reiterations. As *Impact* and *Unravel* unfurled along an ambiguous array of affective trajectories, they unsettled me. Their impressions—remembrances of light, texture, and architecture, of sound and sensation, of ghostly inter(in)animations—continue to expand and challenge my understanding of the gendered lexicons of war and peace, and the tangled extent to which the binary notion of hegemonic masculinities and femininities are deployed as ideological weapons of militarism and nationalism.

Another similarity between *Impact* and *Unravel* is that both projects engage a labour aesthetic. *Impact*'s is most visible in the performance of the tasks of falling and of counting. The repetition of falls in *Impact*, together with its accompanying ritualized ac*counting*, take on a physical and routinized labour-like quality. And while *Impact* was evocative of the regimentation of militarism (as well as industrialized labour regimes), unlike military commemoration's stoically elegiac performance of mourning, my performance sought to expose the vulnerability of loss and the difficult, sweaty, and frequently messy labour of remembering. Though I did not conceive of *Impact* as a masculinized performance, when falling (especially in the winter) I noticed that most of the other people performing physical labour in public outdoor environments (hydro work, construction and road work, snow removal, landscaping, etc.) were men. *Impact*'s perceived masculine aesthetic can also be partially attributed to the fact that I am frequently misread as male. This is especially true during the winter months when the combination of my size (somehow big bones and broad shoulders are deemed male) and my pragmatic attire (also considered male) seems to leave people without the pre-scripted social signifiers to mark me as female. Thus—despite biological sex, gender identity, or intent—I either revert to the dominant norm of unmarked masculinity, or paradoxically become marked as queer.

In contrast, *Unravel*'s labour evokes a decidedly (if not deliberately) feminized aesthetic, one that is grounded in the long-standing historical association of women and cloth. According to Elizabeth Wayland Barber, the gendered nature of women's long history in the invention and development of textile production can be attributed to the fact that historically women were also the primary caretakers of young children: "Spinning, weaving, and sewing," writes Barber, are "repetitive [tasks], easy to pick up at any point, reasonably child-safe, and easily done at home."[11] For a millennium this rationality of caretaking was inextricably woven into cloth's production logic until, as Barber notes, the Industrial Revolution moved textile work "out of the home [and out of the control of its producers] and into large (inherently dangerous) factories."[12] More recently, as the result of "technological, political and economic developments," multinational corporations have largely abandoned factory-based apparel production in favour of global economic networks of subcontracted supply chains.[13] "Homeworkers" are at the end of the chain, the bottom of a bottom-heavy pyramid (or iceberg). The majority work for sub-minimum wages with no benefits and no protection. Health and safety hazards long associated with the garment industry are now part of the homeworkers' home environment. Predominantly women, and largely from the global South or from the global North's internalized "third world" of immigrant and poor women, homeworkers are an isolated and invisible workforce, distanced from both retailer and consumer through long complex chains of subcontracting that are legitimated through discourses of neo-liberal economic rationality. But regardless of the radical shifts in the logics that drive textile production—from home to factory and back to home—the labour relationship between women and cloth remains largely intact.

18 September 2011
Visualeyez 2011, Edmonton
These are buttons and seams that do not easily give way. Pocket corners are especially well reinforced, girded against actions that might cause them to be torn from the uniform's body. Even with the tools intended for their undoing, it's difficult. As I struggle with a particularly well-affixed corner my seam-ripper slips, leaving a

small gash concealed by the uniform's camouflage. A wounding. A violation. A reminder. No matter how ingeniously designed, how painstakingly constructed, no uniform is up to the task of protecting its wearer from weapons intent on destruction.

Despite the increased presence of women in the military, combat fatigues remain an iconic symbol of what R.W. Connell calls "military masculinities."[14] The masculinized symbolism of the military uniform is produced not only by and through war, but also through the myriad of representations that constitute the larger military-industrial entertainment complex—from toy soldiers and G.I. Joes, to blockbuster movies, to performances of mock military manoeuvres at sporting events, to an ever-expanding plethora of video games, including America's Army.[15] As is evident through Paul Gross's big-screen war epics, *Passchendaele* (2008) and *Hyena Road* (2015), Canada has become a producer of the kinds of popular military entertainment that naturalizes militarism.

Just as militarism has a gendered lexicon, so too does peace. For decades, women-led and women-only anti-war and anti-militarist movements have employed essentialist—sometimes strategically framed, other times not—notions of "woman" or "mother," together with their accompanying signs and symbols: Argentina's Las Madres de la Plaza de Mayo, who wore white scarves representing baby diapers as poignant signifiers of the loss of their disappeared children; the Women's Peace Camp at Greenham Commons (UK), where feminist peace activists drew upon the historical associations of women with cloth and caring when they wove themselves to the fence surrounding the base; the transnational anti-war organization, Women in Black, whose use of public symbols of women in mourning, together with their unrelenting call for peaceful solutions, challenges the state's use of memorial for militaristic and nationalistic aims.

From a historical perspective, the gendering of war and peace may well be rooted in the "fact" of the gendered construction of both militaries and (to a lesser extent) peace movements. But as more and more women enlist in national militaries and serve in combat-related positions, feminists are being forced to grapple with the too-easy linkage of women with peace. As Cuban-American artist-scholar Coco Fusco argues, while U.S. feminists have focused on how women within the military have become victims of sexual harassment and sexual violence at the hands of their male comrades, they have been less vigilant in taking seriously the participation of female soldiers in perpetrating sexual violence.[16] For example, when trophy photos of U.S. Army reservist Lynndie England sexually abusing Abu Ghraib detainees went public, white Western feminists were quick to emphasize England's subordinate relationship with her male superior (and lover), U.S. Army specialist Charles Graner, who had a documented history of violent domestic abuse. While Fusco is not suggesting that England was not under pressure from Graner, she argues that by focusing almost exclusively on England's gendered naiveté and institutionally supported gender subordination, feminists contributed to the reproduction of a problematically essentializing gender narrative in which women can only be understood as sexual violence's victims, never its perpetrators.

Within the simulacrum of popular media, with its prolific display of sexual exhibitionism and images of the sexualized female body, England's story unfolded like a racy military soap opera. Through the lens of the dominant media, England's "participation [in] and witnessing of sexualized torture [read] as something else: erotic play and illicit pleasure, for both the viewers and those viewed."[17] Taken together, feminists' downplaying of England's role in the perpetration of sexual aggression and the media's representation of women as sexual objects, not actors, served to "limit the understanding of sexual torture as a calculated practice"—one in which female sexuality is being increasingly strategically deployed by the U.S. military.[18] Equally significant was the astounding extent to which debates over England's innocence and/or guilt diverted attention away from the Arab men in the images who were undeniably the victims of sexual aggression and assault. Dominant (white) feminism's undifferentiated gender narrative masks the degree to which sexual violence is perpetrated on racialized "others."

If our gendered lexicons of war and peace do not, as Fusco asserts, provide us with a language to understand "female sexual aggression as rape," neither do they provide us with a language for comprehending men as victims of sexual violence.[19] In fact, as human rights scholar Lara Stemple writes, "There are well over one hundred uses of the term 'violence against women'—defined to include sexual violence—in U.N. resolutions, treaties, general comments and consensus documents. No human rights instruments explicitly address sexual violence against men."[20] One explanation for the lack of attention to male rape is that women are disproportionately far more likely to be raped than men. But the statistically higher number of women than men who are raped neither accounts for nor excuses our collective participation in the willful denial of men as victims of sexual violence.

With the play *Blasted*, Sarah Kane defies the taboo surrounding male-on-male rape and in the process disrupts the naturalized backdrop of hegemonic military masculinity. Also, by setting the rape of *Blasted*'s female protagonist, Cate, offstage, Kane resists reproducing the eroticization of violence against female-sexed bodies that has become commonplace in both pornographic and popular media. Instead, she complicates conventional narratives that posit rape as an act of sexual assault perpetrated (almost) exclusively against women and girls and reminds us—through excruciatingly affective means—that the sexualized feminization of the other is also a weapon of war and a familiar trope of violent nationalisms. For example, as Diana Taylor asserts in her analysis of Argentina's Dirty War, the military junta's torture scenarios were "organized as . . . sexual encounter[s]" in which both "male- and female-sexed bodies were turned into the penetrable, 'feminine' ones that coincided with the military's idea of a docile social and political body."[21]

What do military transgressions perpetrated by U.S. forces at Abu Ghraib, or by fictional characters in British playwright Sarah Kane's *Blasted*, or by Argentine's military junta have to do with Canada? Just as a binary gender lexicon can facilitate a feminist disavowal of female sexual aggression (and female aggression in militarized zones more broadly), Canada's narrative of peacekeeping and humanitarian militarism can serve as discursive camouflage for the military aggressions and transgressions perpetrated by Canadian Armed Forces while simultaneously allowing Canadians to critique the military aggressions and transgressions of other nations. I include these examples as a means of resisting popular discourses of national innocence and geopolitical exceptionalism, instead situating the Canadian Forces within the broader contexts of global militarism and hegemonic military masculinity.

As a nationalist scenario, military commemoration can also be seen as simultaneously masculinizing and feminizing the dead. Through its homogenizing elegiac narratives of heroism, the dead are remembered as (masculinized) "just warriors." Yet by denying individual voice or narrative to the dead, they are rendered not only physically dead but also politically docile and manipulable (feminized). Without individual voice or agency, they are but pixels in the big picture of both military masculinity and nationalist narratives. Considered this way, rather than honouring the dead, those who shape military commemoration's highly emplotted narratives may well be viewed as "having their way" with the dead. The dictates of hegemonic masculinity—which demands that its male subjects adamantly disavow any attributes considered "feminine" within dominant masculinity's ideological frameworks—ensure that there is little protest from veterans about the manipulation of their fallen comrades.

Violence's feminized sexualization also makes its aesthetic representation risky. As Taylor notes, in their efforts to represent the eroticized and feminized violence perpetrated by the Argentinean military junta, some post-junta theatrical productions problematically reproduced the violent narratives they sought to critically expose. For example, Taylor argues that while the production of Eduardo Pavlovsky's *Paso de dos*—performed by the playwright and (his wife) Susan Evans—exposed the junta's eroticized and feminized perpetrations of violence, it did so by staging "torture as a love story."[22] Unlike *Paso de dos*, Kane's *Blasted* effectively represents the terror of sexualized acts of violence without reproducing the erotic feminization of the violence that is being critiqued. Kane exposes rape as both a mechanism of violent domination and a mechanism of control that uses the sexualized feminization of the other as a weapon. Staged in the context of a queer theatre, *Blasted*'s male-on-male rape further reminds us that sexual violence cannot, and should not, be reduced to a "feminist" issue. Rather, it is part of the warp and weft of hegemonic masculinity.

While I concur with Ouzounian's assertion that the Buddies in Bad Times presentation of *Blasted* was rife with violent excess, I take issue with his dismissive characterization of Kane as "maniacal." Similar to the media's misdirected focus on Colonel Williams's cross-dressing "deviancy," Ouzounian diverts attention from the excesses of violent masculinity and war by conjuring historical echoes of women who are "too much," women who go "too far," "man-hating lesbians," "radical feminists," and all manner of "feminist killjoys," to borrow a term from Sara Ahmed. In contrast to Ouzounian, I applaud both Kane and the Buddies production for their unflinching representation of the excesses of militarism's normalized violent masculinity that is camouflaged by narratives of heroism and humanitarian militarism. In a way, it is odd how disturbing it is to see a dramatic portrayal that affectively conveys violence in our era of both real and media hyper-violence. For me, this is the play's brilliance: it portrays violence as horrific, not as the "death pornography" Geoffrey Gorer writes of (Chapter 1), and sexual violence as a terrorizing act of war, not as an eroticized "fantasy of reciprocal desire."[23]

Blasted also sheds light on how sympathy for victims of sexual violence is differentially allocated. Despite the affectively disturbing quality of his rape, Ian—*Blasted*'s male protagonist—does not come across as a sympathetic character. Within the context of the play, this has to do with his raping of his much younger girlfriend, Cate, and his general unpleasantness. But it is also reflective of sexual violence's victim hierarchy. As Stemple notes, at the top of the hierarchy are "innocent victims"—women (ideally white and either virginal or monogamous) who struggle frantically (but futilely) to resist the assault of a stranger. Women who know their assailant(s) or who are sexually active and non-monogamous rank lower, poor women of colour and sex workers lower yet, and trans women and homosexual men, who—like sex workers—are seen as "asking for it," even lower.

Heterosexual men who are raped are altogether off the chart of sexual violence's victim hierarchy. They are caught in the brittle bind of hegemonic masculinity where, since "'real men' should be able to prevent their own rape," to speak of being raped is to contribute to one's own feminization.[24] Just as Williams's dressing in women's clothes cast him outside of the realm of hegemonic masculinity, thereby absolving both the Canadian Armed Forces and military masculinity of his crimes, so too through their feminization are male rape victims "queered" and therefore cast outside of the realm of masculinity. The brittle fragility of our hegemonic gender binary dictates that masculinity can only be "achieved by the constant process of warding off threats to it."[25] Since being male does not make one impervious to rape, the only means heteronormative men who are raped have of warding off the threat of sexual violation's feminization is through the denial of their rape. Male-on-male rape then becomes a method not only of violation but also of rendering men perverse or queer, of unbecoming their masculinity, and in the process, of rendering them socially unbecoming or deviant.

Moreover, as Stemple notes, since the highest prevalence of male-on-male rape occurs in settings like prisons and conflict zones that are not considered sites of "innocence," there is even less sympathy for the victims. Men belonging to at-risk subgroups or otherized populations are particularly vulnerable to sexual violence. These include "refugees, the internally displaced, migrant workers, disabled men [and men from] a particular racial or ethnic group during armed conflict."[26] The vulnerability of these otherized men is amplified through their interactions with state-sanctioned authorities and associated institutionalized structures of control. Cast outside of the privileged (and unmarked) subjectivity of hegemonic masculinity and nationalistic norms, these are abjected (and marked) "others"—"illegal aliens," "criminals," "terrorists."

Like the male prisoners in Abu Ghraib, the abuse perpetrated on Shidane Arone by his Canadian Forces captors (Chapter 2) bears a remarkable resemblance to the scenarios of the violent perpetration of feminized sexualization discussed by Taylor. There are also similarities between Colonel Russell Williams and Arone's perpetrator, Master Corporal Clayton Matchee, and the crimes they both committed—forced confinement, torture, rape, murder. Perhaps the most obvious similarities between Williams and Matchee are that both were members of the Canadian Forces, both wore a Canadian Forces uniform, and both were cast (in different ways) by the Canadian Forces as anomalous "bad apples," not in any way as representatives of the Canadian military or military masculinity more broadly. In contrast to the similarities between their assailants, the status of Williams's and Matchee's victims within the imaginary of Canadian social memory differs radically. Marie-France Comeau and Jessica Lloyd—with their innocence paradoxically heightened and overshadowed by Williams's spectacularized depravity—rank high on the sexual victim hierarchy. Shidane Arone, to the extent that he ranks at all, does so as an otherized signifier of Canadian shame. Within the Canadian commemorative imagination, Arone has been reduced to the inconvenient dead body that "marred the [Canadian Forces'] otherwise successful deployment" in Somalia.[27]

Why this difference? Comeau and Lloyd were white Canadian women, whereas Arone was a black Somali teenager. Williams perpetrated his assaults in the bucolic setting of Ontario's cottage country on streets with names like Cosy Cove Lane, names coined to convey comfort and safety. Matchee, together with other members of his company, perpetrated their assault in a Canadian Forces camp in Belet Huen, Somalia, deep in the "dark heart" of Africa. Though—like Comeau and Lloyd—in addition to being tortured and murdered Arone was also raped, his assault is not framed as a sexual assault. Just as U.S. military captors sodomized their Abu Ghraib detainees,[28] according to witness accounts Matchee sodomized Arone with a stick.[29] But Arone is understood as neither an "innocent" victim nor a victim of rape. Unlike Comeau's and Lloyd's, Arone's forced confinement is not framed as a kidnapping; it was an authorized imprisonment, marking Arone a suspect.

Nor was there any need for a team of forensic detectives and a months-long investigation to find Arone's abusers and murderer. It is estimated that approximately eighty soldiers could hear Arone's screams throughout his night of torture and abuse. Yet as Razack's detailed account of testimony from soldiers who heard and witnessed Arone's torture illustrates, for the most part they did nothing to stop the abuse. In fact, taken together, their testimonies reveal how the (often sexualized) torture and abuse of the otherized Somali population at the hands of Canadian Forces personnel was disturbingly normalized. Despite the crimes perpetrated against Arone or the silent acquiescence of dozens of members of the Canadian Forces, public outrage over Arone's abduction and rape-murder and its military cover-up has been largely eclipsed by outrage over the defilement of Canada's imagined (and much-beloved) national innocence.

While I seek to resist essentialist notions of the "nature" of both "women" and "men," along with Kane, I believe it behooves us to consider the extent to which rape and war are logical conclusions of men's conditioning in performances of hegemonic masculinity. This is not a question of blame. In fact, as feminist scholars Fusco, Taylor, and Stemple—among others—argue, it is crucial that we look not only at the ways in which militarism enforces male dominance through its construction of a normalized backdrop of hegemonic masculinity, but also at how women and men are both implicated and affected. Connell likewise insists upon a plurality of masculinities. Even within the military, Connell argues, masculinity takes many forms: while some soldiers are trained to obey or to kill on command, some are trained to command others to obey and order others to kill.[30] Moreover, as has become increasingly evident in recent years, not all soldiers who are trained to obey, to kill, or as Fusco points out, to torture or perpetrate acts of sexual abuse on command—nor those who command others to obey, kill, or torture—are men.

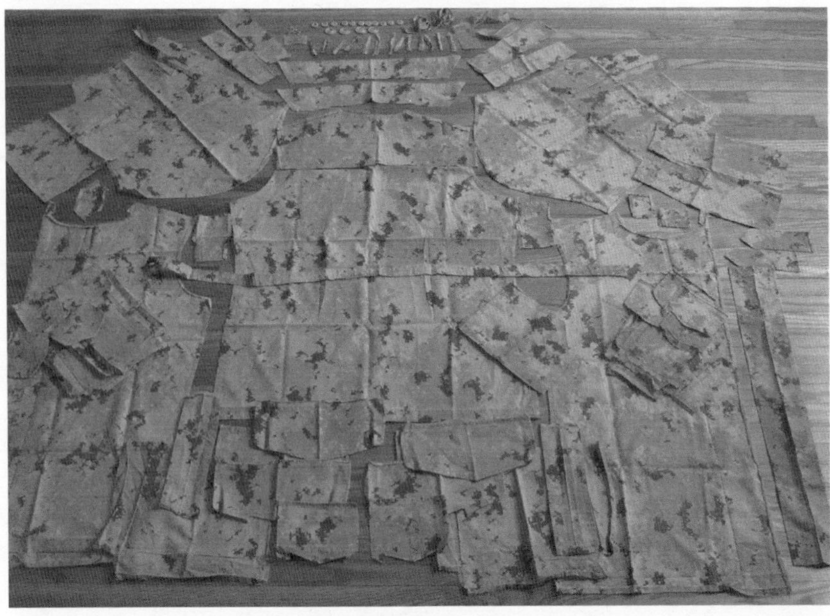

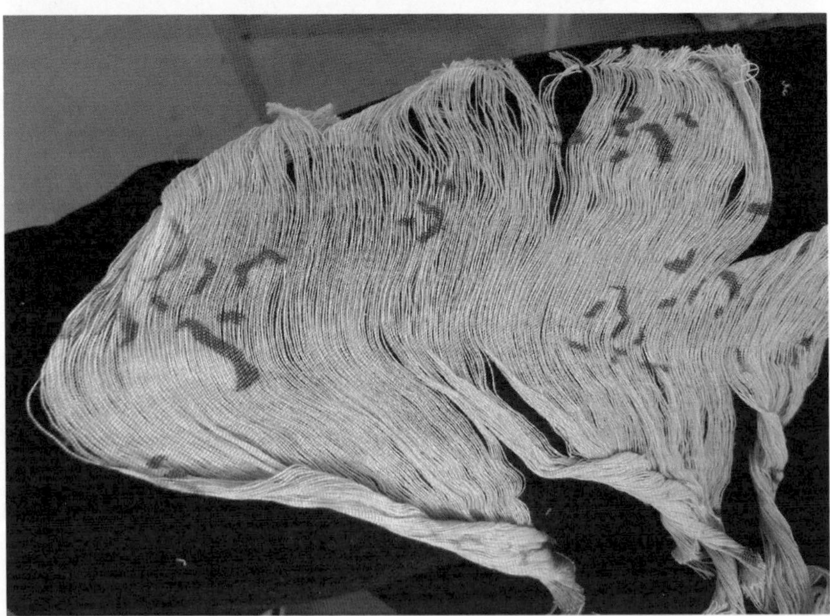

Figure 30. "Jacket," in ninety-four component parts: sixty-four cloth pieces; fifteen buttons (eleven small, four large); six pieces of Velcro (of varying sizes); six grommets; two cords; and one label.
Figure 31. "Ghostly Remains," Latitude 53 Contemporary Visual Culture, Visualeyez 2011.

Threads: From Vibrant Matter to Ghostly Disassemblage

15 September 2011
Visualeyez 2011, Edmonton
As I took the uniform apart at the seams and laid each piece out I found myself involuntarily overcome by feelings of tenderness for the body that bore its weight, for the iconic and iconically grievable soldier (Figure 30). *But the moments that most break my heart come later. When the final weft thread is pulled out and the warp threads remain as ghostly reminders of the hundreds, thousands, millions of history's nameless and forgotten dead who have been rent from the fabric of family, friends, and community, from the weave of life, through the violence of militarism and war* (Figure 31).

From October 2011 through 2014 I worked on deconstructing military uniforms—seam by seam, thread by thread. The first two of the uniforms I unravelled were desert-issue camouflage fatigues. I chose these fatigues as reference both to Canada's engagement in the U.S.-led (and NATO-supported) war in Afghanistan, and to the Canadian Armed Forces' use of the uniform in the images it posts of its Afghan war fallen soldiers.[31] Despite the Canadian military's use of desert-issue fatigues—made highly visible through public relations images and media images of Canadians killed in Afghanistan—the majority of Canadians who witnessed and participated in *Unravel's* (un) sewing circles associated the uniforms with the U.S. military.

I feared that like those who argued that since the militarized hyper-masculinist violence in Kane's *Blasted* was set amidst a fictive war in another place (Leeds, UK), the play had nothing to do with Canadian militarism, those who saw the uniforms I was unravelling as belonging to another military would perceive *Unravel* as having nothing to do with Canadian militarism. I was particularly concerned that *Unravel* might contribute to the popular narrative of Canadian geopolitical exceptionalism with its positioning of Canada as morally superior to our militarized southern neighbour. So for *Unravel's* third uniform I selected the more distinctive Canadian Disruptive Pattern—a computer-generated temperate woodland green camouflage currently used by the Canadian Forces at home.

The tangled remains of the first uniform (unravelled September 2011–May 2012) sit in a wooden bowl in my living room; the remains of the second (unravelled June 2012–March 2013) in a bowl on my porch. From the reverential object of the soldier's uniform, war's effects have become reconstituted in and through the assemblage of materials that went into its construction; in and through the conglomeration of actants involved in the production of thread, cloth, camouflage design, and the military and national identities they once constituted; in and through the tangled mass left in war's wake (Figure 35). From the singularity of the uniform as signifier of the privileged subject of national mourning has come "a polyvalence of sign and symbol," a ghostly disassemblage that makes strange the ritualized familiarity of war's loss, a tangled plurality that beckons one "to imagine the nonmeaning, or the true meaning, of the Thing."[32]

In *Vibrant Matter: A Political Ecology of Things*, Jane Bennett theorizes a vital materiality through which to unmake or unsettle the meaning of things and of the relationship between human and non-human vibrancies. Bennett's central provocation is that matter has its own intrinsic vitality and that life is not bifurcated into animate and inanimate, nature and culture, human and non-human, but is instead made up of a "heterogeneous monism of vibrant bodies."[33] Adopting Bruno Latour's concept of an "actant" as that which is "neither an object nor a subject but an 'intervener,'"[34] and following Deleuze and Guattari, Bennett uses the notion of "assemblage" to explore the ways in which vibrancy resonates not only through isolated things but also through heterogeneous groupings or confederations. Emphasizing "the agentic contributions of nonhuman forces . . . in an attempt to counter the narcissistic reflex of human language and thought," Bennett differentiates her vital materialism from historical materialism as a mechanism for exploring the ways in which matter, human, non-human and the non-human within the human, coexist and inter-animate.[35]

I find myself simultaneously enamoured with and troubled by Bennett's *Vibrant Matter*. Enamoured with the agency she affords to all manner of matter—and by her project of resisting both modernity's disenchantment of the world and critical theory's demystifying reduction of matter to that which is acted upon by human agents. I appreciate as well what Bennett posits as the "political goal of a vital materialism," the move toward a "polity with more channels of communication between its members," which necessitates an "extend[ed] awareness of our interinvolvements and interdependencies."[36]

Indeed, for me *Unravel* became a method of extending my conceptual awareness of the military uniform through engaging with it as an increasingly complex assemblage of vibrant matter. Through the uniform's undoing, the codes woven into the fatigues as a symbol of Every Warrior became undone. Unloosed from the uniform's dominant codes, the intrinsic vitality of the assemblage of materials—threads, buttons, Velcro, zipper, grommets—became more accessible. Through the process of unbecoming, the uniform began to assert an agency that refused the narcissistic control and limitations of my critical analysis. In the process of unravelling the uniforms, I too became undone. I was no longer the thinking human agent, the uniform the object of my analysis. The longer I unravelled, the more interconnected I became with the uniform's unfurled and unfurling warp and weft.

But while indebted to Bennett for her productive theorization of the vitality of matter, I am also troubled by the absences produced by and through her methodological and perspectival approach rooted exclusively within Western theoretical and literary archives. I empathize with (what may have been) the desire to avoid the troubling traps of primitivism and essentialism that haunt Western scholarship of non-Western "others." I am concerned, however, that Bennett's near wholesale omission of the multiple non-Western archival (theoretical and literary) lineages and repertorial practices, in which matter's inherent vibrancy as well as its human–non-human inter-animation is evident, reproduces a Western narrative of newness (by now quite old) and originality and re-performs what Taylor calls the "scenarios of discovery" that are so endemic to both Western scholarship and Western imperialism.[37]

When I first read the title of Bennett's book—*Vibrant Matter*—it reminded me of a line from a song, "Listen more often to things than to beings." "Breaths," the song, by the African American feminist a cappella group Sweet Honey in the Rock, is based on a translation of the poem "Souffles" by Senegalese poet Birago Diop. "The dead are not dead," writes Diop:

> They are in a woman's breast,
> A child's crying, a glowing ember.
> The dead are not beneath the earth,
> They are in the flickering fire,
> In the weeping plant, the groaning rock,
> In the wooded place, the home.
> The dead are not dead.[38]

Diop tells us that the ancestors' breath can be heard in the voices of fire, water, and wind, and in "the sobbing of the trees." Like Bennett, Diop insists on the need to cultivate an expanded sensory discernment in order to listen to the voice of things without their being overshadowed by beings. Unlike Bennett, however, the things to which Diop draws our attention defy notions of Western theoretical newness. They are things cross-temporally inter(in) animated by the spirits of the ancestors as a means by which the past speaks to and through the material present.

I do not doubt the value of Bennett's theorization of vibrant matter for the cultivation in *privileged* subjects of an increased sense of interdependency with things and "to counter the narcissism of humans in charge of the world."[39] But what of the world's majority of non-privileged subjects, especially those living in states of war or other states of extreme dispossession and violence? For populations for whom Western notions of human sovereignty do not apply, the sense of distance between their human subjectivity and the world of things is not nearly so vast.

For example, following Foucault, Cameroonian philosopher and political theorist Achille Mbembe argues that "the ultimate expression of sovereignty resides, to a large degree, in the power and the capacity to dictate who may live and who must die," and that historical considerations of modern terror must "address slavery, which could be considered one of the first instances of biopolitical experimentation."[40] The slave's value as property and as an instrument of production means that the slave was reduced to a thing whose object price and productive value required that they be "kept alive *but in a state of injury*, in a phantom-like world of horrors and intense cruelty and profanity."[41] Just as Nicholas Chare argues that as a result of their subjection to extreme abject conditions, Auschwitz survivors experienced the obliteration of language as a means of symbolic communication,[42] Mbembe notes how from within and "in spite of" an abject state of exception, the slave generates the agency to communicate and create: "Treated as if he or she no longer existed except as a mere tool of production the slave is nevertheless able to draw almost any object, instrument, language, or gesture into a performance and then to stylize it. Breaking with uprootedness and the pure world of things of which he or she is but a fragment the slave is able to demonstrate the protean capabilities of the human bond through music and the very body that was supposedly possessed by another."[43]

Mbembe's description of the slave's relationship with things and with the body as a "thing" possessed is very different from that of Bennett's *humans in charge of the world*. It is a relationship that demands a heightened and intimate sensory awareness of matter, and of all matter of interdependency, while simultaneously requiring a means to break from "the pure world of things."

Bennett's absenting of spirit as an animator of matter is similarly troubling for those whose histories are not archived and monumentalized but who look to cross-temporal inter(in)animation as a mechanism for transmitting cultural memory. As performance studies scholar Joseph Roach argues, for the dead of modernity's "diasporic and genocidal histories,"[44] cross-temporal cultural transmission functions as "restored behavior against a historical archive of scripted record."[45] Just as frames of war can be seen to de-realize populations whose narratives have not made their way into the frames' discursive legitimacy, and military commemoration can be understood to be productive not only of social memory but also of structural forgetfulness, a theory of vibrant matter rooted exclusively in a Western theoretical lineage risks foreclosing against mechanisms critical for the transmission of cultural memories that do not fit within the archival frame of Western theory.

Like the military uniform, the things Diop beckons us to listen to are imbued with a reverentiality; unlike the uniform, Diop's things do not have a singular or fixed identity onto which nationalism has inscribed meaning. Diop's things call for a different reverence, a reverence for that which reaches beyond language's symbolic and archival capacities to accurately represent experience, a reverence that enables the transmission of cultural memory across temporal and geospatial territories, a reverence that seeks to engender an attitude of hospitable reception for the ghosts of the forgotten dead of history. Diop proposes that true meaning involves listening to the material world of things for the voices of the past as they live on, in, and through the present.

Unloosing Obligatory Reverentiality

25 November 2011
Home, Toronto
Since my last visit to the war museum my unravelling sessions
have been filled with rage. Gone is the pretense of a peace—

however ambiguous. I unravel with a vengeance. The impossible task of deconstructing militarism has taken on an oppositional relationship to the impossibility of its deliberate construction and its eradicating omissions. Yesterday, as I was washing the dinner dishes, I heard a CBC news report about the Parliament Hill "celebration" of Canada's "successful" military engagement in Libya. There was a twenty-one-gun salute. Officials—military and government—were downright agog with their congratulatory military display. The Canadian Press has called the mission "a rarity in modern armed combat . . . quick, neat and painless."[46]

I hear the words "no casualties" and I'm dumbfounded. How is it possible that Canadian Forces dropped 600 bombs and there were no casualties? Then I understand. There were no Canadian *military casualties. As with the Afghan war, we don't waste either our airtime or our grief on the casualties of other nations (unless they are being killed by our "enemies" and can be used as ideological fodder).*

Unravelling does nothing to soothe my anger—it merely continues regardless of it.

Unlike the Canadian Armed Forces' incineration of Colonel Williams's uniforms, *Unravel*'s performance of always unbecoming is not intended as an act of exorcism or erasure. It is a cross-temporal evocation of the uniform's signs and symbols. It is a calling forth of the ghosts that haunt military commemoration's dominant nationalist narratives. It is a sticky vehicle for the communication of that which exceeds language's symbolic capacities. Working intimately with the uniform as one of war's ideologically infused material instruments provides a process through which to experience, imagine, and reimagine the vitality and agency of the uniform's assemblage of actants, the hauntedness of its threads, the multiple meanings and non-meanings of the "thing."

Though for the soldiers who wear them, as well as for their families and many members of the general population, military uniforms undoubtedly have multiple, even conflicting, meanings, the overarching narrative inscribed onto Canadian Forces military uniforms through military memorialization is one of heroism, benevolent militarism, and altruistic nationalism. The uniform is essential to military commemoration's discourse of righteous militarism and to its production of a hierarchy of grievability. Military uniforms constitute identities of national authority and reverentiality, signifying that their wearers have been granted not only a licence to kill (and perform other acts of violence) on behalf of the state but also a guaranteed place at the top of the nation's hierarchy of grievability—privileges that, together with a steady paycheque and promises of a post-service college or university education, may be particularly appealing to communities of relatively limited privilege. Those who wear the uniform under the banner of the Canadian flag are elevated to the top of Canada's hierarchy of grievability.

Within the realm of the dominant nationalist and heteronormative nation-state, it is considered unbecoming or deviant to refuse the call to prescribed norms. For example, Sara Ahmed argues that the family sustains its place as a foundational, obligatory "happy object" of Western culture by casting those who refuse to take up its prescriptions of happiness as "affect aliens."[47] "Feminist kill-joys, unhappy queers, and melancholic migrants" are considered destroyers of the family's happiness when they expose its unhappy sexism, heterosexism, and nationalistic racism.[48] I propose that in the same way, those who dare defy military commemoration's code of patriotic silence by questioning the geopolitical conditions that resulted in the loss they are being called upon to reverentially (and unquestioningly) mourn are recast as violators of the nation's heroic dead.

Military commemoration, in this sense, does more than place certain bodies beyond the realm of grievability and push entire histories and historical events to the margins of collective memory. It also obliges us to collude in the violence of nationalism's monumentalized and institutionalized forgetfulness. Instead of being called to participate in a polyvocal chorus of lament and critical reflection, military commemoration interpellates us with its fixed narrative of the nation's archetypal fallen hero. Because of the uniform's role in Canada's reiterated performance of military commemoration for selective losses in selective wars, I propose that as a signifier of the heroic warrior, it acts not only as an object of obligatory reverentiality but also as an object of national melancholia. The uniform bears the sticky trace of a nationalistically inscribed grief that can never be allowed closure, a grief that must be continually re-performed for the ongoing constitution of the nation-state. Moreover, through its participation in the performance of national mourning, the uniform simultaneously bears the affective impressions of the nation's *disavowal* of grief for the lives of "others" killed in the name of the state.

As philosopher and gender theorist Judith Butler and critical race scholar Paul Gilroy both argue, the inability to apprehend, and to therefore give up and grieve, the loss of the disavowed other results in a melancholic identification with the nation-state's disavowed object(s) of mourning. The dominant national community must then project this disavowal of loss, or ungrievability, onto the lives and losses of the nation's internal and external others, thereby producing the frames that justify waging new wars and that obscure the neo-liberal continuations of Canada's violent colonial past. Those bodies that do not serve nationalist discourses of righteous militarism are cast outside of military commemoration's frame of grievability. Within the context of Canadian military commemoration such bodies include (among others) the thousands of Afghan civilians who have died either as a direct result of military action or, indirectly, as a result of the effects of their violent displacement; the Somalis who were tortured to death or shot and killed by Canadian "peacekeepers"; the 600,000 German civilians who were targeted and perished in the Second World War Allied bombing campaign in which 50,000 Canadians took part; the twenty-five First World War Canadian soldiers who were shot by firing squads; the Indigenous populations who perished as a result of the European settlement of Canada (and who continue to perish as a result of institutionalized policies of cultural genocide and resource appropriation).

To successfully bestow its wearers with such troubling but nevertheless exalted privileges, citizen populations must both recognize and be obliged to relate to the uniform as part of a larger assemblage—flag, cannon, poppy, yellow ribbon—of nationalistically inscribed reverential objects. Read in association with the cannon's ritualized ear-splitting twenty-one-gun salute and the poppy, blossoming on jacket lapels of newscasters, politicians, veterans, and civilians, the uniform interpellates Canadians into the annual season of obligatory reverentiality that surrounds Remembrance Day. Situated as part of an ensemble in the performance of national mourning, camouflage fatigues worn by members of the Canadian Forces become differentiated from their role in other decidedly less reverential public displays as an object of entertainment, fashion, or even as an object of anti-military resistance.

This differentiation of the uniform's performance as a reverential object from its other popular cultural performances allows for the management of a range of affective relationships with the uniform. For example, at the Canadian War Museum, in some contexts—like the museum's Royal Canadian Legion Hall of Honour—the uniform is definitively positioned as an object of obligatory reverentiality. In the museum's spectacular and cathartic video *My World: Hope and Peace*, camouflage fatigues are the uniform worn by the soldiers we see bearing arms in peacekeeping missions, serving local communities, and grieving for fallen comrades. In other contexts, however—like the gift boutique or the area where children are invited to try on military attire—the uniform is transformed into an object of consumption and play.

As performance studies scholar Sara Brady notes, the management of the uniform's reverential affect has also been effectively re-deployed by anti-war veterans in the United States who have used their uniforms and other symbols of national military reverentiality in their anti-war struggles.[49] Similarly, many groups engaged in resistance struggles with dominant nation-state militaries also use camouflage fatigues. And throughout the United States and Canada, the presence of homeless veterans wearing their old military fatigues can also be read as a performance that, while not anti-militarist, certainly challenges the state's discourse of reverential regard for its just warriors by exposing the irreverential treatment it affords its discarded veterans.

Despite their reduction to ashes, traces of Williams's uniforms live on as ghostly remains. In our age of digital memory, images of Williams in both casual and formal military dress circulate on the internet—solemnly standing at attention at repatriation ceremonies or saluting as he stands next to Queen Elizabeth II, then prime minister Stephen Harper, and former defence minister Peter MacKay. But while complete erasure was not possible, the Canadian Forces have succeeded in ensuring that Williams's physical uniforms will never be part of commemoration's processes of reflection, that their threads will never be dragged through the weave to animate the silenced voices and stories, of living and dead, from past and present.

The Queer Art of Craft and the Temporal Drag of Unproduction

30 June 2012
Armley Mills, Leeds
Armley Mills, home to the Leeds Industrial Museum, was once the world's largest woollen mill and the primary producer of the cloth used by militaries throughout Europe. According to Barrie, the museum's gifted storyteller-guide, the women who worked at

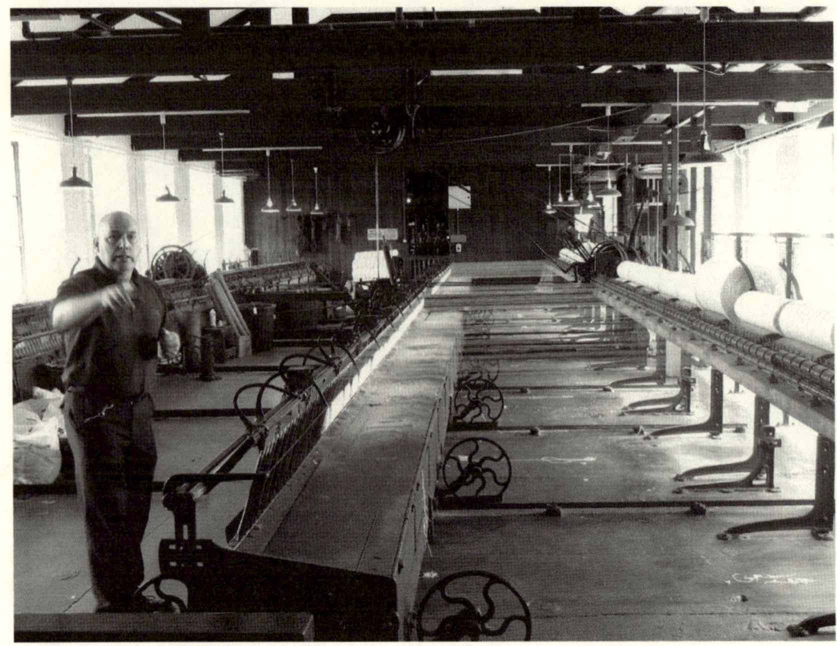

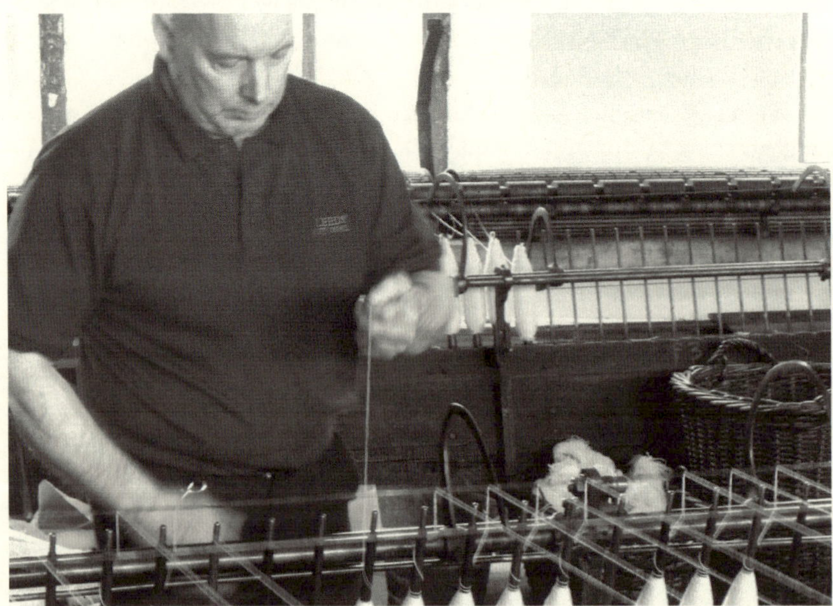

Figures 32 and 33. Barrie, spinning a yarn, and Barrie spinning yarn, Armley Mills, Leeds Industrial Museum.

the mill, in a quiet act of sabotage, once neglected to "set" the dye of a batch of cloth that was to be used to make uniforms for France's troops. When it rained the nation's military colour—blue—bled from the soldiers' coats.

Nestled within a circle of chairs, our table sits across from the massive industrial carding machine in the museum's sunny foyer. The threads from Unravel*'s first—now fully unravelled—uniform are at its centre. They are surrounded by the 191 component parts of the newly fragmented second uniform: 141 cloth pieces; 22 buttons (thirteen small, nine large); ten Velcro pieces; twelve grommets; three cords; one zipper; and two labels* (Figure 30). *From around the corner we can hear Barrie as he alternates his spinning of anecdotal yarns with the spinning of dozens of spools of white thread on the mill's 100-year-old spinning mule, deftly dragging narrative threads from the mill's past into the corporeal present* (Figures 32 and 33). *For three days, accompanied by the clattering din of the mule, a small and shifting group of (un)sewers unravelled* (Figure 34).

In June 2012, as part of the Performance Studies International (PSi) conference and Leeds's Ludus Festival, *Unravel* ventured into the public arena and hosted a three-day (un)sewing circle at Armley Mills, the Leeds Industrial Museum. As with *Unravel*'s inaugural public performance in Edmonton, *Thread-by-Thread* was a porous event that invited participants into an experiential, collective, and conscious re-engagement with the processes, products, and consequences of our collective labour through the task-based performance of unproduction.

Constructed not only of armies of men (and increasingly women), of weapons and their delivery systems, militaries are also made up of the mundane objects needed to nurture and sustain life. Textiles and their manufacture from raw material into cloth, uniforms, bedding, and shelter are an integral component of the military-industrial complex, as are the gestures of globalized industrial labour through which they are produced: gestures shaped through a transnational choreography of technologically enhanced and Taylorized production, with its accompanying ensemble of subcontracted supply chains of increasingly precarious labour; fragmented and abstracted gestures that alienate makers not only from the process and product of their labour but also from its geopolitical consequences.

Despite radical shifts in the logics that drive textile production, the association of women with cloth remains largely intact. The gendered structuring of transnational globalization, on the other hand, is often masked by dominant discourses that frame economics as gender neutral. Connell argues that not only are global markets not gender neutral, they are "inherently, not accidentally, arenas of gender formation and gender politics" that together operate to produce a "world gender order."[50] Connell is not suggesting that this gendered world order is based in a biologically essentialized gender binary of fixed and universalized masculinity and femininity. Rather, he argues that it has been produced by, and is reflective of, the gendered historical processes of imperialism and colonialism that today continue to be manufactured and maintained through networks of economic neo-colonialism interwoven with military and paramilitary expansionism. Our "current growth of world markets and systems of financial control," Connell posits, "has seen gender divisions of labour remade on a massive scale in the 'global factory' (Fuentes & Ehrenreich), as well as the spread of gendered violence alongside Western military technology."[51]

As with the too-easily gendered linkages of war, peace, and piecework, the resurgence of crafting and its use as an alter-globalization and anti-war tactic have stirred feminist debates. While Germaine Greer argues that engaging the gendered lexicon of craft as a political tactic may be counter to feminist goals and that crafting itself is "an exercise in futility [and] heroic pointlessness,"[52] Kristy Robertson suggests that unlike their feminist predecessors of the 1970s and '80s, today's "radical knitters and the Stitch n' Bitchers [have] a sophisticated understanding that the making of any textile is connected to the capitalist system."[53] And drawing on José Esteban Muñoz's theory of disidentification as a performative tactic for "queering traditional identities"—like the gendered identities associated with crafting (and textile manufacturing)—Lacey Jane Roberts proposes a "critical craft theory" that rethinks crafting as a "tactic of ambiguity" and uses queer theory as a framework for negotiating contemporary craft's "identity crisis" impasse.[54] Roberts writes: "By flipping and displacing denigrating and confining stereotypes through tactics of performance and appropriation, craft can reimagine itself. . . . Through the dismantling and reconfiguration of its own stereotypes, craft is positioned as a potent agent to challenge the very systems that create and proliferate stereotypes to maintain hierarchies of visual and material culture."[55]

Anti-militarist crafters enlist craft's gendered lexicon to produce a queer range of crafty challenges to militarism and war. With *antipersonnel*, a series of hand-knit and stuffed replicas of anti-personnel mines, Barb Hunt "juxtaposes the mindfulness and time dedicated to a knitting project with the contemplation of 'knowledge that is otherwise too difficult to bear.'"[56] For her disarming *Pink Tank* project, Marianne Jørgensen collaborated with members of the Cast Off Knitters as well as individual crafters from around the world to "knit and [assemble] over four thousand squares into a covering for a World War II era combat tank as a protest against the ... war in Iraq."[57] And craft artist Liz Collins's Knitting Nation laboriously deploys craft "to question ideas of nationhood through parody."[58] In a "spectacle of craft," Collins and her ensemble of workers labour at knitting machines to produce large-scale installations like the gigantic and unwieldy American flag they created as part of artist Allison Smith's queer civil war re-enactment *The Muster* (2005).[59]

Knitting, crochet, and other handcrafts also stubbornly resist the temporal sensibilities of transnational production. The sedentary hours Hunt spends constructing her pink-hued land mines facilitate a meditation on the ambiguity of production in the face of destruction: "[I will] sit and knit for a few hours and enjoy it a lot, then suddenly realize that during that time about half a dozen people were injured or killed by a land mine somewhere in the world."[60] The temporal vulnerability of the materials in Jørgensen's pink-squared blanket, set in intimate proximity with the hard metallic contours of the tank, brings attention to the precariousness of flesh in its encounter with military weaponry. And as participants in Smith's queer call to arms, Collins's army of knitters deploy their craft with technical skill, in a "spectacle of slowness [that] offers a time-out to the [Civil War re-enactment] audience to observe acts of making usually sequestered from the public gaze."[61]

In her analysis of Smith's *Muster* as an example of the "double-edged politics ... of *affiliating* battle re-enactment with decidedly Left-wing art practices," performance studies scholar Rebecca Schneider "questions what it means to *protest* then, now."[62] Schneider is interested in temporality's sticky slip and slide—the way time and the consequences of its passing (and not passing) "give lie to the Enlightenment mandate that *we head into our futures undetained*."[63] If performative re-doing or re-enactments drag time through time, or make visible the past's present, and if craft's "spectacle of slowness" creates a time out of time, what of the temporality of undoing, of uncrafting, of the unbecoming performance of unproduction?

28 June 2012
Armley Mills, Leeds
On the second of Unravel*'s three-day unsewing circle at Armley, "Mike," a British military veteran who had served in Bosnia, stopped by. Examining the disassembled uniform, Mike tells us that he is currently working as a private contractor for the British Army in Afghanistan. He talks about the many "civilian" deaths in Afghanistan we don't hear about in the media. It takes me a moment to realize that the civilians Mike is talking about aren't those I usually associate with the term collateral damage. Mike is talking about contracted civilian employees of the British, U.S, and NATO ally militaries. Workers who, according to Mike, are made up of a confounding mix of nationalisms—British, Afghan, Filipino, Turkish, Russian, Bosnian, Serbian, Croatian—an army of dispossessed not-so-former "enemies" reassembled to service a war against a newly constituted enemy.*

For three days participants and witnesses passed through *Unravel*'s Armley Mills *Thread-by-Thread* (un)sewing circle. Some unravelled. Some witnessed. Some spoke. Some were silent. Some simply passed by. They were PSi conference goers who made the trek from Leeds University. They were museum visitors who happened upon *Unravel.* They were members of the museum's staff who spent their breaks with us. And they were individuals who learned of the (un)sewing circle through local arts and craft listservs. Those who participated shared stories, reflections, and associations—about war, about peace, about death, about cloth and thread, about labour and art, about pasts, presents, and possible futures.

Many participants and passersby inquired about my plans for the threads. In fact, this is the question I have most frequently been asked since I began unravelling. People offered visions of possible transformation of the threads—a crocheted tablecloth, a nest, friendship bracelets. Members of the knitting circle we shared the museum's sunny craft room with one afternoon expressed their unanimous (and almost lusty) desire to re-spin the threads into yarn. Others were not so interested in the threads. Mike wondered if I'd considered unravelling with veterans as a way of processing their war experiences. And Katja, whom I sat with side by side for three hours on *Thread-by-Thread*'s final day at Armley, was more interested in what the task of unravelling engendered: "*Thread-by-Thread* goes far beyond the produced or un-produced threads. . . . Its temporality *is* the time spent un-producing them; the time of being together and being at times alone with your own thoughts; the minute affects, sensations, reflections, conversations that emerge during this time of creative un-production, which re-appropriates (even if temporarily) the cognitive and affective territories from the dictums of production."[64]

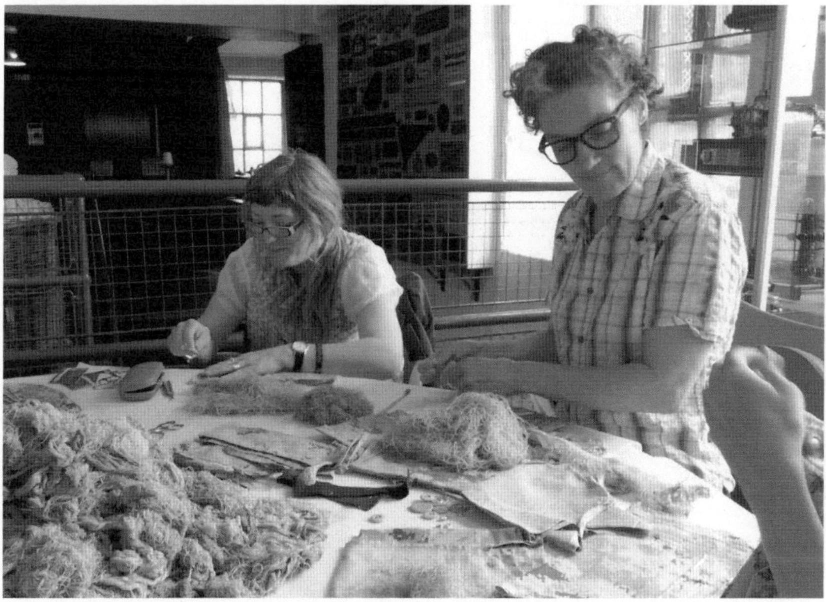

Figure 34. Carrie and Helene, Armley Mills.

I come from a long line of unravellers. Sweaters undone, yarns rewound and re-knit. Wearers—past, present, future—uncannily connected through yarn's intimate encounter with skin, and through the hands that heroically make, unmake, and make again. So I share with many of *Thread-by-Thread*'s participants and witnesses the impulse to redo, to remake, to construct anew. But I am wary of the symmetry the idea of remaking evokes—as though it is possible to *head into our futures undetained* by the messy geopolitical tangles of past and present. Like Katja, I believe that "undoing an economic and military product" is an endeavour potentially requiring an infinite amount of time, a task both born of and seeking to resist "the infinite nature of capital's expansionist logic [which] reveals itself in its most absurd and paradoxical light: we could say that capital needs to produce more wars in order to produce more uniforms in order to produce more wars, etc., etc., ad infinitum."[65] Also like Katja, I do not think of *Unravel* and its *Thread-by-Thread* (un)sewing circles as a "road to some other place" but rather as a commitment to a way of passing time in "revolutionary (unproductive) labour."[66]

Rather than prompting me into redoing, *Unravel* has nurtured my belief in the productive potential of undoing and unbecoming. Like Mike, I imagine an (un)sewing circle of veterans: each with a fragmented segment of their own military uniform cradled in their lap, each engaged in the ambiguous task of pulling thread, after thread, after thread from the fabric's weave. There is conversation. Reflections are shared. There is also silence—or near silence—when all that can be heard is the hiss of threads as they exit cloth's weave. I also imagine (un)sewing circles as durational grieving rituals where spouses, children, parents, friends, and comrades of the deceased gather to collectively dismantle their loved one's uniforms. Sometimes I imagine *Unravel* as a global tactile chorus of lamenters unravelling military uniforms from across a transnational range of violent nationalisms. Unlike the obliging demands of military commemoration's regimented and scripted rituals of remembrance, *Unravel* does not demand that its chorus of (un)sewers disavow the polyvocality of either affect or narratives associated with death. It does not demand grief's allegiance to temporal or geopolitical boundaries.

What if, instead of incinerating Colonel Williams's uniforms, people had been invited to take them apart, seam by seam, thread by thread? What conversations might such an aggravating yet necessarily care-filled task engender? What if, as part of his sentence, Williams was made to sit and engage in the painstaking task of dismantling his own uniforms? What if institutions dedicated to remembering war—like the Canadian War Museum—set up participatory tasks for their visitors, less geared toward entertainment and indoctrination or "transformation" and "reconciliation" and instead focused on facilitating a difficult return through undoing, through an engagement in the critical process of unbecoming? What might be gained by exposing rather than exorcising the war wounds of not only the nation's privileged warriors but of all those who are wounded by war? What if rather than preserving selected trophies from selected wars (while destroying others), we set up dismantling stations as sites of collective reckoning? If instead of dining in the midst of the LeBreton Gallery's artillery, aircraft, and armoured vehicle display, museum guests were invited to take screwdrivers and metal files in hand? What if the time and resources that we currently invest in constructing and maintaining memorialization's spectacle of our perpetually dehistoricized present, we instead invested in the infinite and haunting labour of unproduction?

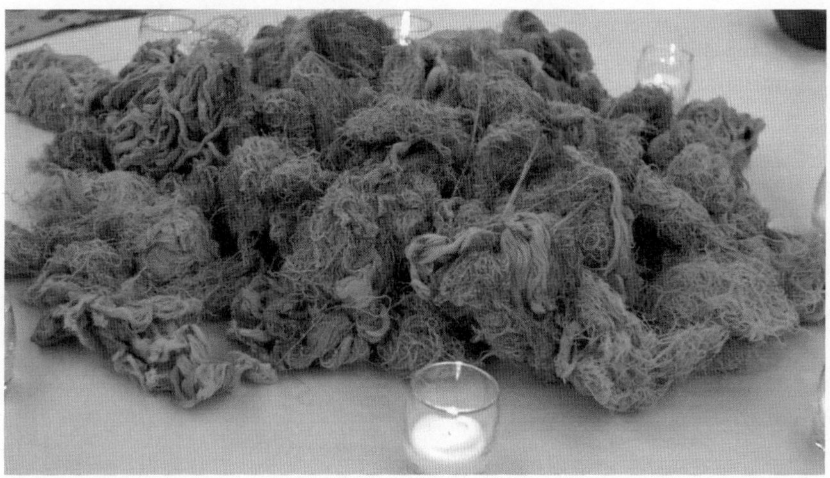

Figure 35. "Threads," Festival of Original Theatre 2012, Toronto.

From the perspective of military and transnational production rationalities, or of history as a dialectical forward momentum, *Unravel* and its (un)sewing circles are undoubtedly queer endeavours. Through the uniform's unbecoming, the plurality of its assemblage is made visible. Undone, the uniform is freed from the obligatory reverential rule of military commemoration's homogenizing discourse and liberated from the burden of elegiac praise and nationalistic loyalty. Through the tactile task of dismantling the uniform, the thread's past inter(in)animates the tangle of thread in the political present. Relationships and histories are "temporally dragged"; participants and witnesses hailed, as thread through weave; the fixedness of militarism, of nationalist identities and ideologies, and of binary masculinized and feminized lexicons unloosed; pasts are unravelled into a present busy with the infinite piece/peace work of unproduction, of unweaving the shroud of militarism's future.

CHAPTER FOUR

THE CANADIAN MUSEUM FOR HUMAN RIGHTS

COLLISIONAL ENCOUNTERS OF UNBECOMING CANADIAN NATIONALISMS

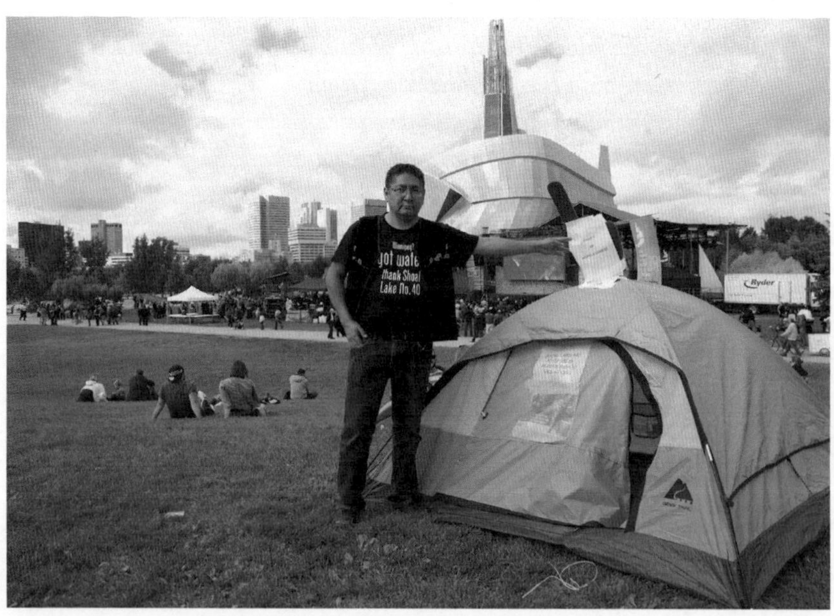

Figure 36. The Canadian Museum for Human Rights (background), and the Shoal Lake 40 First Nation Museum *for* Canadian Human Rights Violations (foreground).

On 19 September 2014 the Canadian Museum for Human Rights opened its doors. Located at The Forks—the meeting point of the Red and Assiniboine Rivers—in Winnipeg, Manitoba, the $351 million national museum occupies a key historic site for the region's Indigenous communities. In *Miracle at the Forks: The Museum That Dares to Make a Difference*, Peter C. Newman and Allan Levine begin their celebratory tale of the museum and its founder, Israel (Izzy) Asper, with a new spin on colonialism's scenario of discovery. "The key to reading this book," they tell readers, "is remaining open to discovery. It is designed to replicate the lively journey of a wanderer traversing the wilderness of the Red River's backcountry and suddenly encountering a palace. The building has no recognizable shape, and seems to be wrapped in candy floss, but it draws the wandering visitor into its vertical embrace through a symbolic 'pillar of fire' that pierces the prairie sky."[1]

On the weekend of the museum's long-awaited launch, members of the Shoal Lake 40 First Nation community offered weary wanderers a pup tent pit stop as they braved the backcountry wilds of The Forks en route to the candy-floss palace with its twenty-three-storey sky-piercing tower (Figure 36). Piggybacking on the Canadian Museum for Human Rights' celebration of benevolent Canadian nationalism, Shoal Lake 40 deployed its performatively disidentificatory and tactically astute Indigenous humour to launch its own museum—the Museum *for* Canadian Human Rights Violations. Community activists passed out brochures and set up camp: along with their mini-museum pup tent, they had a tepee and a fire pit ringed with collapsible camping chairs, thereby creating a hospitable space for critical engagement. Gracing the brochure's cover (Figure 37) is a photo of the human rights museum in all its architectural glory accompanied by the text: "You have heard of the Canadian Museum *for* Human Rights. NOW! 100 years in the making, Shoal Lake 40 is pleased to announce the grand opening of the Canadian Museum *for* Human Rights Violations."[2]

Shoal Lake 40 First Nation is located 100 kilometres east of Winnipeg. In 1916 over 3,000 acres of the community's land was expropriated by the Canadian government in order to supply water to the City of Winnipeg. Forced to relocate to a peninsula, Shoal Lake 40 was cut off from the mainland by a diversion canal for the water supply system. The community's isolation on this man-made island has made travel dangerous and community infrastructure and economic development projects prohibitively expensive. In a creative and tactical diversion of the lexicon of disaster tourism, Shoal

Lake 40's Canadian Museum *for* Human Rights Violations brochure invites visitors to "SEE RIGHTS DENIED" and "EXPERIENCE: Actual Restrictions of Your Own Freedom of Movement!" Beneath the image of the human rights museum's sky-piercing Tower of Hope is a photo of the partially frozen lake that is the community's only access route during Manitoba's long winter months. The cost of entry? Risking one's life to access the museum. "Level of risk," the brochure warns, "may vary by season and weather" (Figure 38).

While it provides drinking water for the City of Winnipeg, Shoal Lake 40 had been on a boil-water alert for over seventeen years at the time of the Canadian Museum for Human Rights' opening launch. It is not surprising, then, that the community took issue with repeated boasts made by the museum's celebrated architect, Antoine Predock, that the building design honours First Nations' relationship to water, as is illustrated in this description I accessed from Predock's website in November 2016: "Like a mirage within the Museum, the Garden of Contemplation is Winnipeg's Winter Garden. Basalt columns emerge from the top surface of the timeless granite monolith. Water and medicinal plants define space and suggest content. The First Nations sacred relationship to water is honored, as a place of healing and solace amidst reflections of earth and sky. The space of the Garden functions as a purifying 'lung' reinforcing the fundamental environmental ethic, which grounds the building."[3]

Lest he was unaware of the injurious material effects of the Government of Canada's water larceny on behalf of the City of Winnipeg, Shoal Lake 40's Chief Steward Redsky wrote to Predock in 2007 to inform him of "a few important facts" to consider before using water as a symbol of "healing and solace."[4] After a detailed listing of the ongoing harmful effects the diversionary canal was having on the Shoal Lake 40 community, Chief Redsky concluded his letter with these words: "So, you see, Mr. Predock, the water available in Winnipeg is hardly a symbol of 'healing and solace' in Canada, in Winnipeg or anywhere else in the world. The water that you would use in your building has, in fact been taken at the *expense* of our community and our human rights. Our friends and family members have literally died in that water. That water is making our people sick and Canada's refusal to stand up for our rights and to correct the isolation they imposed on us is killing our economy and our community."[5]

Electing not to honour Chief Redsky with a response, Predock instead persisted in using the healing waters metaphor on his website for years.

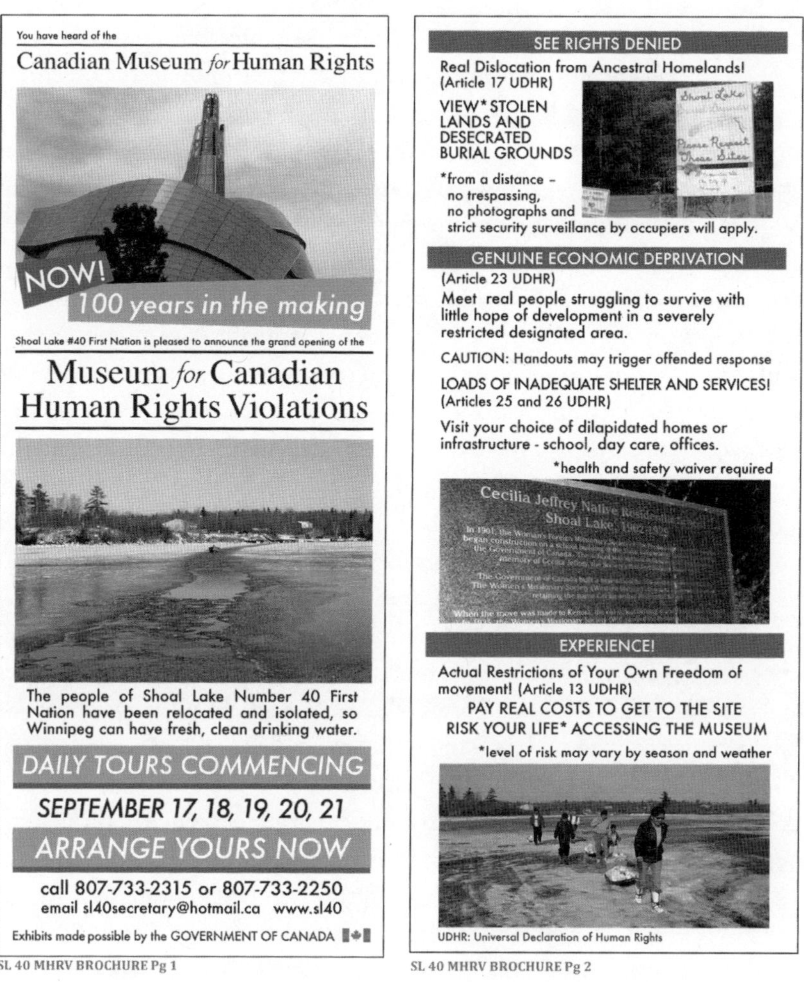

Figures 37 and 38. Shoal Lake 40 Museum *for* Canadian Human Rights Violations brochure.

Undaunted in their efforts to expose the misappropriations of water as both physical and metaphoric resources, four months before the Canadian Museum for Human Rights opened its doors, Shoal Lake 40 issued a press release that contained an open letter addressed to Predock, a letter from Craig Benjamin, campaigner for the Human Rights of Indigenous Peoples with Amnesty International, and copies of previous unanswered letters and emails that had been sent to Predock since 2007. Again, no response—not from Predock, at any rate. Instead, Angela Cassie, the museum's Director of Communications and External Relations, intervened, suggesting that the Shoal Lake 40 community leave Predock alone and direct their communications to the City of Winnipeg. The museum's architect, Cassie explained, "designed the building, he's not responsible for city services."[6] But Shoal Lake 40 activists refused to limit their appeal to a municipal department, to Predock, or to the museum. In addition to their campy pup tent and brochure, community activists made effective use of the human rights museum's spectacular launch as a media event by issuing their own statement, which was picked up by the local and national press: "At the settlers' end of the water pipe there's economic prosperity, clean drinking water and a $350 million building that advertises 'healing' and brags about what a wonderful country Canada is. At our end of the pipe, we have 17 years of boil-water order, no job opportunities and we are forced to risk our lives for basic necessities. It's important that the world have opportunity to see that huge Canadian contradiction."[7]

With its pup tent mini-museum, Shoal Lake 40 did more than mimic and mock the Canadian Museum for Human Rights' architectural extravagance. Together with their letters and press releases, Shoal Lake 40 activists exposed the hypocrisy of Predock's and the museum's metaphoric misappropriation of indigeneity which capitalized on abstracted and reverential narratives of First Nations' historical relationship to the environment while in the material present denying them land rights and customary access to land-based resources. As Eve Tuck and K. Wayne Yang argue, despite its popularization as a discursive gesture, "decolonization is not a metaphor."[8] Accordingly, Predock's and the museum's metaphorization of an ethics of environmental indigeneity does not count as a decolonizing gesture; a meaningful honouring of the First Nations relationship to the environment would demand a redistributive justice process that "brings about the repatriation of Indigenous land and life."[9] In foregrounding water rights, Shoal Lake 40 illuminated a fundamental distinction—and conflict—between human rights and Indigenous rights.

Whereas human rights "reflect a universalizing notion of humanity," writes native studies scholar Peter Kulchyski, "aboriginal rights, by contrast, are rights that only certain people and peoples, indigenous peoples, have by virtue of being indigenous."[10] Rights discourse, explains Kulchyski, operates on conflicting conceptual plateaus with "human rights, citizenship rights, and property rights intersect[ing] on one plateau [while] aboriginal rights, customary rights, and treaty rights operate on another."[11] At the crux of the conflict between human rights and Aboriginal rights is the "incommensurability" of settler-colonial and Indigenous world views in relation to the environment.[12] Since human rights are embedded in Enlightenment narratives of progress, individualism, and scientific reason, an individual's or a corporation's right to own and profit from the environment becomes normalized and protected as "rights."

Based in an ideology of capitalist modernity, settler colonialism sacrifices the environment and Indigenous customary and treaty rights to the logic of capital accumulation, wherein the environment is reduced to a resource to be mined for the production of profit—"healing waters" be dammed. The case of Shoal Lake 40 is not an isolated example of Indigenous rights violations perpetrated by governmental and government-supported corporate bodies. In 2016, Human Rights Watch issued a report stating that there were 133 ongoing boil-water advisories in First Nations communities across Canada.[13] The same logic that resulted in the diversion canal that left Shoal Lake 40 landlocked on a man-made island has also produced the extensive Manitoba Hydro dam projects that provide Winnipeg with electricity (for both its own usage and for export) while severely damaging much of the customary and treaty lands of northern Manitoba First Nations communities. Rivers that once ran clear are now silt-ridden. Fish, once plentiful, are now scarce. Eroding riverbanks spew deadwood into the waters, making them treacherous—often fatally so—to navigate. Hunting grounds and traplines are destroyed as miles of bush are cleared to make way for the towering power lines, and more land is flooded by the massive dams.

In contrast to the intersecting relationships between human rights, citizenship rights, and property rights that form the ideological core of Enlightenment-based rights discourses, "land rights" for Indigenous peoples are not analogous to property ownership, and the measure of the environment's worth is not defined by capitalism's extractive profiteering logic or its totalizing concept of ownership. They are rights of use that demand for their continuance a reciprocal relationship with the environment, a relationship of mutual caring, not exploitative extraction. But as with the unmarked and naturalized role of the heteronormative nuclear family in the (re)production of the nation-state and its armies on display at the Canadian War Museum (Chapter 2), the exploitative and extractive environmental ethic of settler colonialism, neo-liberal nationalism, and capitalism remains normalized and unmarked at the Canadian Museum for Human Rights.

Looked upon as an accidental allegory, Newman and Levine's discovery-themed narration of the miracle at The Forks unreflexively illuminates elements of the collisional encounter of these conflicting world views. They describe a midnight drive Izzy Asper took in 2000 through the streets of Winnipeg, on his quest to find the perfect site on which to build his museum. Asper arrives at an "*unoccupied* gravel parking lot at The Forks" and, despite the late hour, calls Moe Levy, his "confidant, trusted trouble shooter, and *hit man*" to convey his "*orders*": "I found it! I found the land. . . . It's at the Forks, and I want you to tie it up by the end of the week."[14] Given the late hour the parking lot may well have been empty, but The Forks has a history as a site of gathering and seasonal habitation for Indigenous communities. Its reduction to a piece of property available for the taking reflects an ideology of ownership that contradicts principles of customary rights and practice.

While I do not necessarily concur with Asper's assertion that The Forks was the ideal location to build a multi-million-dollar museum with a mandate of addressing issues of human rights, I do believe that the contradictions generated by the placement of Asper's palatial museum are proving uncannily productive in exposing Canada's unbecoming settler-colonial scenario of discovery, and in providing an institutional platform for developing potentially meaningful collaborations. On one side of the contradictory divide, with his bold acquisitional issuance Asper performed a citational repeat of a series of decrees that have for centuries bestowed colonial and corporate dominion over lands deemed "unoccupied," "unproductive," or "empty." Likewise, with its reverential assimilation of the narrative of The Forks as "a historic meeting place" into its lore, the Canadian Museum for Human Rights performs an act of discursive annexation that reframes economic and national occupation as reciprocal encounter.[15] Unlike Shoal Lake 40's nomadic camp, the museum dominates the landscape. It is a citadel constructed to celebrate and promote an amalgamation of Canada-the-good nationalism and neo-liberal modernity.

On the other side of the divide, through its dramatic architectural occupation of The Forks, its celebrated gathering place parable, and its repeated iterations of indigeneity as a metaphor for all things—place, architecture, history—the museum advertently or inadvertently provokes a critical encounter of collisional world views. Whereas the Canadian War Museum's military-cultural memory stakeholders have been highly successful in producing a largely impervious bunker-like discourse of a unified Canadian multicultural nationalism in support of humanitarian militarism, I propose that the Canadian Museum for Human Rights' self-narration is proving far more penetrable and malleable. In particular, the museum's foregrounding of an environmentally reverential indigeneity has set in motion a clash of world views that is generating cracks in its institutional mandate as an instrument of nation building. Left alone, these fissures could be easily glossed over, obscured by the museum's architectural iconography and multimedia spectacles. Instead, an array of tactical creative interventions by an "assemblage" of Indigenous artists, activists, and scholars is skillfully working in, on, and through these cracks, extending and expanding them, so that they propagate rhizomic webs and unbecoming clefts and crannies in the museum's monumental occupation of The Forks, its limiting human rights discourse, and its projection of a benevolently becoming Canadian nationalism.[16]

In Chapter 2, I focused on the Canadian War Museum's representations of Canada's "First Peoples," in its opening exhibit, *Battleground: Wars on Our Soil*, and of Somalia and Rwanda in its closing exhibit, *The Savage Wars of Peace*. These exhibits, which act as colonial and neo-colonial bookends to the museum's main galleries, illustrate how Canada's popular mythologies of multicultural inclusivity and geopolitical moral exceptionalism necessitate the masking of the racism of white settler Canadian nationalism, and the disavowal of Canada's colonial history and its ongoing neo-colonial and neo-liberal enactments. In this chapter, I continue the inquiry into the relationship between institutional representations of Canadian nationalism and the disavowal of settler colonialism through an analysis of the Canadian Museum for Human Rights as an uncanny site of encounter between Indigenous and settler-Canadian world views.

Reading against the grain of the museum's Enlightenment narratives, against the processional flow of its alabaster-lit journey from darkness to the Tower of Hope, I look at the museum as a performance of settler colonialism's ongoing scenario of discovery and exploitative extraction restaged on the contemporized *mise-en-scène* of benevolent Canadian neo-liberal nationalism. As performance studies scholar Diana Taylor argues, despite their migrations across time and space, "performances . . . are always in situ: intelligible in the framework of the immediate environment and issues surrounding them."[17] The Canadian Museum for Human Rights as a performance situates colonialism's discovery scenario within the physical and historical context of The

Forks in Winnipeg, a city born as a contested site of contact and collision and a site on which contemporary discourses and struggles around issues of Canadian nationalism, racism, First Nations redress, resource extraction, and genocide continue to play out.

What are the stories the museum tells about itself and its relationship to Indigenous communities, the environment, The Forks, and the Treaty One land it so unabashedly occupies? What are the contradictions between the story of the museum's architecture and its performance as a material and an iconographic structure? What's left invisible and unmarked through the museum's foregrounding of an architectural metaphor of a naturalized environmental indigeneity? How are Indigenous curators, artists, and activists using the museum's foregrounding of an environmentally reverential indigeneity to generate cracks in its institutional mandate as an instrument of nation building and its accompanying narratives of a Canada as becoming nation?

Discovering the Canadian Museum for Human Rights

17 January 2016
Buhler Hall, Canadian Museum for Human Rights:
Discover the Building tour
It's difficult to hear Sandra's voice against the backdrop of my withheld protestations. But I remain silent. It's not a comfortable, peaceful silence. It's a roiling reserve. A reticence that antagonizes my tongue, my lips—reverberates about my ears. Why not speak up? Why not intervene in Sandra's celebratory tale of the museum and its venerated relationship with Indigenous communities, with the environment, with this Treaty One land? Can my silence be reduced to evidence of a prototypical Canadian-ness? Or, is it that . . . and more? A conditioned performance of settler-Canadian civility—perhaps—but also a product of decades of training in the protocols of obligatory reverentiality. Here, in this palace-shrine with its overwrought compilation of stories of historical violation, genocide, and human rights struggles, do objections themselves become violating infractions? Would dissent be construed as an act of disregard for those whose suffering is represented?

Frenetically recording Sandra's words into my small notepad, I tell myself that my silence is part of a methodology. I'm here to listen. Here to do research, not to engage in civil discourse. I'm here to investigate the stories the Canadian Museum for Human Rights, as an institution, tells about itself in relationship to Indigenous peoples and the land on which the museum is built, to pay attention to what is said and to the silent omissions that lurk in the cracks and crannies of the telling. I can't help but wonder, though, how my methodology, and my silence, contribute to the story.

Sandra, our "Discover the Building" tour guide, begins with a confession: "I thought the building was ugly," she tells us, "but that was before I understood its architecture."[18] Her disclosure is met with a ripple of relieved—or perhaps nervous—laughter. We who share Sandra's dirty secret are off the hook while also having been apprised that our negative assessment of the building's architecture is likely a misguided product of our ignorance. From Sandra's demeanour it is clear: we are about to embark on an enlightening journey that will bestow upon us the information we require to more fully appreciate the architectural wonders of the museum.

We are a group of ten. Five are Winnipeggers, two are from Edmonton, another two from San Francisco, and myself, Winnipeg born and raised but now living in Toronto. The tour begins in Buhler Hall. Along with the museum's boutique and ERA Bistro, the cavernous Buhler Hall is located on the free side of the museum's galleries. These are spaces accessible to those who do not feel up to an encounter with stories of human rights and human wrongs, but who may nonetheless have a desire to "shop with confidence and conscience"; to have a bite to eat at "a gathering place for good food, sharing, and reflection"; or to visit Buhler Hall, the museum's shrine to itself and its makers.[19] "Everyone is welcome" here—a message that is communicated through the hall's large luminous projection wall, where a procession of silhouetted figures write 'welcome' in "twelve indigenous languages and twenty-six international languages."[20]

A second wall hosts another substantial illuminated panel. This one displays a list of museum donors classified by dollar categories. The Donor Wall's upper categories—measured in millions—are sparsely populated. The Aspers have top billing in the $20-million-plus spot. Bonnie and John Buhler share the second ($6-million-plus) position, on par with the Winnipeg

Foundation; and Stuart Clark shares the third ($3-million-plus) spot with the Government of Manitoba. As donation values decrease, categories become more populated. The final two categories to earn a place in the Donor Wall's limelight are $10,000 plus and "Gifts in Kind." Though Sandra assures us that "every donor matters, from the grandmother who gave five dollars to those who gave millions," it appears they do not all matter in quite the same way.

Occupants of the wall's upper echelons not only have donation categories to themselves, they have museum spaces named in their honour. At the museum's pinnacle is the Israel Asper Tower of Hope; the palatial foyer we are standing in is named after the Buhlers; and, for his four million dollars, former Winnipegger and now Calgary-based businessman Stuart Clark purchased naming rights to the museum's Garden of Contemplation. Other high-rolling donors have either lower-profile museum spaces named after them, or they have their names engraved into one of the 3,200 Spanish alabaster tiles from which the museum's labyrinthine ramp—or "ribbon of healing"—is constructed. In addition to the areas of the Canadian Museum for Human Rights for which naming rights have already been procured, the museum has another several dozen for sale, with prices ranging "from $1 million for various facilities up to $7.5 million for naming the main exhibit gallery."[21] Members of the most populated "under $10,000" category have not fared so well. They are not included on the museum's Donor Wall and have no spaces named after them. Instead, their names have been relegated to the less visible "Friends of the Canadian Museum for Human Rights" website.

Accompanying the Donor Wall is an interactive video display where visitors can choose between top donor testimonials and a selection of videos about the museum's history. The first of the history videos begins with the "obvious question... Why Winnipeg?" This is a question that has plagued the museum's miracle-making founders since its conception in 2000. The question gained traction over the years when it became clear that with the project's ever-escalating costs, the museum would require millions in federal funds for the miracle to come to pass. To receive the needed federal dollars, the human rights museum had to be declared a national museum, which necessitated a 2008 amendment to Canada's Museums Act. The first national museum to be built outside of Canada's capital region, the Canadian Museum for Human Rights' final federal price tag came to $100 million in capital funds and an "in perpetuity" commitment of an estimated $22 million in annual operating costs. Curiously, despite their multi-million-dollar value, these federal funds have not earned a spot on the Donor Wall.

The most obvious response to the "Why Winnipeg?" query is simple. Winnipeg is the hometown of the museum's visionary, Israel Asper. The museum, however, has determined that this might not make the most compelling opening for its origin story video. Instead, the Canadian Museum for Human Rights has constructed a narrative that foregrounds Indigenous peoples: "Why Winnipeg? . . . It is because this land, where the Red and the Assiniboine Rivers meet, has been an Aboriginal meeting place for over six thousand years. It is because this land is blessed by Aboriginal elders as a gift to the world. It is because Louis Riel fought to defend Métis land rights here in 1869–1870 when the federal government established Manitoba as a province."[22] The video continues with a mention of Nellie McClung's fight for women's voter rights and a nod to the 1919 Winnipeg General Strike, before concluding with an ode to Asper: "And so, here you are, in what started as the improbable vision in the mind of a Prairie boy, Winnipeg's original and consummate dreamer, Israel Harold Asper."[23]

Unlike the truncated diorama-like exhibits at the Canadian War Museum that ensconced Canada's First Peoples in a dead, static past, at the Canadian Museum for Human Rights indigeneity is foregrounded in multiple arenas of the museum's self-narration. This is perhaps nowhere more evident than in the story of its architecture. After a fierce competition among over five dozen of the world's most prestigious architects, New Mexico–based architect Antoine Predock won the bid to design the museum. "Antoine," our guide Sandra tells us, was awarded the contract because of three aspects of his proposal: first, the way the building would represent the Canadian environment; second, how it would represent "all the people of the world"; and last, but most definitely not least, the way the building design would "represent, and honour, Indigenous peoples."

Much of what Sandra describes in her overview of the building's architecture is quite likely new information for the two San Franciscans on our tour. For most Winnipeggers and many Canadians, on the other hand, what we hear as we gather around the museum's enshrined architectural model at the centre of Buhler Hall has a familiar ring. Stories about the museum's architecture have been widely disseminated and become part of the museum's popular lore. Unlike the Canadian War Museum's dearth of information about the architectural vision of Raymond Moriyama's lilting bunker-like surfaces, the human rights museum has ensured that many of its visitors are well versed in what I think of as the museum's architectural ABCs long before they ever set foot in the building.

"A" is for the Archaeological dig. How the museum commissioned a $550,000 dig—the largest ever in Manitoba. How the dig unearthed over 400,000 artifacts from within its 150-square-metre perimeter, and how the museum took great care to ensure that Indigenous Elders were on hand to conduct ceremonies throughout the construction process. Sandra reiterates these details throughout the tour. In fact, in all of its public relation materials the museum emphasizes these two points in relationship to the archaeological dig: the unprecedented size of the dig within Manitoba, and the performance of ceremonies by Indigenous Elders throughout the dig and the museum's construction. There is no mention, however, of the fact that the dig covered only 3 percent of the site the museum occupies, nor of how the unearthed findings mobilized resistance to the museum's construction on the proposed site, from both Indigenous community members and archaeologists. For example, in a December 2011 CBC interview, Sid Kroker, the archaeologist hired by the museum, reported that the museum's decision makers ignored heritage permits and recommendations for "heritage resource management practices." Kroker retired before the completion of his archaeological report, noting that "making future recommendations would be 'as futile as King Canute railing against the tide.'"[24]

"B" is for the Building's environmental symbolism, represented in its four distinct architectural sections—its prairie-grass-covered Roots that extend out from the base of the building; its Mountain constructed of ancient Manitoba Tyndall limestone; its white-dove-emulating glass Cloud; and, rising gloriously from these natural elements, its sky-piercing Tower of Hope.

"C" is for the miracle of its Construction, which required forty teams from across Canada, the United States, and Europe, and used 3-D design to transmit detailed plans for its material components: glass from Germany, alabaster from Spain, basalt from Mongolia, and limestone and steel from Canada. Sandra reviews these basics, adding anecdotes as she shares with us some of Antoine Predock's design sketches on her tablet. What we need to remember if we are to fully appreciate the museum's architecture, Sandra explains, "is that its design places form over function: The building has a story to tell."

It's not only me. Whether entranced by the museum's architectural mythology, cast under commemoration's hushing spell, or awed by Sandra's weighty inventories—32,000 tons of concrete, 6,000 tons of steel, 3,000 tons of Manitoba Tyndall stone, 600 tons of Mongolian basalt, 3,200 pieces of Spanish alabaster, 1,300 pieces of German glass—we are a largely silent group. We listen and respond appropriately to Sandra's prompts. The exceptions are the two women from San Francisco. As if performing their part in a collective enactment of U.S./Canadian personality stereotypes, they are the ones who ask questions. Questions that nudge Sandra off script. One woman queries, "How does the museum survive financially?"

Though it is a Sunday afternoon, the museum is sparsely populated. There are no lineups. No crowds. This combined with the extravagance of the museum's spectacular construction and its undoubtedly costly upkeep makes her question at least as obvious as "Why Winnipeg?" Sandra explains that the museum has exceeded its projections and "is making money."

Her response momentarily un-silences me. "But aren't the museum's operating costs paid for by the federal government?" I ask.

"Oh, that just covers the cost of salaries," Sandra responds without pause.

I could say more. But I don't.

Apart from the museum's canonized model, the Donor Wall, and the Welcome projections, the only other exhibit in Buhler Hall is titled *Ancestral Land*. The installation has three components: a seven-foot-diameter canvas disk that is mounted onto the wall, and two identical bronzed footprints—one embedded into the floor, the other mounted alongside the explanatory display panel. The panel reads: "The land beneath this museum has always been, and will continue to be, home to Indigenous peoples." The identical bronze footprints are casts of a 750-year-old moccasin print that was unearthed during the archaeological dig. Sandra points out that when we entered the building, we descended. This is because the architect wanted visitors to feel like they were walking into "Mother Earth," she tells us. It is one among many examples we will hear of ways Predock worked to honour Indigenous peoples through his design. This architectural descent also made it possible to position one of the bronze replicas in the exact location from which the original footprint was extracted. It is as though "the moccasin wearer is still travelling," Sandra explains, only "now from the past into the present and future." A third bronze replica of the footprint is located in the Indigenous Perspectives gallery at the interpretive rail overlooking the "ceremonial terrace" and The Forks.

Though the footprint has been assiduously integrated into the museum's mythology, the disk with radiating shades of black and brown is new to me. After quizzing us on what we think the disk might represent—"a fire circle," "the sun"—Sandra explains that the artist created the installation by stretching a membrane over a seven-foot drum. He then placed earth and sweetgrass on top, and they were drummed into place. While the informational panel that accompanies the Ancestral Land installation reiterates the story of the legendary moccasin footprint, it offers no explanation for the drum. There is no artist statement, only the words "circle element" and the artist's name, David Gordon Thomas. I wonder whose decision this is. I want to think it is Thomas's; that the disk is intended as an aesthetic embodiment of Indigenous people's repertorial practices; that through its lack of textual narrative, it defies being appropriated into the museum's public relations discourse, while haunting the physical space with the "inter(in)animation" of its drummers, its activated medicines and earth, its silent echo.[25]

Tricia Logan, former curator for Indigenous content at the Canadian Museum for Human Rights, may not share my hopeful fantasy about productive potential of the limited information the museum provided about Thomas's piece or that of other Indigenous artists throughout the museum. In 2013, Logan resigned from her curatorial position at the museum after being told to remove the terms genocide and cultural genocide from all Indigenous exhibits.[26] According to the editors of *The Idea of a Human Rights Museum*, Logan was also compelled to withdraw her submission to their collection because it did not comply with the museum's "policy concerning publication of curators' work pertaining to the museum."[27] In a post-resignation article she published about her experiences at the museum, Logan describes being "consistently reminded that every mention of state-perpetrated atrocity against Indigenous peoples in Canada must be matched with a 'balanced' statement that indicates reconciliation, apology or compensation provided by the government."[28]

Logan was not alone in her departure. As Helen Fallding writes, "Six of the original team of eight researchers and curators hired in 2010 had left by the end of 2013, before the museum opened."[29] While museum spokesperson Angela Cassie attributes the mass departures to concerns of job security in the face of museum funding shortfalls, Fallding goes on to note that "a week before the museum opened . . . fears of political interference resurface[d] when [then] Minister of Heritage Shelly Glover asked to review all content that mention[ed] the Canadian government."[30]

Like Shoal Lake 40's Museum *for* Canadian Human Rights Violations, Logan's article offers a glimpse into tensions between the positive spin that the Canadian Museum for Human Rights endeavours to instill in its representation of Canadian settler–Indigenous relationships and the lived experience of many Indigenous community members and the struggles of curators of Indigenous exhibits within the museum. Taken together, Shoal Lake 40's activist intervention, Logan's resignation, Thomas's drum, and *Trace*—an original artwork by Anishinaabe artist Rebecca Belmore, commissioned by the museum in 2011, which I will discuss later in this chapter—all attest to the range of vocabularies and insurgent tactics that are being used to expand the discursive contact zones generated by the museum.

As Diana Taylor asserts, writing and logocentric textual narrative has long served "as a strategy for repudiating and foreclosing the very embodiedness it claims to describe."[31] This strategy is illustrated in the Canadian Museum for Human Rights' ubiquitous narrations about Indigenous communities' centuries-long relationship to The Forks. The museum's textual representations often problematically reduce notions of gathering place, land, and home to disembodied concepts that are then mined for their symbolic value. For example, through a discursive sleight of hand, the museum is able to celebrate Indigenous peoples' relationship to The Forks, land which "has always been, and will continue to be [their] home," while simultaneously obscuring and normalizing its colonization of that same land/home. The same strategy is also evidenced through the tale of the anonymous footprint bearer that is reiterated throughout the museum and in its public relations materials. Extracted—like the limestone, basalt, and alabaster that constitute the museum's physical construction—the footprint has become part of the discursive material on which the museum's architectural symbolism is built. Along with the bronze replicas, the repeated tale of the once-embodied footprint ensconces Indigenous people's celebrated relationship to the land that the museum now occupies in a distant past, and positions the museum as rescuing this weary traveller from the darkness of the past, and setting them on the museum's path toward an enlightened future. The museum's public celebration of the footprint as an archaeological trophy obfuscates the disregard its miracle makers showed when, despite urgings from Indigenous community members as well as their own archaeological consultants, they refused to halt construction so that the dig could extend beyond its limited sample area. Hundreds of thousands of artifacts remain buried beneath the building, Sandra informs us, and there is a door somewhere in the museum's foundation (she has not seen it) that was added to the design to facilitate future archeological access should it be deemed necessary.

We forego the Escher-like alabaster ramp and bypass the museum's lower galleries to ascend, via elevator, to the next stop on our architectural tour—the Stuart Clark Garden of Contemplation. Despite our presence in the "healing waters" garden, Sandra makes no mention of Shoal Lake 40's protest, their Museum for *Canadian Human Rights Violations, their cease and desist letters to Predock, or their media campaign. Instead, she tells us that the garden's waters have been blessed by traditional Elders; that the garden is constructed of over 600 tons of basalt from Inner Mongolia; and that its basalt-paved floor is made to resemble the back of the turtle. According to the "seven sacred teachings" Predock has incorporated into the building, "turtles teach us about truth in relationship to time."*

We also learn that—like the Canadian War Museum's LeBreton Gallery—the Garden of Contemplation, along with Buhler Hall and other museum spaces, can be rented for weddings and other social events. I wonder what would it be like to celebrate here, around the corner from the museum's Examining the Holocaust gallery, in this space designed to facilitate contemplation about truth and memory.

Thus far, what I've been able to glean about the building's "fundamental environmental ethic" from Sandra's scripted tour is largely based on the museum's honorific narratives about Indigenous peoples' sacred relationship to the land. But just as the tour is about to conclude, Sandra takes a few moments to point out some of the museum's more material environmentally friendly design aspects. Standing atop the turtle's mighty basalt back,

Sandra invites us to look up at the massive glass cloud and informs us that the high-quality construction and southern exposure of the windows help to warm the building during Winnipeg's long winter months, while ensuring that during the summer months they avoid the sun's direct rays. A sensible architectural consideration to be sure, but still, as a former Winnipegger, I have a hard time fathoming the costs of heating a building the size of the Canadian Museum for Human Rights with such massive windows. While I'm grappling with this, Sandra continues with her testimonial of the elements that contribute to the building's environmental ethic, like the alabaster ramp's 10,000 LED lights, and the cisterns that capture water in the summer months that is then used to flush the museum's toilets. The cisterns, she tells us, were installed with Shoal Lake 40 in mind, "to help decrease stress on that Indigenous community."

Stories, like memory, reveal and conceal. The Canadian Museum for Human Rights is a building designed to tell a story about honouring Indigenous peoples' relationship to the land through an abstracted environmental ethic that obscures the material effects of the building's environmental and social impacts. With its Discover the Building tour, the museum integrates Predock's architectural symbolism into an origin story that celebrates The Forks as a land that "has always been, and will continue to be, home to Indigenous peoples" while shifting attention away from the museum's larger political, economic, social, and environmental implications. What if, instead of asking "Why Winnipeg?", we were to ask, "Why the Canadian Museum for Human Rights with its spectacular architecture and its $350 million (and still counting) price tag? Why the immense extraction of material resources to construct a building that claims an indigenized environmental ethic? Why this monumental (re)occupation of these ancestral lands?

When Israel Asper publicly announced his plans for the museum in 2003, he boldly declared before a select audience of invited dignitaries gathered at The Forks that "the [Canadian Museum for Human Rights] would put Winnipeg on the world map."[32] Asper, who died of a heart attack months later, did not live to see the extent to which his pronouncement would come to pass. From the start, however, he was critically aware of the role the museum's architecture would play in achieving its global notoriety. Asper envisioned a design of such magnificence that it would "mimic the 'Bilbao effect' of Frank Gehry's Guggenheim Museum in that once-obscure Spanish city."[33] When Gail Asper took up the torch after her father's death she expanded on his vision of the museum's future notoriety, exclaiming: "When people think of Canada they'll think of this building."[34] The significance of the building's iconographic architecture was perhaps most bluntly stated by Charles Coffey, a museum supporter and then executive vice president of the Royal Bank of Canada: "The Canadian Museum for Human Rights is an opportunity for Canada to brand human rights leadership on both the national and international stage."[35]

From the outset, the museum was plagued by debates over both which human rights atrocities it would foreground and the language it would use to frame these historic violations. Despite Asper's efforts to promote "tolerance" and "human rights" as the conceptual axis of the museum, a 2002 *Winnipeg Free Press* article dubbed the project a "Holocaust Museum." Soon after, the Ukrainian Civil Liberties Association and the Ukrainian Canadian Congress launched campaigns arguing that the "museum should not elevate one group's suffering over another and that it was unacceptable that the permanent Holocaust gallery should be given more space than the Holodomor."[36] A coalition of forty-seven Ukrainian Canadian member organizations formed Canadians for a Genocide Museum to promote key demands organized around the "twin principles of inclusivity and equity."[37] While it is beyond the scope of this chapter to fully explore the complexity of the opposition that stakeholders in the Ukrainian Canadian community posed to the museum, I want to draw attention to one aspect of the debate that I will return to in the final section of this chapter: the profound differences in the tactical approaches used by stakeholders in the Ukrainian Canadian community and the eclectic assemblage of Indigenous rights activists, artists, and scholars in response the human rights museum.

Amidst a decade of media reports on the contentious debates—almost two-thirds of which, according to Fallding, were preoccupied with the Holodomor debate—the museum's architecture served as a diversionary lightning rod. Alternately reviled and revered, it has been the museum's most consistent attention-grabbing feature. An article published in *The Walrus* one month after the museum's inauguration described the building as a "behemoth," a "white elephant," and a "human rights theme park."[38] Author Adele Weder goes on to challenge the originality of Predock's design, noting that it bears remarkable resemblance to his "unbuilt 1994 scheme for the Atlantis Hotel and Casino in Las Vegas, Nevada."[39] Similarly, in a *Globe and Mail* article, Alex Bozikovic writes that the museum is "inexcusably clumsy," an incoherent "monolith of mixed metaphors."[40] Alternately, the museum has been described as "iconic," "world class," and "monumental."[41] Love it or hate it, the museum's "iconomy" is indeed earning Winnipeg—and Canada—a degree of global notoriety.[42] For example, in its "Best Trips 2016" list of twenty go-to destinations, *National Geographic* credits the Canadian Museum for Human Rights with putting Winnipeg on the international radar.

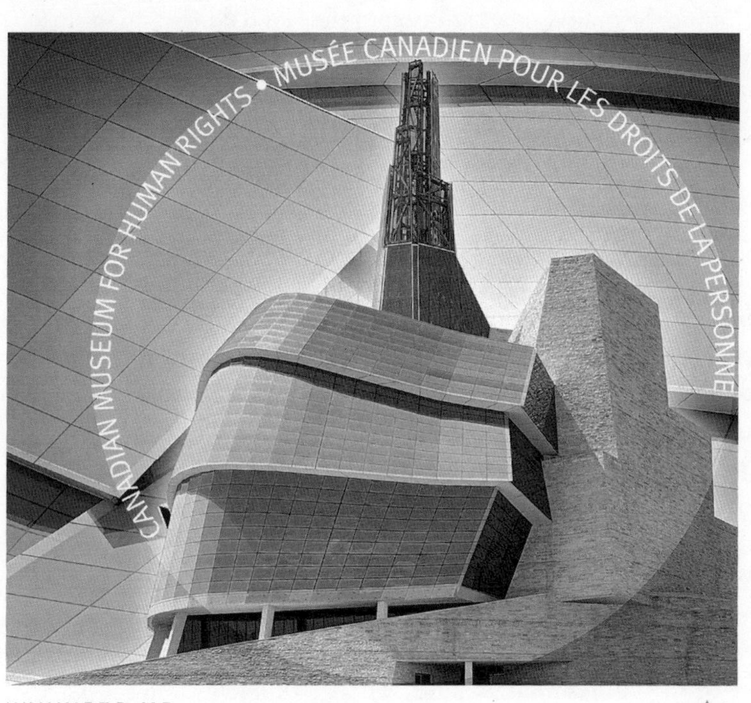

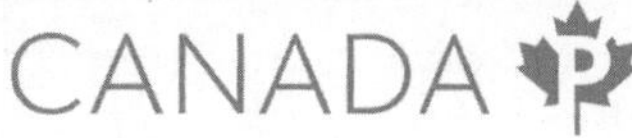

Figure 39. Canadian Museum for Human Rights postage stamp.

For those unable to make the journey to Winnipeg, Canada Post has issued a stamp that delivers the museum to destinations across the nation and around the world (Figure 39). Unlike the Discover the Building tour and many of the museum's self-produced promotional materials and museum displays that use Predock's architecture to help foreground the intersecting themes of The Forks as a historic meeting place and Indigenous peoples' relationship to the land, on the Canada Post stamp the building's spectacular architecture totally eclipses the environment it is purported to honour. A lithographed image of the museum fills the stamp's foreground. Behind its Roots, Mountain, Cloud, and Tower, in the place where one might expect to glimpse the prairie sky that inspired the cloud design, we see instead an enlarged echo of the lithographed glass cloud. No longer merely a symbol for the environment, Predock's building exceeds its own architectural parameters to overwhelm and replace earth and sky. A halo of ethereal white font encircles the museum with the text CANADIAN MUSEUM FOR HUMAN RIGHTS—MUSÉE CANADIEN POUR LES DROITS DE LA PERSONNE. Fulfilling Asper's proclamation, the brand is then linked back to place with the text WINNIPEG, MB, printed onto lower left side of stamp's ripple-edged frame while in larger font, CANADA and Canada Post's trademark maple leaf occupy the lower right. The museum's environmental and human rights leadership ethics have morphed from embodied practices to symbolic abstractions to brand.

Like the "purifying lung" of Predock's Garden of Contemplation, the Canadian Museum for Human Rights' brand places Winnipeg and Canada under the percepticidal halo of benevolent Canadian nationalism. In her analysis of military violence during Argentina's "Dirty War" (1975–83), Taylor argues that large-scale social percepticide was produced wherein the general population denied what they saw and thereby colluded in the violent nationalism of Argentina's military junta. Though different from the percepticide enacted through militarized performances of violent nationalism, I propose that the cumulative effect of Canada's spectacular performances of national goodness have a "snowblinding" effect that shields the general populace from the historical and contemporary acts of state violence—physical, cultural, and institutional—perpetrated on Canada's Indigenous populations.[43]

Cast outside the metonymic frame of the museum's brand are chains of unremarked-upon signs and signifiers. How the reiterated tale of the building's environmental symbolism masks the social and environmental impacts of the extractive practices that were necessary to meet the material demands of the museum's colossal architecture. How these extractive practices are part of the overarching capitalist logic on which Canada as a settler-colonial nation is founded and upon which it continues to rely. How, as the hundreds of thousands of unearthed artifacts—and the many hundreds of thousands more buried beneath the museum—reveal, the environment on which settler colonialism is founded was richly inhabited. How the museum's (re)occupation of The Forks is reflective of centuries of settler colonialism, with its royal and governmental decrees and land grabs that for their successful enforcement also necessitated genocidal policies and actions enacted at the behest of the nation-state. How beyond the discursive frame of the museum's celebration of Indigenous relationship to the land, the normalized exploitative relationship of Canadian settler colonialism and capitalist modernity remain unmarked and continue unabated.

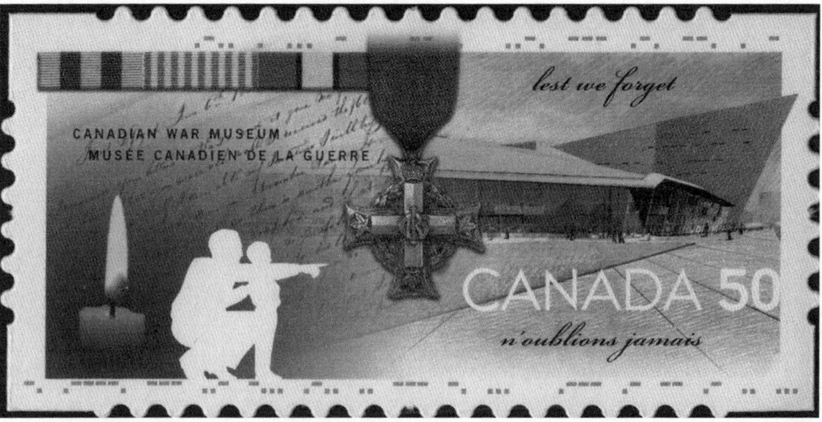

Figure 40. Canadian War Museum postage stamp.

As another national museum, the Canadian War Museum has also been allotted a Canada Post stamp (Figure 40). But unlike the dominance of Predock's architecture on the human rights museum's stamp, on the war museum's stamp, Raymond Moriyama's building is a fragment consigned to a corner in the stamp's upper right rear. Based on one of Moriyama's architectural sketches, the building is pictured in back of an expansive green lawn and paved terrace. Afloat in the colour-pencilled blue sky above the building is the refrain *lest we forget*, which has itself become a brand for Canada's ever-expanding military commemoration projects. The stamp's central image is the Memorial Cross, more popularly known as the Silver Cross, a medal that is awarded to the mothers and wives of Canada's fallen military personnel

(Chapter 1). Sandwiched behind the Silver Cross and in front of the obscured portion of Moriyama's building is a translucent "handwritten" letter. The stamp's other two images are a burning candle, and the ghostly white silhouette of a man crouched beside a young child and pointing toward the museum.

Read side by side, the two stamps reveal something about a fundamental difference between the two museums and their most dominant stakeholder communities. For the Canadian Museum for Human Rights' miracle makers, the building's architecture is central and has always been seen as a critical feature in achieving one of its key mandates—a notoriety that would brand Winnipeg, and Canada, as centres of human rights leadership. Stakeholders in Canada's military-cultural memory network, on the other hand, were less interested in the symbolism that Moriyama poured into his architecture, or even in promoting a national brand. Their central mandate has been the production of an honorific narrative of Canada's military history and control over its epistemological dissemination to future generations.

While on its home front at The Forks the human rights museum reiterates its tale of reverence for the land and the Indigenous peoples for whom it is "home," the museum's brand is also projected outward to cast its iconographic spell on the national and international imagination. But there are stories other than the one told by the museum and its brand. Stories transmitted through vocabularies that refuse the limiting logics of a universalized human rights discourse, of capitalist modernity's iconography, of logocentric textual narration. Stories that "give lie to the Enlightenment mandate that *we head into our futures undetained*" and insist instead on the sticky slip and slide of time.[44] Stories that haunt like the silent echoing beat of Thomas's drum with its activated and activating earth and sweetgrass. A kind of haunting that sociologist Avery Gordon describes as "an animated state in which a repressed or unresolved social violence is making itself known, sometimes very directly, sometimes more obliquely."[45] These are the haunting stories contained in the medicine bundles placed by Indigenous Elders into the earth beneath the museum. Stories told *by* those who live and have always lived on this land. Stories told by an assemblage of Indigenous activists, artists, and scholars who have long been engaged in the critical project of restoring Indigenous history into social and archival memory and of exposing the structural mechanisms through which colonialism's past continues in our corporeal present. Stories of settler colonialism's unbecoming hospitalities.

A Blanket Returned: Unbecoming Settler-Colonial Hospitalities

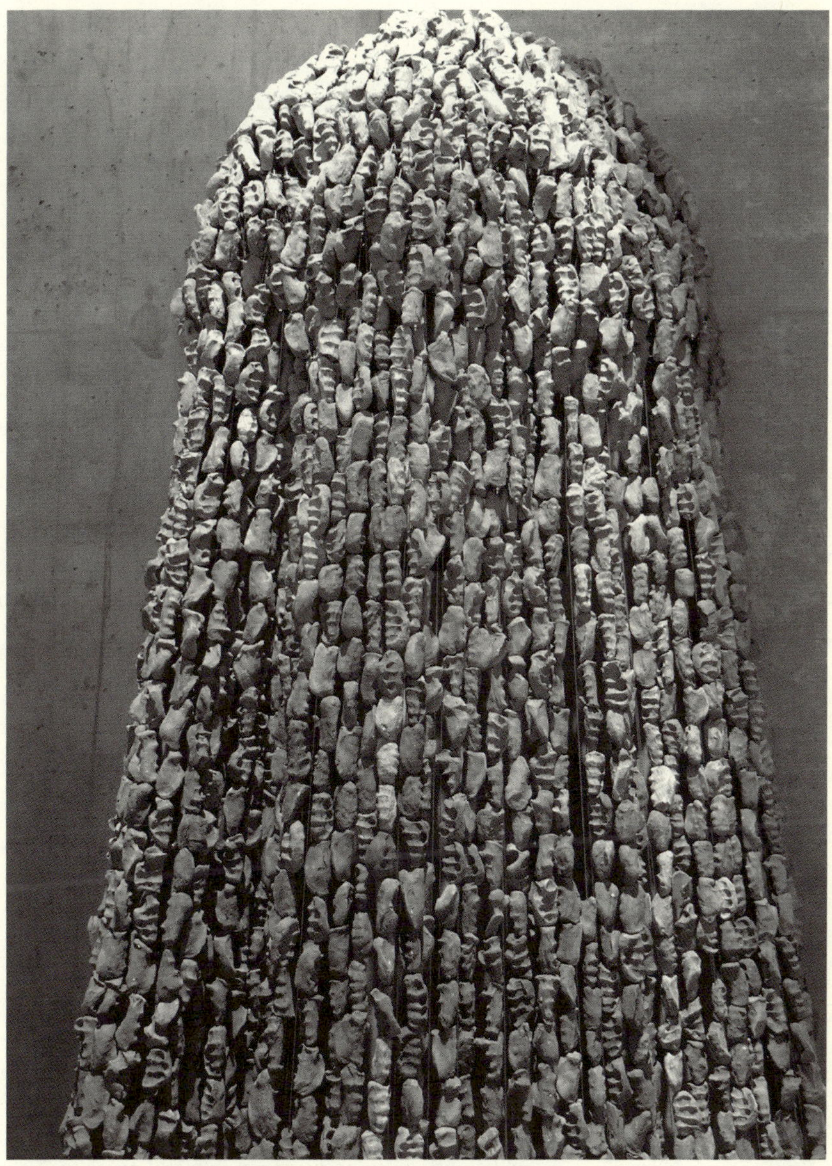

Figure 41. Finger imprints in clay beads. *Trace*, by Rebecca Belmore, Actions Count Gallery, Canadian Museum for Human Rights.

19 September 2016
Indigenous Perspectives gallery, Canadian
Museum for Human Rights

There is an uncanny, almost grotesque, beauty to the blanket. Something obscene about its gargantuan scale. Its inhospitable materiality. The sharp edges of its 14,000 fire-hardened clay beads. Each bead carrying the imprint of the soft interior of a clenched fist (Figure 41). *It is an embodiment of excess, constructed of Red River clay gumbo removed from beneath Winnipeg's streets and sidewalks to make way for the city's revamped sewer lines. A blanket made of waste extracted to make way for the conveyance of city inhabitants' waste.*

It's funny, and not. Funny because it's true, and not—for the same reason.

Is it possible to tell a scatological joke inside a national museum dedicated to the commemoration of historical violence and the promotion of human rights? Is it possible to shit in a "candy-floss" palace? In her essay "In a Wilderness Garden," Rebecca Belmore recounts a lecture on performance art that she delivered during a 1997 residency at the Banff Centre. Belmore gathered her inspiration from a story in Ramsay Cook's chapbook *1492 and All That, Making a Garden out of a Wilderness.*[46] The story, told by a Mi'kmaq man, recorded by a Baptist minister, and retold by Belmore, goes like this: "A Mi'kmaq man was taken to France where he was placed in a wilderness garden with a deer. There, he was told he was to perform for an audience of nobility: he was expected to kill the deer with a bow and arrow, skin and dress the carcass, then cook and eat it. According to the Mi'kmaq, wrote the missionary, the man adhered to their instructions but took the liberty of expanding on their idea of his performance by 'easing himself before them all.' I took this to mean [Belmore writes] that he shat upon the ground."[47]

Reflecting on her location within Banff National Forest, with its mandate of protecting the remains of the "Canadian wilderness," Belmore identified with the Mi'kmaq man and saw herself as "trapped in a 'wild' garden."[48] Moved by the man's performative manoeuvre, the day before her lecture Belmore eased herself in bushes behind her studio. Returning the following day she gathered her shit in a jar and, in a second jar, collected excremental remains from Banff's plentiful—seemingly tame, but still wild—elk population.

Belmore arrived to deliver her lecture carrying the jars in two paper bags. She stood at the lectern with her paper bags while video footage of her clearing a path through the forest with a leaf blower was projected onto a screen. When the video ended, Belmore removed the jars from their modest containment and shared the story of the Mi'kmaq man. Before continuing with her lecture, she took the fecal specimens—hers and the elks'—to the washroom where she flushed them down the toilet, sending them on a comingled journey through the civilizing sewers of Canadian modernity. She returned and delivered the remainder of her lecture accompanied by a second video—this one of Belmore running through the forest with "hands bound, an escaped captive Indian."[49]

Like Cuban-American performance artist and scholar Coco Fusco, Belmore contests the dominant Western origin story of performance art with its roots in Europe's Dada movement.[50] Instead, Fusco and Belmore map out a more damning scenario of performance art being rooted in the colonial practice of capturing Indigenous "specimens" and displaying them "for aesthetic contemplation, scientific analysis, and entertainment."[51] With both her essay and performance lecture, Belmore also reveals another critical performance lineage—that of performance as resistance; performance as a method of "tactical inversion," a means of performing escape while living under dominating conditions.[52] Similar to her Mi'kmaq predecessor, through her performance and arts practices, Belmore deploys what Julia Emberley calls an "aboriginal uncanny,"[53] or what queer and performance studies theorist José Esteban Muñoz has dubbed disidentification—a strategy for the critical negotiation of toxic identities. The uncanny disidentification of the Mi'kmaq man's performance is in how he neither directly opposes nor allows himself to be assimilated by the essentializing narrative of otherized wildness placed on display as an object for colonial consumption. Rather, while adhering to the French aristocracy's toxic script of captive otherness, with improvisational flair the Mi'kmaq man adds a touch of realism to his wilderness diorama. Neither captive nor free, he performs his unbecoming disidentificatory escape.

Akin to her Mi'kmaq predecessor, Belmore takes liberties. Who else would fashion a blanket—a symbol of warmth and comfort—out of Red River "muck" to hang in a prairie palace built of some of the finest materials money can buy—Spanish alabaster, German glass, Mongolian basalt? Like Shoal Lake 40 First Nation, Belmore matches and mocks the museum's iconomy with her monumental blanket's inversions of materiality and scale. Constructed from discarded traces of Treaty One land, Belmore's oversized clay-bead blanket adds a touch of material Indigenous realism to the Canadian Museum for Human Rights' universalizing human rights script. She muddies the museum's Enlightenment narrative of ever-forward-moving progress by exposing the consumptive practices of colonization and neo-liberalism that extract not only land and land-based resources but also art and spirituality from Indigenous communities while ignoring the day-to-day lived conditions of those same communities, conditions that are part of the ongoing violent effects of Canadian settler colonization. With *Trace*, Belmore instills into the museum's human rights archive a testimony of place, of indigeneity, and of the incommensurability of reconciliatory hope without material redress.

Belmore took her inspiration for *Trace* from the museum's excavation process, which exhumed over 400,000 pre-contact artifacts including ceremonial pipes, pottery shards, tools, bison skulls, and 191 fire pits. The unearthed artifacts have become property of the Province of Manitoba's Historic Resources Branch. Classified and archived, the artifacts become indicators of a pastness that can live in the present only as objects that mark their very pastness. Like Shoal Lake 40's fire pit that was part of their museum launch campsite, Belmore's repurposing of Red River clay into contemporary art marks a refusal to relegate history to an archival past, or the land on which the Canadian Museum for Human Rights and the city of Winnipeg are built to a previously unoccupied wilderness in need of colonial intervention. "There's two great rivers here," Belmore reminds us; "it was an amazing site to gather long before Winnipeg existed."[54] Winnipeg's cast-off muck is recast as an aesthetic interlocutor in a discourse about land, indigeneity, and limitations to the notion of human rights. Belmore collapses the divide between object and waste, between archival past and living present through the "act of pressing this clay, this land," she explains, "and at the same time thinking about the future. The people who help create this blanket or sculpture will leave their trace for those [yet to come]."[55]

While the body is a constant presence in Belmore's work, in the case of *Trace*, it is an uncanny presence. Individually, each bead bears physical traces (finger imprints, body oils, skin cells) of the person who pressed the raw gritty clay into shape. And as a whole, the blanket carries the collective traces of the thousands of makers who remain a haunting presence despite having faded back into the social world from which the project is born. Unlike the majority of the museum's exhibits that rely on textual narrative, *Trace* speaks another language, in another voice. *Trace* provides no story line. No beginning, middle, end. *Trace* also resists the museum's high-tech delivery systems. There are no buttons to press, no screens to swipe. Even the museum's self-guiding app offers no additional narration for *Trace*. Like Thomas's drum piece, *Trace* haunts the space with a testimonial presence that is amplified both through the absence of narrative and of the bodies and repertorial actions that went into its making.[56] Through the process of its making, and as an affectively imprinted material artifact, *Trace* embodies the concept not only of a meeting or gathering place, but also of Indigenous communities' ongoing collective relationship to land. *Trace* is an aesthetic and physicalized acknowledgement that The Forks, this place where the Red and the Assiniboine Rivers meet, where the human rights museum in all its architectural glory now reigns, is a place where Indigenous communities have gathered for thousands of years and continue to gather today.

Along with the recurring themes of meeting place and collective labour in Belmore's work is the concept of The Forks as a site of collision between Canada's Indigenous and white settler populations. In 1992, Belmore brought *Ayumm-ee-aawach Oomama-mowan: Speaking to Their Mother* to the place where the now-revitalized Forks exists. The project consisted of a two-metre-wide wooden megaphone which Belmore took to First Nations reserves, rural communities, and urban centres across Canada. Indigenous community members were invited to speak into the megaphone, sending their voices echoing out across the various landscapes the project visited. While at The Forks in Winnipeg, as speakers sent their voices out over the rivers they were heckled by "angry passers-by. . . . It made me think," Belmore recalls, "about Louis Riel's much-quoted words about how art has the potential to move people: 'My people will sleep for 100 years and when they awake, it will be the artists who give them back their spirit.'"[57]

Visitors to the Canadian Museum for Human Rights first encounter Belmore's ceramic blanket in the Indigenous Perspectives gallery where it is accompanied by a plaque:

> *Trace* honours the memory of the original inhabitants of the land upon which this museum stands.
>
> To acknowledge the depth of Indigenous history, the artist used raw earth from deep beneath the city of Winnipeg.

> The "beads" made from this clay carry the hand imprints of many local children and adults who collaborated with the artist in the realization of this work.[58]

Though Belmore fashioned *Trace* after "a blanket on a hook," the museum's description of the work makes no reference to the sculpture as a blanket.[59] This is a curiously glaring omission for two reasons. First, in addition to Belmore's consistent reference to the sculpture as a blanket, the blanket has long been a motif in the artist's work. For example, similarly to *Trace*, Belmore's 1994 *a blanket for Sarah* offered little in the way of physical hospitality. Made in memory of a homeless Indigenous woman who froze to death on the streets of Sioux Lookout, the twelve panels that comprise the installation are laboriously constructed of over 800,000 pine needles poked through the tiny holes of wire mesh and stretched over steel frames.[60] With her 2002 *Blood on the Snow*, Belmore unsettles the romanticized association of snow with a purified Canadian settler identity. A white chair sits at the centre of the installation's large white quilted blanket. The blood that seeps down the chair makes visible not only the violence of settler colonialism but also the coldness of white indifference.

The second reason the omission of any reference to *Trace* as a blanket seems suspect is the museum's location at The Forks—where blankets were a staple of trade during the Hudson's Bay Company's fur trade monopoly—and mere blocks away from Winnipeg's historic Hudson's Bay department store—where today the iconic blanket is sold as a collectable. In fact, the same year the museum commissioned *Trace*, Belmore presented her video installation *The Blanket* (2011) as part of *Close Encounters: The Next 500 Years*, an exhibit at Winnipeg's Plug In gallery, located across the street from the Hudson's Bay store. In the video, Winnipeg dance and performance artist Ming Hon performs a death dance in a prairie snowscape while wrapped in a red Hudson's Bay blanket. *The Blanket* recalls the role of smallpox-infected blankets in the decimation of Indigenous communities across North America. As *Close Encounters* curator Lee-Ann Martin told audience members at the exhibition's opening, "The deliberate impregnation of the smallpox virus into government-issued blankets distributed to aboriginal people in the 18th century represents one of the most horrific stratagems perpetrated against aboriginal peoples."[61]

A blanket returned, *Trace* is impregnated, not with traces of a disease intended to annihilate but with a history intended to haunt, to provoke, to call witnesses to the necessary labour of critical reflection. It is a blanket that recalls genocidal acts perpetrated against First Nations populations. In light of the Canadian Museum for Human Rights' proximity to the Hudson's Bay Company department store, it is also a blanket that recalls the royal charter issued by King Charles II in 1670 that facilitated the company's theft of lands stretching from the Hudson Bay to The Forks. By omitting any reference to the blanket or stolen lands in its "honorific narrative of peaceful collaboration," Angela Failler argues, the human rights museum diffuses "the critical force of *Trace*."[62] Similar to architect Antoine Predock's designation of the museum's Garden of Contemplation as representative of First Nations' "sacred" relationship to healing waters, the museum's narrative of *Trace* simultaneously celebrates and neutralizes First Nations relationship to the land the museum now occupies.

19 September 2016
Actions Count gallery, Canadian Museum for Human Rights
Where does Trace *begin? Is it in the museum's architectural Roots, its earthy base, where the Indigenous Perspectives gallery is located and where museum visitors catch their first glimpse of the blanket? Is it in the community workshops where the clay is pressed into beads? In the city's trenches where construction workers dig? In the signing of Treaty One? In King Charles II's issuing of the 1670 royal charter? In the hearths dug up and archived, or in those left behind and sacrificed to the gods of architectural Enlightenment? In the violently annihilating gestures of colonial contact—resource extraction, blankets, residential schools—wrapped in narratives of progress, hospitality, and paternalistic care?*

After many switchbacks on the illuminated alabaster ramp, I arrive at the place where the clay-beaded blanket and its supporting frame are affixed to the wall, the place from which its weighty beaded folds cascade down. Here, the imprints of the fingers that tightened around the stiff gritty clay are visible (Figure 41). *Unlike the hidden labour of the construction workers who excavated the clay, or those who toiled to construct the museum, or those who laid the pipes that deliver "healing" waters to the*

Garden of Contemplation and usher away visitors' waste, the labour of the beads' construction remains palpable. With it, the relationship between resistance, labour, and endurance are also rendered visible. Though many, the individual beads and their makers do not compete with one another or with the museum's overwrought cacophony of voices. They are exquisitely silent in their inter(in)animated haunting of presence with absence. Action made into object.

Intentional or not, it strikes me as elegantly ironic that *Trace* makes its most intimate contact with the museum and is most accessible to visitors not in the Indigenous Perspectives gallery, with its honorific plaque, but in the Actions Count gallery. Here is the hook on which Belmore hangs her blanket. From here *Trace* travels against the grain of time. Traversing down to the museum's earthy realms where indigeneity is architecturally rooted, it unbecomes the linearity of Predock's processional choreography that propels visitors on an ever-upward journey from "darkness to light," along the alabaster "ribbon of healing" toward the Tower of Hope.[63] Working with and against the museum's universalizing human rights discourse, *Trace* unbecomes its naturalized association with an Enlightenment narrative of unidirectional progress that renders the past primitive and archival. The blanket's hard folds cascade down through the museum's galleries, crossing time with time. With her use of earth from this Treaty One land and the clenched fists of the beads' makers, Belmore reminds visitors that actions—past, present, future—do indeed count. That past actions count in the present and into the future. Even, perhaps, that present and future actions might count in the past.

Though *Trace* successfully functions as both art object and artifact, I read it as a performance. A performance that takes place upon a number of differently located stages—historical, community, media, arts. A performance that takes place against a backdrop of contemporary national debates around the contested framings of Canadian and Indigenous history, Indigenous rights, genocide, resource extraction, and treaty rights. A performance that brings bodies, objects, and narratives of pasts, presents, and futures into an inter(in)animating dialogue. But though a performance, through its weighty presence *Trace* uncannily defies performance's ephemerality, refusing disappearance. With *Trace* Belmore insists upon the heaviness of our collective historical relationship to the Treaty One land that lies beneath the Canadian Museum for

Human Rights' spectacular stately architecture, beneath Winnipeg's streets and sidewalks. Like the 400,000 First Nations artifacts excavated from the grounds over which the museum reigns, which are now ensconced in provincial archives, *Trace*'s 14,000 beads are here to stay; unlike the hundreds of thousands more artifacts buried beneath the prairie palace, *Trace*'s beads throw off the forgetful shroud of benevolent settler-Canadian nationalism.

Freedom Road: More Than a Metaphor

19 September 2016
Osborne Bridge, Winnipeg
GOT WATER? THANK SHOAL LAKE! *I encounter the graffiti stencilled message crossing the Osborne Bridge on my way home from the human rights museum* (Figure 42). *The message has taken on a meme-like quality. Like the ubiquity of the water it draws attention to, it's everywhere. During my brief stay in Winnipeg I see it painted onto sidewalks, bridges, street signs, walls. It's also been making the rounds through photos shared on social media networks, where instead of graffiti stencil it is printed onto T-shirts worn by community activists at political protests, Idle No More events, and lobbying actions.*

But Got Water? *isn't the only Shoal Lake 40–generated meme in town. The message—*WE SUPPORT SHOAL LAKE 40 FREEDOM ROAD*—is spelled out in block letters on the signboards that occupy church lawns across the city and province* (Figure 43). *Whereas the graffiti and T-shirts belong to an activist lexicon, these signboards speak the language of another constituency. As I travel to and from my parent's home in the largely white (and conservative-leaning) suburb of Charleswood, I am delighted to see the message displayed on the lawn of the Charleswood United Church.*

On 17 December 2015—fifteen months after Shoal Lake 40 community activists launched their Museum *for* Canadian Human Rights Violations and pitched their mini-museum pup tent in front of the Canadian Museum for Human Rights—municipal, provincial, and federal government

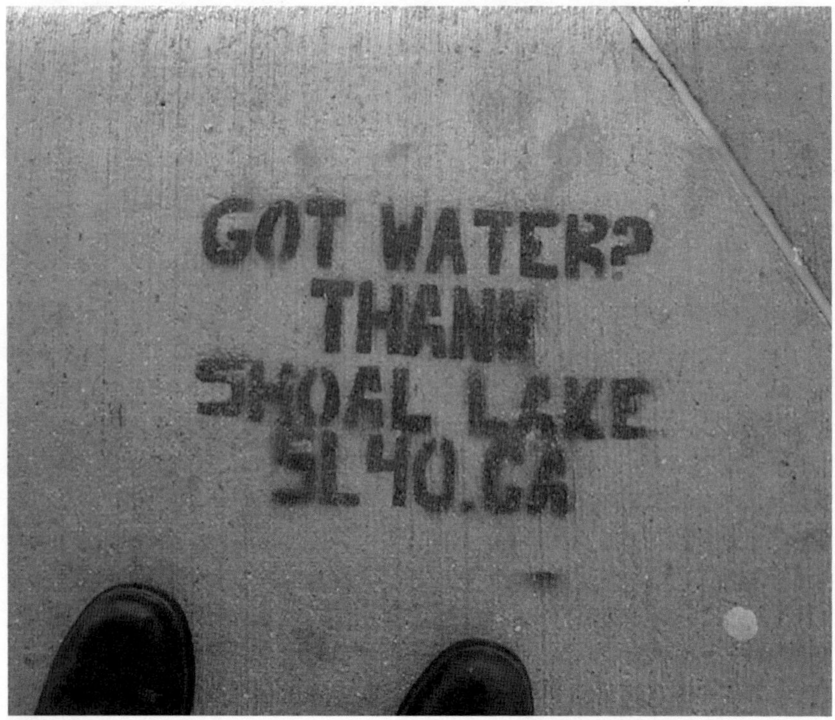

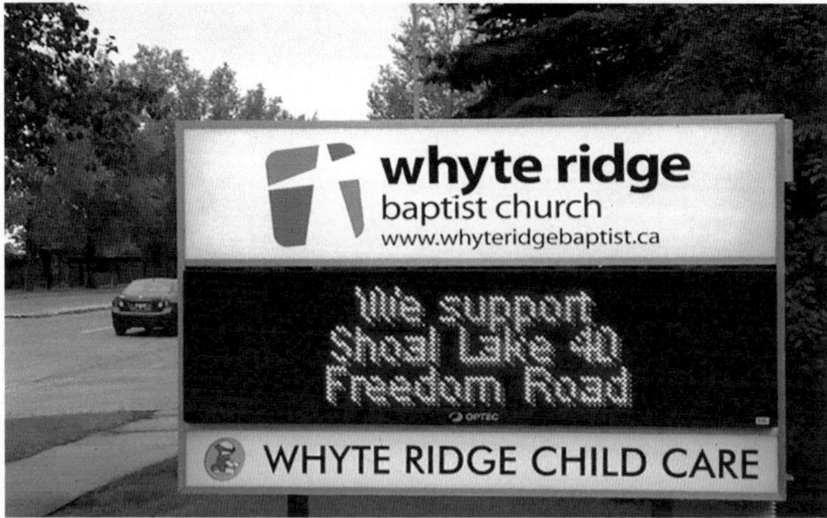

Figure 42. "Got Water? Thank Shoal Lake," graffiti stencil, Osborne Bridge.
Figure 43. "We Support Shoal Lake 40 Freedom Road" church signboard, Whyte Ridge Baptist Church.

representatives gathered in Winnipeg to officially announce their joint commitment to funding Shoal Lake 40's Freedom Road. Since the community was cut off from the mainland over 100 years ago by an aqueduct constructed by the federal government to carry fresh water to Winnipeg, Shoal Lake 40 First Nation has dealt with consequences that include social and economic isolation, dangerous—at times lethal—travel conditions, and a decades-long boil-water advisory. Construction on Freedom Road—the 24-kilometre stretch of all-season highway needed to connect Shoal Lake 40 to the Trans-Canada Highway—began in 2017 and the project is scheduled for completion in June 2019.

Shoal Lake 40's tactics as well as its measures of success differ significantly from those of other constituencies that have organized themselves in response to the museum and the perceived limitations of its curatorial vision and human rights mandate. The most vocal of these groups has been a coalition of forty-seven Ukrainian Canadian organizations that formed under the umbrella group Canadians for a Genocide Museum. With a campaign organized around the "twin principles of inclusivity and equity," the group fought for territory within the museum.[64] Though unsuccessful in gaining "equitable" square footage to that of the human rights museum's Holocaust gallery, the campaign succeeded on at least two fronts: first, the Canadian Museum for Human Rights created a permanent Breaking the Silence gallery dedicated to the five genocides officially recognized by Canada—the Ukrainian Holodomor, the Armenian genocide, the Holocaust, the Rwandan genocide, and the Srebrenica genocide in Bosnia; and second, the museum has produced *Covering the Holodomor: Memory Eternal*, a film critically examining the international media's role in covering up the Holodomor, and included it as a permanent exhibit within the Breaking the Silence gallery.

Shoal Lake 40 First Nation, on the other hand, did not wage a battle based on "inclusivity and equity" or what critical memory scholar Michael Rothberg calls "memory wars," wherein communities compete with one another over limited space within the public sphere.[65] In contrast to how both Jewish Canadian and Ukrainian Canadian groups lobbied the museum "to reconsider the genocide and Holocaust galleries," former curator Tricia Logan writes, "Indigenous groups in Canada have focused their rights struggles 'on the ground.'"[66] This strategy is born both of necessity as well as distrust on the part of many Indigenous scholars and activists of the contemporary "politics of recognition" in Canada, which, Dene political scientist Glen Coulthard argues, "promises to reproduce the very configurations of colonial power that Indigenous Peoples' demands for recognition have historically sought to transcend."[67]

Unlike the Ukrainian Canadian community's success in having an expanded gallery dedicated to the Holodomor genocide, Shoal Lake 40 has so far not succeeded in convincing Predock (or the museum) to desist in disseminating his "healing waters" narrative (though Predock has since removed from his website the assertion that "First Nations sacred relationship to water is honoured" in the museum's Garden of Contemplation). What they did achieve was far greater, both in terms of discursive and material effect.

Rather than seek territory *within* the museum, with their Museum *for* Canadian Human Rights Violations, Shoal Lake 40 facilitated a process of what Gilles Deleuze refers to as the "deterritorialization" and "reterritorialization" of space. Shoal Lake 40 deterritorialized the museum's discourses around human rights, and Indigenous and settler relationships to the environment, thereby taking the conversation out of the discursive control of the national museum and reterritorializing it within the broader social sphere.

Instead of limiting their appeal to the museum's decision makers, Shoal Lake 40 community activists invited Winnipeggers to come and gather around a fire pit. This simple gesture of creating a convivial gathering space served as a reminder that The Forks and its unearthed and buried hearths are not something to be archived in a distant past. They also invited people to come visit the Shoal Lake 40 territory as a living Museum *for* Canadian Human Rights Violations, to witness and learn about the conditions of the waters the Shoal Lake 40 community has been forced to live with as a result of the aqueduct that supplies Winnipeg with its water. Hundreds of school, church, government, and community groups took Shoal Lake 40 up on their invitation. In the process, Shoal Lake 40 activists not only succeeded in gaining the long overdue funding needed to build Freedom Road, they also engendered a process of collective critical engagement about the relationships between settler Canadian communities' naturalized relationship to environmental resource extraction, and the Indigenous communities from whom those resources have been and continue to be extracted.[68]

Shoal Lake 40's actions facilitated for many a conscious re-engagement with the consequences of our day-to-day relationship to the water we consume. Winnipeg's water (and more broadly, that of all urban communities) does not miraculously flow from taps by some magic of capitalist modernity. Like the hundreds of tons of basalt, limestone, steel, concrete, and alabaster that went into the museum's construction, our water is extracted, and its extraction has consequences for the environment and for the communities who live in and with that environment. Like The Forks, the environment from which our water is extracted was not and is not an uninhabited empty wilderness. It is a land on which Indigenous peoples live and have lived for thousands of years. With its human rights violations museum and its Got Water? and Freedom Road campaigns, Shoal Lake 40 demetaphorized the Canadian Museum for Human Rights' public relations narrative of healing waters and environmental indigeneity and instead grounded it in a material here and now, a present that is intimately linked to equally corporeal pasts and futures.

Freedom Road is not a metaphor. It is both an infrastructural necessity and a way. As a physical structure, Freedom Road is needed for the community to build a water treatment facility, for community members to freely and safely engage in economic opportunities on and off the reserve, for on-reserve community members to access medical and other services, and for off-reserve community members to be able to return home at will. Like the Red and Assiniboine Rivers and the hundreds of other waterways that served as the original living thoroughfares for Indigenous peoples of this land now called Canada, Freedom Road is also more than a material resource. It is a way for community members to sustain their ongoing lived relationship to place.

With their uncanny embrace of the Canadian Museum for Human Rights' celebrated human rights narrative, Shoal Lake 40 took the story of the community's governmentally manufactured water crisis and isolation out of the percepticidal realm of settler-colonial obscurity and rendered it apprehensible to a broad range of local, national, and international constituencies. Like the Canadian Museum for Human Rights brand, Shoal Lake 40's campaign to expose the museum's hypocrisy has extended far beyond the localized terrain of its pup-tent launch. A broad range of communities mobilized across the city, the province, the nation, and beyond in the struggle to mobilize federal dollars to build Freedom Road.[69] There were Students for Freedom Road, Churches for Freedom Road, 10 Days for Shoal Lake, a Road to Reconciliation crowdfunding campaign, a Human Rights Watch investigation, and an Amnesty International Justice for Shoal Lake Campaign. Hashtags proliferate: #FreedomRoad, #BoilNoMore, #Shoalidarity, #HonourTheSource, #ChurchesForFreedomRoad, #FriendsofSL40.

The Canadian Museum for Human Rights, like The Forks, is a contact zone, a place of encounter, a site where world views collide. As queer theorist Jasbir Puar proposes, thinking about power through the concept of assemblages captures the complex complicities of privilege's production of normative world views and practices of exploitation and domination. Likewise, thinking of struggles of resistance through the concept of "always already assemblages . . . open[s] up new avenues of thinking, speaking, organizing, doing politics—lines of flight, affective eruptions, affect, energies, forces, temporalities, contagions, contingencies, and the inexplicable."[70] In contrast to the vertical embrace of the museum's sky-piercing Tower of Hope or its architecturally choreographed journey of enlightenment, Shoal Lake 40 is part of a horizontal, rhizomic, and cross-temporal assemblage engaged in multi-faceted and inter(in)animating performances of resistance to a world view that supports the domination and exploitation of Indigenous peoples and the environment.

Like David Gordon Thomas and his silently echoing drum, like the Mi'kmaq man who performed his unbecoming escape before his aristocratic captor audience, like Rebecca Belmore and her unbecoming blanket, Shoal Lake 40's activist performances pull back the curtain on the complicities of settler colonialism, capitalist modernity, and neo-liberalism that are obscured by the museum's metaphoric misappropriations, its universalizing human rights discourse, its architectural iconography, and its logocentric textual narratives. To the extent that the Canadian Museum for Human Rights can be considered a place of "hope," it is a hope that is not located within the museum's monumental architecture and Enlightenment human rights narratives, but rather in the ways the museum is being taken up. Hope lies in the Indigenous community's uncanny and disidentificatory work in, on, through, and against the museum.

Unlike the museum's contact zones that operate as spaces of managed transcultural exchange, designed to facilitate what Stó:lō First Nation scholar Dylan Robinson has theorized as "reconciliatory affect," artists and activists like Thomas, Belmore, and Shoal Lake 40 (among so many others) create a living contact zone that reminds the museum and its visitors of their ongoing responsibilities and of the incommensurability of hope without redress.[71] A contact zone organized around material effects. A contact zone that shifts the discourse from universal and individualized notions of human rights and instead focuses on the ongoing effects of land, water, and other resource thefts. A contact zone that mines the fissures of misappropriated metaphor within the Canadian Museum for Human Rights to unbecome abstracted notions of benevolent settler-Canadian nationalism.

CHAPTER FIVE

UNBECOMING CANADA 150

BY MANY MEANS NECESSARY

> How to stop a story that is always being told? Or, how to change a story that is always being told? The story that settler-colonial nation-states tend to tell about themselves is that they are new; they are beneficent; they have successfully "settled" all issues prior to their beginning.
>
> — Audra Simpson[1]

Beneath the dazzle and beyond the din of Canada 150's spectacular fireworks displays are stories. Unlike military commemoration, whose reverential fortifications affectively ward off dissent to produce a univocal and elegiac narrative, celebratory Canadian nationalism's story of multicultural inclusivity accommodates difference with a diffusive and proliferating flair. With folkloric tales of cultural diversity as the hallmark of Canada's sesquicentennial celebrations, 2017 became a year in which it was nearly impossible to access any form of media—television, radio, social media—without encountering a story about what it means to be Canadian.

CBC began preparing for Canada 150 celebrations as far back as 2013, when it launched its "2017 Starts Now" work kit instructing Canadians on how they could help "to incubate and inspire ideas for celebrations." The national broadcasting corporation issued invitations to Canadians to share their stories, from which it then constructed a multicultural media mosaic of Canadian-ness. The plethora of story-themed programs under CBC's "20!7 Canada 150" tagline included the snapshot series *What's Your Story?*, where Canadians shared personal vignettes about what defines Canada for them;[2] *Canada: The Story of Us*, which offered viewers a more elaborated and enthralling engagement with Canadian history in a ten-hour drama-documentary series featuring "exciting action-adventure narratives told through dramatic recreation and 3D animation";[3] and *We Are Canada*, which celebrated "the next generation of talented and passionate change-makers whose works are shaping and defining our future in imaginative ways."[4] *Becoming Canadian* "[captured] the life-changing moment when individuals [became] new citizens";[5] while *We Are the Best* was for those interested in exploring "the extraordinary richness of Canada's culinary heritage";[6] and *CBC Short Docs: Indigenous*, because "as Canada celebrates 150 years since Confederation, CBC wants Indigenous voices and perspectives to tell a more robust story of our collective nationhood."[7]

CBC's programming may have offered a dizzying celebration of Canadian diversity, but as Mohawk scholar Audra Simpson asserts, there are three intersecting narratives at the crux of the story that settler-colonial nation-states tell about themselves: first, *they are new*; second, *they are beneficent*; and third, *they have "settled" all issues prior to their beginning*. Regardless of the multicultural nuances that are integrated into its national birthday narrative, the Canada 150 celebrations tell a story about the legitimacy of Canada's becoming, the benevolence of the contemporary Canadian nation, and the pastness of what came before. It is a repeat of a repeat of a repeat. It is colonialism's oft-told story of "enlightened" development that is based on the foundational "concepts used to justify European sovereignty over Indigenous peoples and lands, such as the Doctrine of Discovery and *terra nullius*."[8]

At its core, the story of Canada, and more pointedly, the celebration of Canada 150, relies on the naturalization of Canadian settler-colonial nationalism and the nation-state it constructs. Settler colonialism is naturalized through a scenario of discovery that posits the landscape as empty and wasted prior to European intervention; it is naturalized through the eradication from social memory of the rich cultural, economic, and political histories of Indigenous societies that inhabited and continue to inhabit these lands now called Canada, and through the ongoing denial of Indigenous sovereignty; it is naturalized through updated renditions of narratives of progress—civilizing missions, resource development, multiculturalism, reconciliation. As a naturalized entity, the Canadian nation can apologize for "past" mistakes and issue calls for reconciliation without jeopardizing its totalizing presence.

Speaking at Toronto's Massey Hall, at a public panel hosted by CBC's Matt Galloway, Michif (Métis) artist and activist Christi Belcourt vehemently refused acquiescence to the dominion of Canadian nationalism and its celebrated multicultural national identity: "Do not refer to Indigenous people as Canadians. Do not think that we can come under the umbrella of Canada."[9] Belcourt went on to denaturalize the very notion of the nation-state:

> I am a Michif woman. I am a Metis woman. I am an Indigenous woman. There are over fifty Indigenous nations—*Nations*—in this country. . . . My ancestors were buffalo hunters, buffalo people. We have ceremonies, songs, and respect for the buffalo, so much so that we refer to the buffalo as a nation. We consider the birds to be nations. We consider the trees to be nations. Our view of nations is so much bigger and so different than just to assume that human beings are the only ones. We always assume human beings are at the top of the food chain, and yet, we are at the bottom. We are at the bottom because nothing needs us to survive and we need absolutely everything else.[10]

Shifting the discourse away from "the nation" as an unquestioned and totalizing entity, Belcourt tells another story, one that foregrounds a world view in which there are a multiplicity of nations—human and non-human—each with sovereign rights. Critically, Belcourt's depiction of multiple nations bears no resemblance to Canada's celebrated multiculturalism. By recognizing the nationhood of over fifty Indigenous nations, of the buffalo, of the birds, of the trees, Belcourt asserts a web of nation-to-nation relations in which no single nation has jurisdiction over another.

Just as Canada's celebrated multiculturalism bears no resemblance to Belcourt's multi-nations, the grassroots approach of Idle No More and the assemblage of artists, activists, and cultural producers who are working to unbecome Canada 150's celebratory settler-colonial refrain carries no resemblance to the Highway of Heroes' much acclaimed grassroots emergence. Whereas the former is informed by a decentralized nation-to-nation logic of relationality and by a rich history of diverse practices of rebellion and resistance, the latter is informed by nationalism's totalizing logic and draws upon

Canada's century-long reiteration of a militarist poetics of elegiac commemoration and obligatory reverentiality.

Though voiced via an ever-diversifying chorus, the overarching tenor of the Canada 150 refrain delivered through official events and the mainstream media remained surprisingly univocal. An effective technique of Canadian settler-colonial governmentality, multiculturalism also serves as an effective narrative device for the always-told story of settler-Canadian beneficence. How then to resist? How do artists, activists, and cultural producers work against the purifying optics of the settler-Canadian myth of multicultural inclusivity? Rather than offering a single answer to Simpson's question—*How do you change a story that is always being told?*—this chapter focuses on some of the diverse strategies of artists, activists, and cultural producers who are engaged in the ongoing work of unbecoming the narrative of celebratory settler-Canadian nationalism that Canada 150 heralded.

Kent Monkman, Miss Chief, and the Bearing of Canadian History

> I could not think of any history paintings that conveyed or authorized Indigenous experience into the canon of art history. Where were the paintings from the nineteenth century that recounted, with passion and empathy, the dispossession, starvation, incarceration and genocide of Indigenous people here on Turtle Island?
>
> — Kent Monkman, *Shame and Prejudice: A Story of Resilience*[11]

Social memory—like gender—is performative, meaning it is constructed through a series of reiterations. Two-spirit Cree artist Kent Monkman, in queer fashion, inserts slippages into the repeats of the Canadian settler-colonial story that is told over, and over, and over again. Similar to Shoal Lake 40's Museum *for* Canadian Human Rights Violations and to *Trace*, Rebecca Belmore's blanket returned, with his monumental Canada 150 counter-memorial solo exhibition Monkman both mimics and mocks the original as he tells a story about the story that is always being told. Though *Shame and Prejudice: A Story of Resilience* (2017) was created under the aegis of Canada 150 funding, as a nationally (and internationally) renowned artist, Monkman's party-crashing intervention exceeds the temporal confines of Canada 150 and will live on in the canon of art history long after the celebration's fireworks have fizzled and the hot dogs and birthday cake have been consumed.

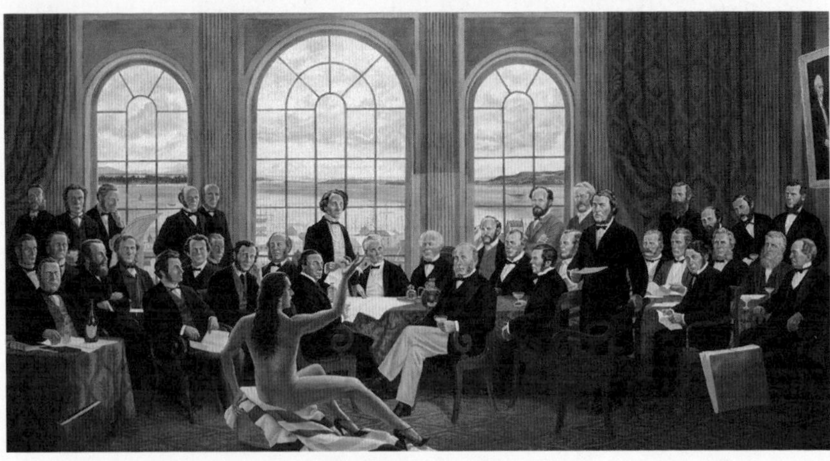

Figure 44. *The Daddies* (2016), by Kent Monkman.

Unlike the many Indigenous artists who have issued public statements of refusal to produce work under Canada's sesquicentennial banner, when Monkman was approached to create a project for Canada 150, "he leapt at the possibility."[12] It was an opportunity, as Monkman explained in conversation with Rosanna Deerchild, host of the CBC radio program *Unreserved*, "to create a body of work that would be critical of this last 150 years of Canada, something to counter the celebrations that will be happening this year. I wanted people to reflect on what have the last 150 years meant to Indigenous people."[13]

Commissioned by the Art Museum at the University of Toronto, the exhibition—which is also curated by Monkman—places the artist's paintings, drawings, and sculptural installations in dialogue with historical artworks and artifacts borrowed from museums and private collections across Canada. Miss Chief Eagle Testickle—Monkman's gender-bending, time-travelling alter-ego—acts as *Shame and Prejudice*'s narrator and guide. Using the many tongues of gesture, image, form, and language, she speaks to and through the historical characters within the artworks, as well as to her contemporary and future audiences.

Miss Chief Eagle Testickle is holding court. Seated atop a wooden crate draped with a Hudson's Bay blanket, she's naked save for a single visible earring, black stiletto slingbacks, and long dark hair that cascades down her muscled back. Her right arm is raised, hand open, and fingers turned elegantly upward—a gesture made all the more exquisite by its contrast to the stodgy dullness of the thirty-seven Fathers of Confederation she faces. "Perched in all of her naked splendour and showing her junk to all of the Fathers,"[14] *Miss Chief is giving them a piece of her mind. Or perhaps she's singing an aria—suitably silent for willfully deaf ears. Dressed in their portrait dandies, the "Daddies" feign disinterest.*

Maybe it's not the "Daddies" she's come to confront. Adept at the temporal drag of time travel, Miss Chief has landed simultaneously at the tableau of the faux Charlottetown Conference of 1864—painted in 1883 by Robert Harris, destroyed in the Parliament building fire of 1916, resurrected by Rex Woods for Canada's 1967 Centennial—and here in 2017, a.k.a. Canada 150. Her back is turned to us, her contemporary audience.

I wonder what she might be saying. To aid myself in this act of imagining, I try on her posture. I sit on a plastic milk crate covered in an orange and white wool blanket brought from Holland by my mom. The blanket tickles and itches. No stilettos (I don't own any heels). No earrings (ditto). I reach my left hand back and rest it on the crate behind me, raise my head, broaden my back, lift my right hand and turn my fingers skyward. But I'm not Miss Chief. Nor am I a Daddy. I am a second-generation Canadian, born and raised on Treaty One territory, who grew up without having the slightest clue of what that meant. I remember learning the C-A-N-A-D-A song in school for Canada's 1967 centennial celebration. I remember the flag waving. I remember the pioneer dress my mom made me. I don't remember the hot dogs, or the fireworks, or the other centennial birthday treats, but I'm sure they were there, and that I partook.

I don't know what Miss Chief is saying, but I'm glad she's come to crash the party.

At over nine feet wide and five feet high, *The Daddies* (2016) is a centrepiece of *Shame and Prejudice*. The portrait acts as signifying marker for both Canada 150's erasure of the years preceding the "event" of Confederation, and the purification of the 150 years of Canadian settler colonialism that have come in its wake. With *The Daddies*, Monkman draws our attention to the racialized and gendered conception of Canadian nationalism—or baby Canada. *The Daddies* together with its historical predecessors—Robert Harris's portrait of *The Fathers of Confederation*, and its 1967 reincarnation by Rex Woods—can be read as an allegory for Canadian social memory. *The Daddies* tells a story about a story constructed of additions, revisions, and omissions. A story about the story the Canadian nation-state tells and retells about itself. A story about the historical authorization of inclusion and exclusion. A story about the role of art, and art's historical canon, in the making of history, and in the becoming and unbecoming of myths of the Canadian nation.

Like *The Daddies*—and the *Shame and Prejudice* exhibition as a whole—the iconic *Fathers of Confederation* painting on which *The Daddies* is modelled is a child born of the communion of Canadian arts funding and Canadian nationalism. In fact, the impetus for *The Fathers* did not come from Canada's fledgling federal government. It was the brainchild of Lucius R. O'Brien, then president of Canada's Royal Academy of the Arts. In what proved to be a bold move that resulted in increased visibility and political viability for the newly founded Academy, O'Brien issued a memorandum to the government proposing that it commission a painting to commemorate "the meeting of the Conference at which the foundation was laid for the Confederation of the Provinces constituting the Dominion of Canada."[15]

So it followed that in 1883, the federal government commissioned Robert Harris to paint a portrait of the twenty-three delegates who had gathered at the 1864 Charlottetown Conference. After some political manoeuvring, Harris was compelled to change the venue to the Quebec Conference and to incorporate delegates from both conferences into the painting—raising the Daddy total to thirty-three (democratically including secretary Hewitt Bernard). After the original painting was destroyed in the Parliament Building fire of 1916, *The Fathers* were left to rest in peace until 1967, when Rex Woods resurrected them in a painting commissioned by the Confederation Life Assurance Company in celebration of Canada's 100th Anniversary of Confederation. The new painting grew in both stature and population, with two metres added to its overall dimensions and three Fathers joining Canada's already Daddy-heavy national birth narrative. Despite the negotiated inclusions, *The*

Fathers of Confederation remained a decidedly exclusive—white, heteronormative male—crew until Miss Chief Eagle Testickle entered the scene.

Not satisfied with a seat at the table, in *The Bears of Confederation* (2016) Miss Chief removes the Daddies from their historically fixed seats of power to take them out for a little back-to-nature wilderness romp. Exiting the staid scene of emergent Canadian governmentality, Monkman's *Bears* is a "frolicking huge landscape" where Monkman imagines in painterly fashion "all of those Fathers—or all those Daddies—as 'bears' running around frolicking with real bears, and Miss Chief is this dominatrix and she's summoning the spirit power of those bears to help her seduce or take control of these Daddies."[16]

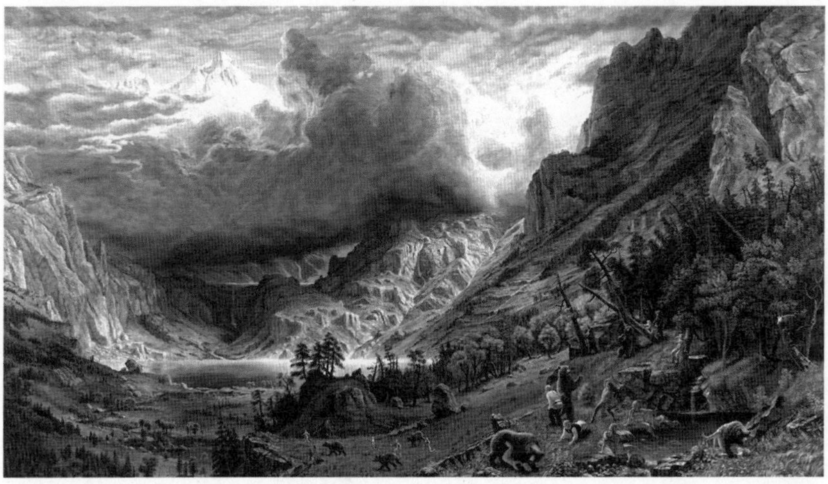

Figure 45. *The Bears of Confederation* (2016) by Kent Monkman.

It's the Daddies who are bare-assed now. And Miss Chief is running the show. She traded in her classy black slingbacks for a pair of thigh-high red leather stilettos. Her junk is now draped in a sheer red loincloth that whirls like a ghostly flaming serpent between her legs. Her eyes are ablaze and her teeth bared. In one hand she's got a Daddy on a leash. Her other whip-wielding arm is cocked above and behind her head, the whip hovering on the brink of release. Its target is leashed-Daddy's exposed bottom. A second Daddy sits nearby. Watching. Waiting his turn, I imagine.

The Daddy-bears appear to be enjoying their humiliations and servicings at the hand of Miss Chief and her Spirit Bears. Only one seems to be resisting domination. He's climbed a tree. His Spirit Bear stands on its hind legs at the tree's base. Maybe it's not escape Daddy-bear seeks. Maybe he's taking a climbing lesson from his Spirit Bear. While most of the bears—Daddy and Spirit—are in the painting's foreground where they are either copulating or relaxing around a small clear pond, others are meandering off into the painting's landscape backdrop. Many of the Daddies have already disappeared into the vast wilderness.

While the content of Monkman's work is overtly subversive, his choice of form is covertly insurgent in its deployment of aesthetic conventions that were influential in shaping European ideas of America and "Indianness." Through his paintings and diorama-like sculptural works, Monkman engages the powerful and pervasive narrative of the American West and its Indigenous inhabitants that was created through Euro-American art movements: neoclassicism, landscape painting, and American western art. For example, through the use of a naturalistic style, which assumes a kind of neutrality, facticity, or realism, nineteenth-century landscape paintings introduced Europe to an America that was "a vast wilderness, relatively empty of human occupants."[17] These aesthetic renditions of the land as uninhabited reinforced legalistic concepts like *terra nullius* and the Doctrine of Discovery, thereby helping to legitimate European encroachment and masking the brutality of the colonization of the Americas. If the land is empty, settlers are simply filling a void. If no one is there to begin with, no one is being violently dispossessed.

Using the long-established aesthetic codes of these movements to disrupt these same codes, Monkman produces what performance studies scholar Rebecca Schneider (after Vivian Patraka) refers to as "binary terror." Schneider writes: "The terror that accompanies the dissolution of a binary habit of sense-making and self-fashioning is directly proportionate to the social safety insured in the maintenance of such apparatus of sense."[18] In Monkman's works, the "imaginary Indian" that these art movements construct—an "Indian" or "Indianness" that, as Melissa Elston writes, is in "a state of disappearance, dependence and savagery" collides with Indigenous peoples as a living presence.

In both *The Daddies* and *Bears*, Miss Chief is the only Indigenous human present. In *The Daddies*, her presence before the all-male white delegates marks the absence of any Indigenous participation in the political negotiations that the celebrated Fathers of Confederation undertook for the juridical conception of Canada as a nation-state. Her positioning between the painting's thirty-seven *Daddies* and her contemporary audience produces a temporal collision between Canada's national birth story and its spectacularized sesquicentennial celebration. No longer dispossessed and peripheral, Miss Chief has taken centre stage where, in her naked splendour, she lays bare the settler-colonial nation's naturalized and hierarchical social binaries—male/female, white/Indigenous, civilized/primitive, present/past—and blows a hole in the story of Canadian national innocence and beneficence.

In *Bears*, Miss Chief is not only the only Indigenous presence. She is also the one wielding power, through her whip and her connection to the non-human world of the Spirit Bears. Whereas, as Elston notes, "neoclassical subject painting was a common visual means of regulating gender," landscape paintings can be seen as a visual means of regulating geography by defining space as empty and therefore available for the taking.[19] By reconfiguring the conventions of neoclassical iconography and landscape painting, Monkman creates what Elston calls a "genre-blending ruckus" in which he "deregulates the gender *and* geographic restrictions which silently commingle and mutually reinforce one another in dominant Euro-American visual culture."[20]

With Miss Chief as his drag-doppelgänger, Monkman flips the racial and gender codes of the historical Eurocentric archive. In the process, he shifts the aesthetically encoded status of Indigenous peoples in art history "from object-status to subject-status, from victimhood to action, from elegiac absence to living presence."[21] Formatted to resemble a historical journal, the *Shame and Prejudice* brochure is a critical element of Monkman's code-shifting. The faux leather-bound front cover is embossed in gold with two beseeching winged beavers. Following Monkman's foreword, the brochure's nine chapters are framed as excerpts from the "Memoirs of Miss Chief Eagle Testickle."

As is the dictate of galleries and other forms of cultural production, a page is dedicated to acknowledgements of support. And so it is that the last word of Miss Chief's Memoirs goes to the Canada Council for the Arts with its mandated logo and pre-scripted bilingual message in English and French. Following the conventional acknowledgement of "the support of the Canada Council for the Arts," the message continues, "which last year invested $153 million to bring the arts to Canadians throughout the country."[22] There is something uncanny about the placement. Like Jane Austen's Bennett sisters—after whom Monkman has fashioned Miss Chief's narrative—who, as women without financial means of their own, do what they must to secure social status, it is as though Miss Chief is acknowledging not only the Council's financial support, but also what it takes to get a seat at the settler-colonial table. As Monkman—Miss Chief—writes: "When the stakes are high and our enemies mighty, it behooves us to do what we can in order to tip the scales in our favour."[23]

Strategic Refusal as Resistance and Resurgence: Christi Belcourt and the Onaman Collective

> These nation-states have the gall, the mendacity, and the hyperbolic influence to call and then imagine themselves as something other than dispossessing, occupying, and juridically dubious.
>
> — Audra Simpson[24]

Canada is a nation whose continued becoming relies on reiterating the story of the beneficent nation and masking the violence of its originary and ongoing becoming. One way this violence is enacted is through institutionally supported performances of celebratory nationalism—like Canada 150—that serve to manufacture and maintain a national process of settler-Canadian forgetfulness. For many in Canada's Indigenous communities (and beyond), the national invitation to celebrate the 150th anniversary of Canada's Confederation was—in the words of Christi Belcourt—nothing short of "insulting": "We have 15,000 years of ancestry. Our ancestors are buried in these lands. It's like a bunch of us jumped in a boat and went over to England, and decided we were going to rename everything, put our languages on everything, forget everybody that lived there, take over the space with our laws, then make a declaration and then the following year, celebrate the one-year anniversary of our declaration of taking over those lands. It's just really—it's an insult. And it's sad, and it hinders the ability for us to move forward."[25]

Social memory is a frame with material consequences. Just as Canadian military commemoration produces a "differential allocation of grief" by allotting "grievable humans" with institutionally supported venues for "celebrated public grieving" while disavowing the grievability of "others'" lives, performances of Canadian celebratory commemoration produce a structural forgetfulness that has violent effects.[26] Beneath the two intersecting demands that Canadian military commemoration issues to the nation's "civilian soldiers"—silence and reverential engagement—is the more egregious agenda of quelling dissent. I propose that the repercussions of Canadians' century-long indoctrination into the protocols of military memorialization extend beyond the rituals of military commemoration. As a population, settler Canadians have become conditioned to sideline their dissent during moments of national spectacle both reverential *and* celebratory. During national "moments" of commemoration, which in practice are often both durational and sequential, it is considered unbecoming to criticize. Bad-mannered at best, and disrespectful at worst. In short, it is quintessentially un-Canadian.

But to uncritically take part in Canada 150 celebrations—as Minister of Canadian Heritage Mélanie Joly so enthusiastically called on Canadians to do—adds injury to insult. Celebratory participation in Canada 150 events affirmed the national social blindness to the 15,000 pre-Confederation years of Indigenous ancestry in what is now called Canada. Uncritical celebratory participation perpetuates an attitude of indifference to the conditions through which Indigenous peoples have been (and continue to be) dispossessed of their lands and resources, and to the resulting socio-economic conditions of Indigenous peoples in contemporary post-Confederation Canada.[27]

Whereas Monkman/Miss Chief took a seat at the Canada 150 table in order to interrogate and alter—for posterity—the settler-colonial story that is always being told, for Belcourt, refusing to participate in the rituals of its continued telling is the way to change the story. When asked by CBC host Matt Galloway how she would be spending Canada Day 2017, Belcourt responded: "I'm going to be in the bush building a Culture Camp Forever[28] . . . and we are going to be completely ignoring Canada Day celebrations that are going on because they are ignoring Indigenous people so we're just going to go do what we need to do to try and rebuild."[29]

In 2014, together with Anishinaabe traditional storyteller Isaac Murdoch and Métis/Cree visual and media artist Erin Konsmo, Belcourt formed the Onaman Collective with the mandate of "finding ways to converge land-based art creation with traditional knowledge, youth, Elders and Anishinaabemowin and Cree languages."[30] Since its inception, the Collective has hosted culture camps and community workshops that combine traditional arts, storytelling, and language immersion with contemporary social arts practices. From the outset, the Collective established a land fund to purchase a site and build a permanent camp where "youth and Elders can connect on the land to share traditional skills and speak the language."[31] The camp, Nimkii Aazhibikong (which means Village of Thunder Mountain in Anishinaabemowin, the Ojibwe language), is located by Ompa Lake, northern Ontario, in traditional Anishinaabe territory.[32]

More than a reactive "No," Belcourt's and the Onaman Collective's refusal is an equally resounding and affirmative "Yes."[33] More than a turning away, it is a turning toward. As Audra Simpson writes, "Contorting oneself in a fundamental space of misrecognition is not just about subject formation; it is about historical formation."[34] By refusing to contort to Canada 150's space of insulting misrecognition, Belcourt and the Onaman Collective assert a historical accounting that precedes and exceeds Canadian Confederation, the settler-Canadian nation-state, and Canada 150—an accounting that is asserted not only discursively but through community actions and practices that embody "resistance, resilience, and resurgence."[35] As Murdoch says of Nimkii Aazhibikong, "This is a camp of resurgence. . . . We want it to be for the environment, for the waters and to start getting out on the land and occupying our traditional spaces. Our resurgence is the resistance."[36]

The Onaman Collective does not accept government funding and instead turns to the community as its sole means of support. In addition to a GoFundMe campaign (which as of May 2018 had raised almost $16,000), a key fundraising strategy has been participatory Auctions for Action that the Collective hosts on Facebook several times a year. While this strategy could be perceived as placing a burden on a community that is already confronted with what Pamela Palmater describes as "crisis-level socio-economic conditions,"[37] Michi Saagiig Nishnaabeg (Anishinaabe) scholar and activist Leanne Betasamosake Simpson asserts: "It is time to admit that colonizing governments and private corporate foundations are not going to fund our decolonization, because the colonial relationship serves their interests and they remain the beneficiaries of colonialism."[38]

Whereas the contemporary institutionalized social movement model—sometimes referred to as the "non-profit industrial complex model"—has a tendency to reduce participation to forwarding emails, sharing posts, signing petitions, and of course, donating money, the Onaman Collective's Auctions for Action ask for and give more. Financially, the auctions have proved highly successful—a single auction held from 12 through 30 March 2018 raised $20,000. But the auctions' measure of success transcends monetary terms. The auctions reveal and extend community connections. They are sites of celebration, generosity, resurgence, and palpably vital creative social engagement in a way that is reflective of the praxis of resurgence and community engagement that Nimkii Aazhibikong fosters.

The Auctions for Action follow a simple structure. It is also one that generates reciprocal engagement, distributes responsibility, and helps to build an arts-based community gathered around shared social and environmental values. Donors post an image of the item to be auctioned, along with relevant information about its medium, dimensions, or history, and who—donor or high bidder—will pay for shipping. Items put up for auction include original art—well-known artists like Belcourt, Murdoch, and Sherry Farrell Racette (among others) participate alongside lesser-known artists; activist T-shirts and posters; hand-crafted jewellery, drums, baskets, moccasins, blankets, ribbon skirts; soaps and medicinal salves; books. When the auction comes to a close, winning bidders send their money via e-transfer or cheque directly to the Onaman Collective, and the donor and bidder work out the details of delivery. It is a structure that makes evident existing community values and capacities while simultaneously building new ones.

Taken together, the Auctions for Action and the Culture Camp they are set up to support engage what Glen Sean Coulthard calls a prefigurative praxis in "the sense that they build the skills and social relationships (including those with the land) that are required within and among Indigenous communities to construct alternatives to the colonial relationship in the long run."[39] Rather than becoming hindered by the piecemeal structure of arts funding grants or Canada 150 as the latest installment in Canada's serials of national commemoration events, with Nimkii Aazhibikong the Onaman Collective refuses Canadian setter-colonialism's old story and instead tell their own story, on their own terms, on their own land, in their own language(s). They are quite literally doing what they need to do to rebuild.

Rather than quietly turning her back on Canada's sesquicentennial spectacle, however, Belcourt deployed her "refusal" in a profoundly effective tactic of resistance, availing herself of the Canada 150 backdrop as an activist stage from which to contest settler colonialism's always-told story. She launched the year 2017 with a YouTube circulation of her by-now iconic video poem "Canada, I can cite for you, 150," which reads in part:

> Lists of the dead
> 150 languages no longer spoken
> 150 rivers poisoned
> 150 Indigenous children taken into care last month
> 150 Indigenous communities without water
> 150 grieving in a hotel in Winnipeg
> 150 times a million lies
> told to our faces
> to steal our lands.[40]

As the year unfolded, Belcourt was a frequent guest on CBC, where she continued to voice her critiques of Canada 150 while asserting the sovereignty of a multiplicity of Indigenous and non-human nations.[41]

Like Monkman's paintings, Belcourt's poem and refusals have outlived Canada 150. Refusal in this sense cannot be mistaken for the apathetic disempowerment that is all too common among settler Canadians whose relative privilege includes that of political disinvestment. It is a refusal that pulls back the curtain of celebratory nationalism to expose its behind-the-scenes ideological wizardry. Moreover, it is a turning toward that is part of a broader movement of "Oshkimaadiziig, the New People."[42] According to Nishnaabeg prophecy, "it is the Oshkimaadiziig," writes Leanne Betasamosake Simpson, "whose responsibilities involve reviving our language, philosophies, political and economic traditions, our ways of knowing, and our culture."[43] The responsibility and the approach that Simpson articulates are evident in Belcourt's refusal, and in Nimkii Aazhibikong and the Onaman Collective. As Leanne Simpson writes of the contributors to the collection *Lighting the Eighth Fire*: "While recognizing that community- and nation-based activists may be forced to negotiate with settler governments and the legal system to immediately protect their citizens and territories . . . this cannot be the *emphasis* of our work."[44]

Through the assertion of multiple tactical modes of resistance ranging from infiltration and subversion, artists, activists, and cultural producers challenge not only the totalizing effects of Canadian nationalism but also its totalizing mechanisms. Though Monkman's and Belcourt's approaches—engagement and refusal—may appear to contradict one another, it would be reductive and reflective of the statist world view that their work resists to view their methods as oppositional. As Kahnawà:ke Mohawk political scientist Taiaiake Alfred argues in *Peace, Power, Righteousness: An Indigenous Manifesto*, contrary to nation-states, in traditional Indigenous governing practices "there is no absolute authority, no coercive enforcement of decisions, no hierarchy and no separate ruling entity."[45] Using a by-many-means-necessary approach to disrupting the always-told story, assemblages of Indigenous artists, activists, and cultural producers have been particularly effective in engaging in the ongoing praxis of redress and unbecoming performances of settler-Canadian nationalism. As Leanne Simpson asserts of Idle No More, the strength in the movement's decentralized approach is that it eschews a top-down leadership: "We now have hundreds of leaders from different Indigenous nations emerging all over Mikinakong (the Place [of] the Turtle). We now have hundreds of eloquent spokespeople, seasoned organizers, writers, thinkers and artists acting on their own ideas in anyway and everyway possible. This is the beauty of our movement."[46]

Every. Now. Then. Postcolonial Melancholia in the Dominion of Canada

> Dominion [d*uh*-**min**-y*uh* n]
> 1. the power or right of governing and controlling; sovereign authority.
> 2. rule; control; domination.
> 3. a territory, usually of considerable size, in which a single rulership holds sway.

28 June 2017
Art Gallery of Ontario, Toronto:
Every. Now. Then. Reframing Nationhood exhibition
I step into one of the smaller display spaces. Occupying one side of the room is Dominion *(2001–ongoing), a model of an imaginary*

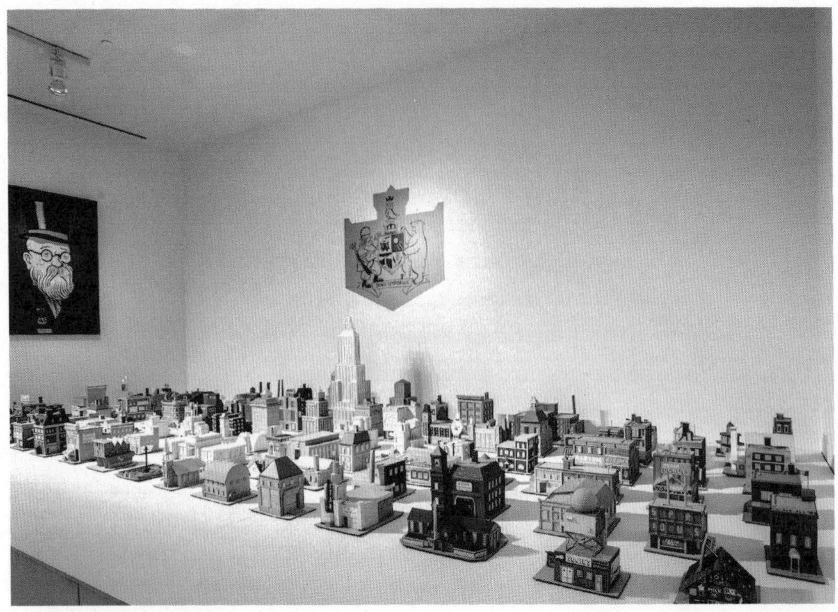

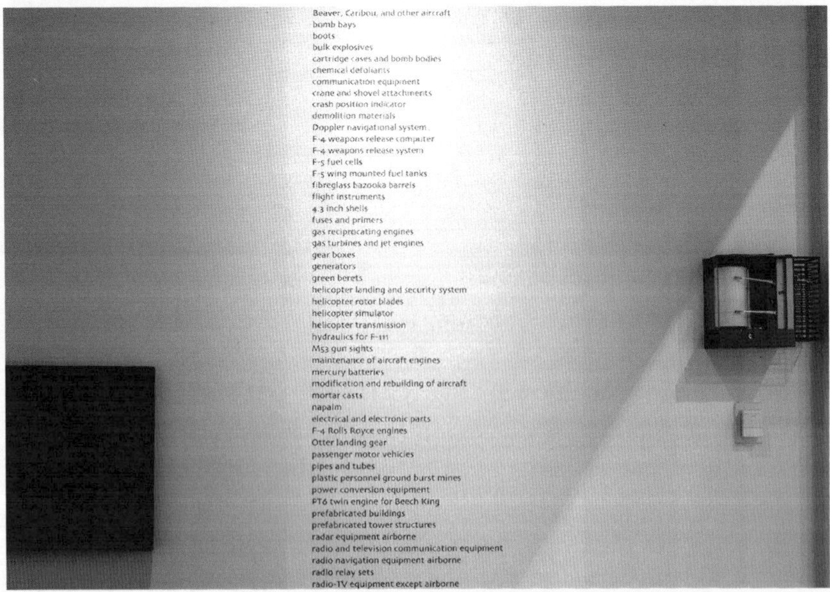

Figure 46. Seth, *Dominion*, 2000–ongoing. Installation view, *Every. Now. Then: Reframing Nationhood.*

Figure 47. List of military components sold to U.S. during Vietnam War, Lisa Steele and Kim Tomczak, *The afternoon knows what the morning never suspected* (Swedish proverb), 2017. Installation view, *Every. Now. Then: Reframing Nationhood.*

city created by graphic novelist—a.k.a a comic book creator—Seth (Figure 46). *On the other side of the room is* The afternoon knows what the morning never suspected *(2017), a three-channel video exhibit by Lisa Steele and Kim Tomczak that looks at Canada's role in the Vietnam War.* Dominion*—a bucolic mid-century Ontario model city (more of a town really)—stands eerily quiet, while across the room, televised footage from the Vietnam War sporadically explodes across the screens and over the shoulders of the two young women who are the video's narrators, go-betweens of a past unfolding war and its rememoration in the unfolding present.*

There's a viewing bench in front of the screens, but the steady flow of visitors passing through the exhibit and the joviality of the gallery's opening night atmosphere make sitting to watch the twenty-minute video somewhat untenable. Instead I'm drawn to the text that cascades down the length of wall to the right of the screens. It's a list of seventy-eight products Canada supplied to the U.S. for use in the Vietnam War—an alphabetically ordered ode to the intersecting economics of global militarism and nationalism (Figure 47). *Items range from the apparently innocuous—boots, pipes and tubes, rye whiskey, trucks and tractors—to those designed for the sole purpose of inflicting harm—anti-personnel grenades, bulk explosives, F-4 weapons release system, fibreglass bazooka barrels. Included on the list are two items—green berets and napalm—that have become iconic signifiers of the Vietnam War. Though the information is new to me, my surprise quickly dissolves into "ah-ha" resignation. Of course we sold weapons and war-related materials to the U.S. As the more recent example of Canada's multi-billion-dollar arms export deal with Saudi Arabia makes clear, even in the land of Canada the good, economics trump ethics.*[47]

Dominion *is a grid of downtown core buildings with signs to signal the activities of those who once frequented the now empty establishments: Violet's Flowers, Sugie's Bait Shop, Saint Henri of the Woods Chop House, Dominion Telegraph Building, Mining Exchange, No Style Beauty Salon, Canadian Toboggan Works, The King Lunch Spot. A water tower stands at the town's centre. Looking out over the uninhabited cardboard city, I am left to imagine its wee denizens. I wonder if they are seated in their homes, somewhere on the outskirts of town, watching in dismay as the Vietnam War and the anti-war protests south of the border erupt across the screens of their tiny black and white television sets. I wonder if tomorrow, they will wake up and go to work at a factory that contributes to the production of one of the seventy-eight products that will be shipped to the U.S. for use in Vietnam.*

It is the opening night of the Art Gallery of Ontario's *Every. Now. Then. Reframing Nationhood* exhibition (2017). The overarching mood is vibrant, alive, buoyant even. A celebration of unbecoming. It is an atmosphere that belies "killjoy" critiques often waged against those who refuse to join the Canada 150 party or other nationalist revelries. Like Shoal Lake 40's campy protest, Miss Chief's riotous historical romp, or Belcourt and the Onaman's Collective's resurgent refusal, this night is a reminder that resistance is not the antithesis of festivity and conviviality. Though resistance requires sustained commitments and can be dangerous—especially for populations who are targets of colonial and imperial aggressions, police violence, institutionalized racism, sexism, homophobia, transphobia (the list goes on)—it can also be joyful.

While Indigenous artists, activists, scholars, and public intellectuals have been at the forefront of the resistance to Canada 150's ahistorical celebratory narrative of multicultural inclusivity and national innocence, *Every. Now. Then.* is an important reminder that critiques of and resistance to dominant narratives of Canadian nationalism are multiple and multiply situated. The exhibition is eclectic in terms of mediums, approaches, and content, with thirty-five projects representing the work of fifty-five artists. Each work is in conversation with the overarching theme of "reframing nationhood" through a critical engagement with the "idea of Canada."

Unlike the univocal and elegiac refrain of Canadian military commemoration, or the celebratory multiculturalism of Canada 150, the artists in *Every. Now. Then.* together constitute a temporary polyvocal chorus that speaks out across the complex geographies, migrations, identities, concerns, and relationships to the Canadian nation that their works animate. Camal Pirbhai and Camille Turner's *Wanted* series (2016) uses performance and contemporary fashion photography to restore the humanity of enslaved subjects of "runaway slave" newspaper ads posted by Canadian slave owners in the early 1900s by portraying them as "people performing freedom." Father and daughter Xiong Gu and Yu Gu's adjoining digital photography and video installations make connections between Niagara Falls' migrant farm workers and Xiong Gu's experience as an urban youth in China who was sent to the countryside to be re-educated as a farmer. The larger-than-life pencil-sketched portraits in Syrus Marcus Ware's *Baby Don't Worry, You Know That We Got You* (2017) act as moving tributes or "love letters" to Black activists working on the front lines of political struggle. *Don't Breathe, Don't Drink*, Ruth Cuthand's beaded blue tarps and floating magnified replicas of the bacterium and parasites found in First Nation communities under boil-water advisories brings attention to the crisis-level living conditions of many Indigenous communities in Canada.

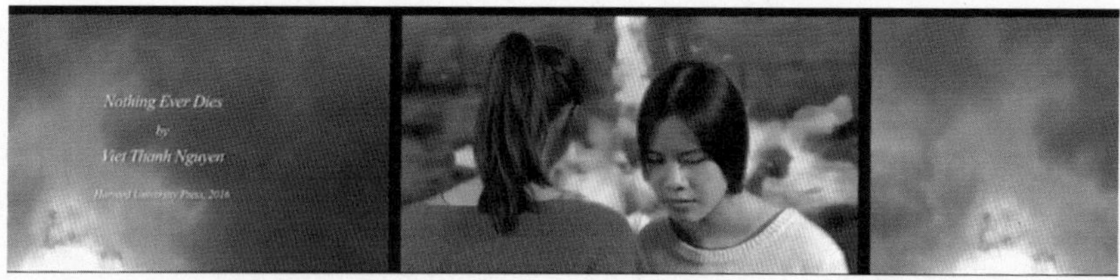

Figure 48. Lisa Steele and Kim Tomczak, *The afternoon knows what the morning never suspected* (Swedish proverb), 2017.

20 August 2017
Art Gallery of Ontario, Toronto: *The afternoon knows what the morning never suspected* and *Dominion*
*It's a month before I return to revisit the exhibition and to watch Steele and Tomczak's video. It opens with a wind chime soundscape. Across the three screens clouds reveal small sections of blue sky. The film's two narrators appear in the centre screen. One faces toward the viewer, but her gaze is averted, her eyes downcast. The other is turned away. "This is a book on war, memory, and identity," she reads, as the source—*Nothing Ever Dies, *by Viet Thanh Nguyen—appears in text on the screen to her left: "It proceeds from the idea that all wars are fought twice, the first time on the battlefield, the second time in memory."*[48] *Behind them, the clouds and blue sky are gone. In their place is footage taken from the air of bombs detonating on the ground below. An inverted fireworks display* (Figure 48).

Throughout the video the setting that the two women occupy changes. Sometimes they are in a kind of home space where they sit, quietly read, and occasionally narrate from. Other times they are oddly afloat as they alternate between looking out toward their future viewers and back across space and time at the shifting backdrops of documentary footage from the Vietnam War, the wars that led up to it, and speeches by politicians legitimizing it. In their hovering presence, I feel an uncanny sense of place and placelessness, time and timelessness.

With images of Toronto's City Hall towers and an October 1966 Financial Post *report that Orenda would be building U.S. jet engines in Toronto, the video's second part—"stories we forget"—brings the war "home." Owned by Hawker Siddley Canada, Orenda engines were used in the A-37 Dragonfly that was flown by both the U.S. and South Vietnamese air forces. As data is displayed on the screens to the right and left of our narrators, they tell us that between 1965 and 1973 Canada furnished $2.47 billion in war materials to the U.S.; that Canada's GDP grew by more that 6 percent in each of the years 1964, 1965, and 1966; that Canada's unemployment rate fell from 5.5 percent in 1963 to 4.7 percent in 1964, to 3.9 percent in 1965, and remained below 5 percent through 1969; and, by way of comparison, that Canada's unemployment rate in 2016 was 6.6 percent.*

I stay to watch the video three times. After each showing, there is a pause of several minutes during which I get up, stretch my legs and look out over the town of Dominion.

Though rarely referred to as such in contemporary discourse, "Dominion of Canada" is Canada's official name—a name bestowed on the nation in 1867 by the "Fathers" who took part in the conferences and negotiations that brought about Confederation. After "Kingdom of Canada," the name choice put forward by John A. Macdonald, was nixed by the British government over concerns that the imperial-sounding moniker "would offend the Americans,"[49] Sir Leonard Tilly suggested that the newly constituted nation be christened "Dominion of Canada." According to popular lore, Tilly took his inspiration from the Bible's Psalm 72:8: "He shall have dominion also from sea to sea, and from the river unto the ends of the earth." No matter that the Psalm was referring to an omnipotent creator-being, the Daddies liked the name, Britain approved, and "so mote it be."[50]

Like the many Colonization Roads that traverse Indigenous territories throughout Canada, the name Dominion of Canada reveals much about the nation. It is a title that links Canada to the larger geopolitical projects of dominion, colonization, and conquest that preceded its formation as a nation-state, and has proceeded, and continues to proceed, from it. Projects that both define and defy national borders. Projects that are executed through the varied tools and gestures of dominion and colonization—military, legislative, economic. Projects produced, sustained, and masked through the "stories history tells" and "the stories we forget."[51]

"When it comes to war," writes Vietnamese-American novelist and ethnic studies scholar Viet Thanh Nguyen, "the basic dialectic of memory and amnesia is . . . not only about remembering and forgetting certain events or people. The basic dialectic of memory and amnesia is instead more fundamentally about remembering our humanity and forgetting our inhumanity, while conversely remembering the inhumanity of others and forgetting their humanity."[52] The irrefutable goodness that is continually re-inscribed through reiterated narratives of Canadian humanitarian militarism, multicultural inclusivity, and national innocence divert attention from the nation's neo-liberal continuation of the legacies of dominion and colonization. These include resource extraction projects—pipelines, hydro dams, mining—that dispossess Indigenous communities within and beyond the nation's borders from their lands and resources; police and militarized aggressions waged against land and water protectors and against all those struggling to resist the nation-state's various forms of control and domination; the legal mechanisms that legitimate dispossession; webs of economic activity that alienate workers not only from the products of their labour but also from the geopolitical consequences; and continuing military engagements in multiple "postcolonial" conflicts.

At first, I'm not sure why I am so drawn to the small gallery space that houses Steele and Tomczak's *The afternoon knows what the morning never suspected* and Seth's *Dominion*. Nor am I sure of the curators' intentions in juxtaposing these two works. The more time I spend in the space, however, the more I am struck by how, taken together, Steele and Tomczak's installation and Seth's cardboard city act as an uncanny cipher for the two threads of this book—becoming and unbecoming performances of Canada's military and settler-colonial commemorations. Together the pieces conjure a nostalgic dissonance. A space of longing and aversion, of wanting to look, wanting to look away.

With *The afternoon knows what the morning never suspected*, Steele and Tomczak construct an affective collision of what it is like to remember our humanity and *re*-remember our inhumanity. It is a story that is both familiar and unfamiliar. Familiar in the sense of what is known and remembered—like Canada's role in taking in tens of thousands of U.S. draft dodgers during the Vietnam War. Unfamiliar in the sense of what is also known but not widely remembered—like Blair Seaborn's role in carrying messages at the behest of the U.S., or the extent to which Canada profited from the Vietnam War on economic as well as moral grounds. Familiar in the sense that the information Steele and Tomczak reanimate is not new, it was and is readily available: in newspaper reports like the 1967 *Maclean's* headline "We're Making Millions Out of Vietnam" that the video's narrators read; on library shelves filled with texts that critically examine Canada's involvement in the Vietnam War, like Charles Taylor's *Snow Job: Canada, the United States and Vietnam*; in popular public media productions like CBC's 2015 documentary *Vietnam: Canada's Shadow War*. In restaging this fifty-year-old story of memory and willful amnesia, Steele and Tomczak raise the question: "What contemporary contradictions are Canadians living with right now?"

I feel a different kind of longing-aversion when I look out over *Dominion*. A longing for the pleasure born of familiarity, even a fictive or fantasy familiarity. Though I have only ever driven through towns that look like *Dominion*, there is something about its model buildings, its shops and factories, its water tower that evokes in me, a second-generation settler Canadian, an affective familiarity that brings with it an involuntary (and paradoxically sad) kind of pleasure. Like places and objects, whether real or fictive, repeated stories can also engender familiarity and trigger a pleasure reflex. For its maintenance, however, this pleasure demands a continued process of selective remembering, a process akin to what critical race scholar Paul Gilroy calls "postcolonial melancholia." Writing about Great Britain, Gilroy applies Freud's concept of melancholia to a geopolitical context to argue that white subjects of colonial nations, in their refusal to grieve the "loss of a fantasy of omnipotence,"[53] must continually fend off any narrative that threatens the privileged subjects' sense of rightness and right. Rightness of actions, rightness of history, rightness of privilege. Right to colonize, right to extract, right to expand, right to settle, right to profit, right to celebrate.

Across the three video screens, footage of Yonge Street passes by. As a viewer, I'm positioned in the car as it travels south. It's dawn and the trash bins are still out. Traffic is sparse—mostly taxis. One of the video's narrators hovers in the centre screen. Her gaze is direct. The second narrator, now a disembodied voice, tells me—her future viewer—that the hovering woman is Ivana Dizdar. That both of her parents are half Serbian, half Croatian. That when the civil war started, this was a problem in the former Yugoslavia: "It was the kind of situation where you would go to Belgrade and they'd slap you on the right cheek, and you'd go to Zagreb in Croatia and they'd slap you on the left cheek." That they immigrated to South Africa when Ivana's mother was eight months pregnant with her. That neither of Ivana's parents knew anyone in South Africa. That they didn't know any English at all. That Ivana was born in South Africa but the family came to Canada when she was a couple of months old. That now, here she is, over twenty years later, in Toronto.

They trade places. Ivana, now the disembodied voice, introduces her co-narrator, Julia Huynh. Like Ivana before her, Julia looks directly out at her viewer. Ivana tells me that Julia is second generation Vietnamese-Canadian. That her parents fled South Vietnam as one of the hundreds of thousands of "boat people." That her dad and uncle had to flee from the police and her mother made the eight-day boat journey without them. That the wooden boat began to crack as they reached the refugee camp in Malaysia. That Julia's father eventually made his way to the camp and was reunited with her mother. That they lived in the camp for two years until they were accepted into Canada. That they arrived in Montreal. That when they were driving to Peterborough at night, they were scared, they had never seen farms before. And now, here Julia is, in Toronto.

When Senator Lynn Beyak suggested that the best way to heal is "to move forward . . . , to not live in the past," what did she really mean?[54] I doubt that she was suggesting that Canadians should refrain from reverentially commemorating Canada's past military engagements or celebrating commemorative events like Canada 150. Perhaps she was expressing a longing for a different past. A longing for a place-time, a Canada, when the stories history told did not include words like colonization, settler-colonialism, residential schools—or if they did, they were spoken without shame, with a sense of rightness. A place-time when the divine omnipotence of the Dominion of Canada and the crimes of its ongoing becoming went unquestioned, when "killing the Indian in the child" was not called genocide, but rather was a "good deed" performed by "kindly and well-intentioned men and women."[55] A place-time whose memory necessitates a willful amnesia.

Listening to Ivana's and Julia's inherited memories of their parents' experiences of war, dispossession, and migration, I imagine a continuum of projects of dominion—wars and war profiteering, colonial conquests, land theft, resource appropriation—falling into and out of view, like the shifting architectural landscape of Yonge Street as it passes away on the screens to my left and right. Once out of view, they become conveniently located in a historical past from which narratives of the becoming actions of a becoming nation are revised and revisited. When acknowledged at all, the stories that reveal Canada's unbecoming underbelly, on the other hand, are shelved and moved on from. The colonization of Canada, War of 1812, North-West Rebellion, Boer War, First World War, Second World War, Korean War, Vietnam War, Bosnian War, Somalia, Gulf War(s), Iraq War, the war in Afghanistan, wars Canada fought in or profited from. Wars selectively remembered and re-remembered, selectively forgotten and re-forgotten, through performances of military and celebratory nationalist commemoration designed to purge acts of inhumanity from national memory while elevating narratives of national goodness. Wars that are part of a naturalized project of dominion that reaches back and forward through time.

Before I leave the gallery, I take a last look out over Dominion. *If* Dominion *were inhabited and contemporized, I wonder: Would its settler-citizens recite territorial acknowledgements? If so, would they do it out of obligation, or as a way of unbecoming?*

Could Dominion *be Winnipeg? It's smaller for sure, but some of the architecture is reminiscent of Winnipeg's Exchange District, with its own story of dispossession. If* Dominion *were inhabited, where would its water come from?*

I am struck by the contrasting affective responses I've had while researching and writing about the aesthetic and activist projects discussed throughout this chapter. Writing about Kent Monkman and Miss Chief, Christi Belcourt and the Onaman Collective (or even my brief description of *Every. Now. Then.*) evokes a feeling of satisfaction I attribute to engaging with performances that work to unbecome dominant narratives of Canadian nationalism. I'm grateful for this, and to the many artists and activists who have shared their works and their voices throughout this year (2017) of ahistorical nationalist commemoration.

As a settler Canadian I am also wary, however, that I may be problematically conflating my affective experiences of viewing projects by Indigenous artists and activists with what Stó:lō First Nation scholar Dylan Robinson calls "reconciliatory affect." As Robinson writes of aesthetic works, "they may have strikingly different efficacies for Indigenous and settler audience members."[56] This divergence in efficacy also corresponds to differences in collective investment. As Jesse Wente wrote days before 2017 came to a close, "The wearying toll that 2017 has had on the First Nations, Métis and Inuit people I talk to is unlikely to drain away with the champagne at midnight on December 31."[57] The prolific by-many-means-necessary aesthetic and activist acts of Indigenous resistance that have been so brilliantly evident before, throughout, and since 2017 are not the actions of isolated individuals. They are the actions of people who are part of a much larger assemblage of Indigenous artists, activists, and scholars working to unsettle narratives and the corresponding practices of Canadian settler-colonial nationalism through an ongoing, intergenerational praxis of redress.

In contrast to the collective resistance that underscores the prolific by-many-means-necessary aesthetic and activist acts of Indigenous resistance that were so evident throughout 2017, *Dominion* and *The afternoon knows what the morning never suspected* feel like lonely, isolated works. The more time I spent looking out over *Dominion*'s uninhabited cardboard buildings, the more I felt caught in a vortex of settler-Canadian postcolonial melancholia; the more time I spent viewing *The afternoon knows what the morning never suspected*, on the other hand, the more cognizant I became of what an anomaly the project is, of how little collective resistance there is to Canada's role in global militarism. Rather than celebrations of unbecoming, Seth's *Dominion* and Steele and Tomczak's *The afternoon knows* are haunting reminders in very different ways of the work still to be done to unbecome settler-Canada's melancholic attachments to narratives of national and geopolitical innocence.

ACKNOWLEDGEMENTS

This book was made possible through an uncanny assemblage of generosities and influences. The initial ideas for the book were developed during my time as PhD student in York University's Theatre and Performance Studies program. Without Laura Levin's ardent commitment to performance-based research, this project would not have been possible. Laura's Performance Art and Performance Lab seminars were spaces of intellectual and creative inspiration. As my dissertation supervisor Laura was an astute guide and a passionate supporter of my work. My dissertation committee members, Honor Ford-Smith and Natalie Alvarez, provided intelligent, insightful, and enthusiastic support. Honor's cultural production seminar was a breath of fresh air with its alchemical mix of critical inquiry, play, artistry, and social engagement. Meeting Natalie in conference seminar on "War and Wartime Performance" was a stroke of good fortune. She provided invaluable feedback on what eventually became the first chapter of this book. Others at York also graciously supported my work. Belarie Zatzman's reflections on my performance praxis helped me to embrace and name its labour aesthetic. Marlis Schweitzer provided steadfast mentorship and initiated an oh-so-important dissertation-writing group. Gratitude as well to my fellow travellers in the group—Kimberley McLeod, David Owen, and Marlene Mendonça. An extra special thanks to Kim for being such an amazing and fun academic and artistic collaborator.

I owe a great debt of gratitude to the multitude of artists whose works inspire me to think in new ways. Some are identified in the pages of this book. To the named and the unnamed thank you for your labour in bringing ideas into form. A special thanks to Guillermo Gómez-Peña for the path-altering nudge and to the artist collectives I have been fortunate to participate in: *Life and Limb*—Saul Garcia Lopez, Beyhan Farhadi, Bradley High, Tara Ostiguy, Marlene Mendonça, and Cassie Scott; *Queen's Beavers*—Kimberley McLeod and Laura Levin; and *CONSTELACIONES*—Roewan Crowe, Doris

Difarnecio, Christina Hajjar, and Monica Martinez. Huge gratitude to all who fell, unraveled, stitched, or otherwise took part in the counter-memorial performance meditations that informed my thinking throughout the writing of this book—*Impact Afghanistan War*; *Unravel: A Meditation on the Warp and Weft of Militarism*; *Flag of Tears: Lament for the Stains of a Nation*; and *Stitch-by-Stitch*.

Institutional funding supports and recognitions have been instrumental in bringing this book to fruition. At York, my research was supported by scholarships from the Social Sciences and Humanities Research Council of Canada (SSHRC), the Province of Ontario, York University's Theatre and Performance Studies Program, the Graduate Students' Union, the Canadian Union of Public Service Employees Local 3903, an Armand and Denise LaBarge Graduate Scholarship in Multiculturalism, and the Centre for Feminist Research's Mary McEwan Memorial Award. The Canadian Association for Theatre Research supported my research into the politics of military commemoration with a Theatre Practice and Performance Research Award, a Robert G. Lawrence Prize, and a Heather McCallum Scholarship.

I am immensely grateful to the Canadian Consortium on Performance and Politics in the Americas (CCPPA) and SSHRC for the two postdoctoral fellowships that made it possible for me to extend my dissertation research beyond the scope of military commemoration to look at a broader range of Canadian national memory projects. These fellowships enabled me to engage with an exciting range of national and international scholars, artists, and activists working at intersections of performance, nationalism, and social memory. As socially engaged scholars my CCPPA and SSHRC postdoctoral supervisors, Diana Taylor and Peter Kulchyski, were role models par excellence. Diana's writing about the dissonant logics of the archive and the repertoire as vehicles for the transmission of social memory proved not only foundational to my investigations of Canadian military commemoration, but also played an inspirational role in my decision to embrace embodied inquiry as a method through which to "perform" a philosophy of praxis and socially engaged scholarship. Peter's scholarship on Indigenous culture, history, politics, and law and his praxis-based research into the impacts of hydro development on Indigenous communities in northern Manitoba has been inspirational. Peter's feedback on early drafts of my book proposal was instrumental in helping me to extend beyond the limitations of my white settler knowledge base.

The editors and staff at the University of Manitoba Press (UMP) have been a delight to work with. From my first informal conversations with Jill McConkey I knew I was in excellent hands. Jill, thank you for your support, sage advice, and wry humour as you ushered me through every stage of the submission and review process. Thanks to UMP managing editor Glenn Bergen for your responsiveness and for expertly overseeing the book's publication, to Maureen Epp for your meticulous copy-editing of the manuscript, to Jess Koroscil for your design, and to everyone else at UMP for the many labours you have contributed to the production of this book.

As feminists have long argued, life's greatest generosities—the myriad of everyday actions and labours that sustain life—are often the least visible. Thanks to my parents, two of the most generous people I know, and my family who continue to teach me that love is measured in actions and that labour can and does exist outside of the limiting and exploitative logic of capitalism. A special thanks to two activists who have greatly influenced my life, my mom, Antonia (Toni) Vosters, and my mother-in-law, Maylie Scott. Each in her own steady way has taught me the importance of learning how to turn toward suffering, how to bear witness, and how to engage—despite ambiguity and regardless of outcome—in the ongoing, and often aggravating, labours of caring for a world beyond the limiting social horizons of family, identity, or nation. Most of all, thanks to my beloved partner, Cassie Scott. Your love, wisdom, laughter, poetry, and your myriad of roll-up-your sleeves pragmatic support has sustained me and ensured that the journey was an adventure.

NOTES

INTRODUCTION: LEST WE FORGET: THE CONTESTED TERRAIN OF CANADIAN SOCIAL MEMORY

1 I embroidered this flag with the #ReadTheTRCReport hashtag as a response to Senator Lynn Beyak's statements about residential schools. Inspired by Métis writer and lawyer Chelsea Vowel, who called on all Canadians to read the TRC report, #ReadTheTRCReport is a video reading project in which Indigenous activists, scholars, journalists, lawyers, and community members read sections of the TRC report. The project was conceived by Erika Lee, a Plains Cree student in Saskatoon, and co-organized with Metis writer Zoe Todd and Inuk lawyer Joseph-Murdoch Flowers.

2 CBC, CBC News/Windsor, "Windsor Law Professor Calls on Senator Beyak to Educate Herself about Residential Schools."

3 Canadian Newswire, "Government of Canada to Mark 100th Anniversary of the Battle of Vimy Ridge."

4 Joly, "Canada 150: Kick-Off Celebrations."

5 Palmater, "Canada 150 Is a Celebration of Indigenous Genocide."

6 The Tallest Poppy Artist Residency is curated by Synonym Art Consultation.

7 Truth and Reconciliation Commission of Canada, *Final Report: Honouring the Truth, Reconciling the Future*, vol. 1.

8 TRC, *Final Report*, 184.

9 Tasker, "Conservative Senator Defends 'Well-Intentioned' Residential School System."

10 Tasker, "Senator Lynn Beyak Says She Has 'Suffered' with Residential School Survivors."

11 CBC, CBC News, "Senator Murray Sinclair Responds to Lynn Beyak's Defence of Residential Schools."

12 Jago, "Why Is Senator Lynn Beyak Publishing Racist Letters on Her Website?"

13 Chase, "Ottawa Spends More on Military History amid Criticism over Support for Veterans."

14 Ibid.

15 McCready, *Yellow Ribbons*, 15.

16 Leblanc and Chase, "Ottawa Lays Out $62-Billion in New Military Spending over 20 Years."

17 See Canada, Government of Canada, Veterans Affairs Canada, "Civilian Shoes to Combat Boots" for an example of one of a multitude of military history lesson plans designed by Canadian Forces and Veterans groups and distributed to schools and cadet groups.

18 Butler, "New Year's Eve Twin Fireworks Display to Cost More Than $200K."

19 Government of Canada, Ken McDonald, MP, "Canada 150—Join the Celebration!"

20 CBC Arts. AGO Creative Minds at Massey Hall: "Art and Nationhood." *Art Gallery of Ontario,* 21 April 2017. http://www.cbc.ca/news/canada/toronto/ago-creative-minds-1.4081401.[Belcourt is quoted in the embedded video.]

21 Palmater, "Canada 150 Is a Celebration of Indigenous Genocide."

22 Anderson, *Imagined Communities.*

23 Coulthard, *Red Skin, White Masks*, 6–7. Emphasis in original.

24 Ibid., 15.

25 Ibid., 125.

26 Razack, *Dark Threats and White Knights*, 7.

27 Spivak, "Nationalism and the Imagination," 86.

28 Findlay, "Redress Rehearsals."

29 Ibid., 218. Emphasis in original.

30 Feldman, "Memory Theatres, Virtual Witnessing, and the Trauma-Aesthetic," 172.

31 Canada, Royal Commission on National Development in the Arts, Letters and Sciences 1941–1951, *Report of the Royal Commission*, 275.

32 Stewart, "Massey Commission."

33 Fremeth, "Searching for the Militarization of Canadian Culture," 53.

34 *Star*, "Top General's Comments Anger Liberals."

35 Canada, Parliament, Senate, *The Valour and the Horror*, 15.

36 Bradshaw, "Study Reveals Erosion in Arts Funding."

37 Teigrob, *Living with War*, 4.

38 See Puar, *Terrorist Assemblages*. Following Puar's analysis of queer assemblages, I am using "assemblage" here as a way of reading Aboriginal community activism not as something in need of creation but as something that already always exists through uncanny and often inexplicable webs of connection (see Introduction). As with José Esteban Muñoz's theorization of disidentification, reading activism through the lens of an assemblage resists the binary between oppositionality and complicity, and instead allows for multiple contingencies and more flexible ways of working in, on, and through dominant systems of representational and material control.

39 Belcourt, "Canada, I can cite for you, 150."

40 Isaac and Nagam, "Reverberations, Vibrations, Echoes That Invigorate the Stone Fortress," 14.

41 Muñoz, *Disidentifications*, 5.

42 Simpson, *Mohawk Interruptus*, 21. Emphasis in original.

43 Townsend-Gault, "Rebecca Belmore and James Luna on Location at Venice," 734.

44 Wente, "Canada Can't Look Away after 2017. We Won't Let It."

45 Palmater, "Trans Mountain Pipeline Crisis Is a Watershed Moment."

46 Abma, "Budget Boosts Funding to Canada Council, CBC."

47 *Guardian*, "Canada to Boost Military Budget by 70% after Pressure from US to Spend More."

48 Dwight Conquergood, quoted in Schechner, *Performance Studies*, 24.

49 See Smith, *Decolonizing Methodologies* for a critical analysis of the intersections of imperialism and research. Also Taylor, *The Archive and the Repertoire* for an analysis of the critical role of embodied

performance in the transmission of social memory and knowledge; and Kadi, *Thinking Class* for a critical analysis of how abstracted academic vocabularies are used and misused to simultaneously distort and take ownership of the commonplace actions and understandings of working-class peoples.

50 Taylor, *The Archive and the Repertoire.*

51 Garneau, "Imaginary Spaces of Conciliation and Reconciliation," 24.

52 Ibid., 30, 31.

53 See Althusser, "Ideology and Ideological State Apparatuses (Notes towards an Investigation)." Althusser uses the term "hailing' to describe the process through which the state interpellates individuals as national subjects.

CHAPTER 1: BEYOND THE HIGHWAY OF HEROES: FROM REVERENTIAL SILENCE TOWARD A PERIPHERAL POETICS OF LAMENT

1 This chapter is an elaboration of two previously published articles: Vosters, "Beyond Heroism and towards Shared Vulnerability: Re-Imagining Canada's Affective Deployments of Mourning in Response to Afghan War Deaths"; and Vosters, "Between Worlds: Reflections on a Year of Falling."

2 The italicized sections throughout the first part of this chapter are based on blog entries made during the year I performed the counter-memorial project *Impact Afganistan War*. I will introduce and discuss *Impact* in greater detail later in the chapter.

3 By the end of my year of falling, the number of Canadian military personnel who died while serving in the Afghanistan war had risen to 158. With each death I used a Sharpie pen to alter the number on the flag, and cards dedicated my first fall of the day to the fallen Canadian soldier.

4 Butler, *Frames of War*, xiii.

5 Butler, *Precarious Life*, 33.

6 Ibid., 37.

7 Butler, "Violence, Mourning, Politics," 9.

8 Butler, *Precarious Life*, 40.

9 McCready, *Yellow Ribbons*, 13.

10 Coulon and Liégeois, *Whatever Happened to Peacekeeping? The Future of a Tradition*, 3, 50.

11 See Thobani, "White Innocence, Western Supremacy" for a critical analysis of Butler's post-9/11 writings on the geopolitics of mourning.

12 Butler, *Frames of War*, 47. Emphasis is Butler's.

13 Fremeth, "Searching for the Militarization of Canadian Culture," 52.

14 Fisher, *Highway of Heroes*, 20.

15 Ibid., 27.

16 An under-analyzed aspect of the Highway of Heroes origin story is the fact that Canada's first four Afghanistan casualties were killed by U.S. "friendly fire." Though most reports about the Highway of Heroes (including Fisher's) briefly outline the facts surrounding the Canadian soldiers' deaths, few explore the possibility that there might be a connection between how these soldiers died and the "spontaneous" public display of patriotic memorialization in response to their deaths.

17 Though often attributed to George W. Bush, the U.S. ban was initiated in 1991 during the Gulf War by the George H.W. Bush administration.

18 Thompson, "Should the Military Return to Counting Bodies?"

19 Teigrob, *Living with War*, 4.

20 Ibid., 4.

21 Razack, *Dark Threats and White Knights*, 18.

22 Royal Canadian Legion, "Teachers Guide."

23 McKay and Swift, *Warrior Nation*, 69.

24 Ibid., 73.

25 See Chapters 2 and 3 for two examples of how the Canadian Armed Forces also exorcises its inconvenient killers.

26 Gorer, *Death, Grief and Mourning*, 18.

27 Ibid., xxi.

28 Bergen, *Censorship; the Canadian News Media and Afghanistan*, 5.

29 Ibid., 1.

30 Engler, "A Propaganda System: How Canada's Government, Corporations, Media and Academia Sell War and Exploitation."

31 I learned this detail about the management of military families' grief at a staged reading by Montreal's Teesri Duniya Theatre of James Forsythe's "Safer Ground?" (2012). The production I attended was a work-in-progress reading of excerpts of a verbatim play derived from interviews Forsythe conducted with Canadian soldiers returning from Afghanistan, their families, and members of Montreal's Afghan community. In one excerpt, a soldier's spouse explains the surreal process of writing a brief statement to be released to the press in the case of their partner's death.

32 See Althusser, "Ideology and Ideological State Apparatuses (Notes towards an Investigation)." Althusser describes interpellation as the processes through which individuals are recruited, or hailed as subjects by state and other ideological institutions.

33 Orr, "The Militarization of Inner Space," 452.

34 Massumi, "Fear (the Spectrum Said)."

35 Ruddick, "The Rationality of Care," 242.

36 Ibid., 242–43. Note 22 references Elaine Scarry.

37 CBC, CBC News/World, "Canadian Soldier Killed in Afghanistan," 11 April 2010.

38 CBC, CBC News/World, "Canadian Soldier Killed in Afghanistan," 20 July 2010.

39 Hockey, "Women in Grief."

40 Carr, "War, History, and the Education of (Canadian) Memory," 69.

41 Seremetakis, *The Last Word*, 1.

42 Bourke, "More in Anger Than in Sorrow," 175.

43 Holst-Warhaft, *The Cue for Passion*, 4.

44 Bourke, "More in Anger Than in Sorrow."

45 Feldman, "Memory Theatres, Virtual Witnessing, and the Trauma-Aesthetic," 172.

46 Henderson and Wakeham, *Reconciling Canada*, 19. See the Truth and Reconciliation Commission of Canada, *Final Report: Honouring the Truth, Reconciling the Future*, for examples of the work the Commission has done in resisting the de-historicizing containment of residential schools. See also Coulthard, *Red Skin, White Masks,* for a critical analysis of the "colonial politics of recognition."

47 Holst-Warhaft, *The Cue for Passion*, 4.

48 Holst-Warhaft, *Dangerous Voices*, 3.

49 Holst-Warhaft, *The Cue for Passion*, 34.

50 Ibid., 37.

51 Mukta, "The 'Civilizing Mission.'"

52 Ibid., 27.

53 Connell, "Globalization, Imperialism, and Masculinities," 72.

54 Klassen and Albo, *Empire's Ally*.

55 Hanieh, "A 'Single War,'" 74.

56 Joya, "Failed States and Canada's 3D Policy in Afghanistan," 285–86.

57 Ibid., 287.

58 CTV News/Kitchener, "Canada in Afghanistan: From Digging Trenches to Digging Mines?"

59 Skinner, "Canadian Mining Companies Make the Big Move into Afghanistan."

60 Ed Fast, as quoted in Skinner, "The Empire of Capital and the Latest Inning of the Great Game," 127.

61 Canada, Government of Canada, National Defence and the Canadian Armed Forces, "The Canadian Armed Forces in Afghanistan."

62 Coulthard, *Red Skin, White Masks*, 125. Emphasis in original.

63 Simpson, *Mohawk Interruptus*, 156.

64 Pearce documented 824 missing and murdered Aboriginal women and girls, over 300 more than previously recognized "official" figures, "An Awkward Silence," 22.

CHAPTER 2: THE CANADIAN WAR MUSEUM: IMAGINING THE CANADIAN NATION THROUGH MILITARY COMMEMORATION

1 Quoted in Graham Carr, "War, History, and the Education of (Canadian) Memory," 63. The resurgent popularity of this image is not unique to the Canadian War Museum. Brian McKenna and Terence McKenna used the same image for the opening sequence of their docudrama 1992 *The Valour and the Horror*, and on 4 October 2014 a bronze statue, a commemorative stamp, and special edition two-dollar coin immortalizing the image were unveiled at a ceremony in New Westminster, BC.

2 Quoted in Carr, "War, History, and the Education of (Canadian) Memory," 58–59.

3 Ibid., 58.

4 Ibid.

5 Ibid.

6 Simon, Rosenberg, and Eppert, introduction to *Between Hope and Despair*, 3. Emphasis in original.

7 Ibid., 4.

8 Ibid., 5.

9 Garneau, "Imaginary Spaces of Conciliation and Reconciliation," 30.

10 Rukszto, "Haunted Spaces, Ghostly Memories," 743.

11 Razack, *Dark Threats and White Knights*, 18.

12 Greenberg, "Constructing the Canadian War Museum/Constructing the Landscape of a Canadian Identity."

13 Ibid, 185–86.

14 Canada, Parliament, *Guarding History*.

15 Ibid. A Holocaust exhibit figures prominently in Winnipeg's Canadian Museum for Human Rights that opened 20 September 2014 (see Chapter 4), and on 27 September 2017 the $8 million National Holocaust Monument was unveiled in Ottawa on a 0.79-acre site across from the Canadian War Museum.

16 Greenberg, "Constructing the Canadian War Museum/Constructing the Landscape of a Canadian Identity," 186. My focus in this chapter is limited to the museum's interior. In contrast, Greenberg's analysis examines how architect Raymond Moriyama's design functions as part of a broader memorial landscape through the creation of a war-peacekeeping walking experience between the Canadian War Museum, the National War Monument, and the Parliament Buildings. Since the completion of the museum, this route has been used for Remembrance Day and other military commemoration processional ceremonies.

17 Canadian Museum of History, Canadian War Museum, "Summary of the Corporate Plan." Since the Canadian War Museum and the Canadian Museum of History (formerly the Canadian Museum of Civilization) come under the same Crown corporation, the actual governmental cost of the Canadian War Museum can be somewhat elusive. It is also important to note the amounts identified above are operating costs and do not include additional funding allotted to special exhibits and other projects.

18 Moriyama, *In Search of a Soul*, 13.

19 Ibid., 48.

20 Ibid., 57.

21 Levinas, "Cities of Refuge," 40. Levinas draws on the Judaic concept of half guilt, half innocence in the founding of cities of refuge intended to safeguard unintentional criminals from acts of vengeance. Importantly, these safe havens were not intended as spaces of escape from accountability but rather as sites for critical reflection and learning.

22 Gordon, *Ghostly Matters*, 195.

23 Ibid., 8, 195.

24 Memorial Hall was originally called the Hall of Remembrance and is referred to as such by Moriyama.

25 Moriyama, *In Search of a Soul*, 22.

26 Ibid., 64. While Moriyama does not indicate how the decision was arrived at, as the example of struggles over the Bomber Command display illustrates, the issue of how decisions regarding the Canadian War Museum are made, and by whom, is a recurring one. See Ward, "War Museum, Vets Reach Compromise."

27 Ibid., 64.

28 Ibid., 48.

29 Rukszto, "Haunted Spaces, Ghostly Memories," 743.

30 Phillips, "Re-Placing Objects," 83, 85. Other examples of this investment in Canadian museums include Winnipeg's Canadian Museum for Human Rights, which will be discussed in Chapter 4, and Toronto's Royal Ontario Museum and Art Gallery of Ontario.

31 Boast, "Neocolonial Collaboration," 64.

32 Schneider, *Performing Remains*, 127. Here Schneider departs from Richard Schechner's delineation between performances that "make believe" and those that "make belief" by asserting that historical re-enactments deploy "make believe" as a means of "making belief," or the "*making* of ideological investment" (127).

33 Clifford, quoted in Boast, "Neocolonial Collaboration," 61.

34 Schneider, *Performing Remains*.

35 Simon, Rosenberg, and Eppert, *Between Hope and Despair*, 4.

36 Boast, "Neocolonial Collaboration," 59.

37 Ibid., 56.

38 Ibid., 67.

39 Fremeth, "Searching for the Militarization of Canadian Culture," 65.

40 Evans, "The Scout Series."

41 In an email message Thomas explained, "the 'FBI' photo is a composite of two images. The man on the left is not identified, but is part of the Spotted Tail delegation of 1872 [to Washington, DC. The] photographer is Charles Milton Bell. The two men, centre and right, are from an 1875 [delegation] to Washington, DC; the centre man may be Swift Bear (1827–1909) and on the right is Spotted Tail, (1823–1881), the photographer is Frank F. Currier." Thomas, email message to author, 28 July 2018.

42 Hill "Jeff Thomas: Working Histories," 13–14.

43 Phillips, "Settler Monuments, Indigenous Memory," 345.

44 Thomas, Champlain Series: 2000–2011.

45 Hill, "Jeff Thomas: Working Histories," 13.

46 Lonetree, *Decolonizing Museums*, 62.

47 Ibid., 15–16.

48 Razack, "Introduction: When Place Becomes Race," 2. Emphasis in original.

49 Ibid.

50 Emphasis is mine.

51 Emphasis is mine.

52 Simpson, *Mohawk Interruptus*, 147–48.

53 Ibid., 152.

54 Razack, *Dark Threats and White Knights*, 35.

55 Moriyama, *In Search of a Soul*, 24.

56 For examples of some of the interactive technologies the museum uses as pedagogical tools to teach the history of this reclaimed Canadian origin story, see the Canadian War Museum's online "micro site," *1812: Virtual Exhibition*.

57 Bradshaw, "Study Reveals Erosion in Arts Funding." See also Filewod, "National Theatre, National Obsession."

58 Simpson, *Mohawk Interruptus*, 155.

59 See Asch, *On Being Here to Stay,* for a detailed contestation of Flanagan's thesis, 34–38. See also Kulchyski, *Aboriginal Rights Are Not Human Rights,* for an articulation of the significance of the legal distinctions between the concepts of human rights and Aboriginal rights.

60 Asch, *On Being Here to Stay*, 35.

61 Simpson, *Mohawk Interruptus*, 7.

62 Taylor, *The Archive and the Repertoire.*

63 Der Derian, *Virtuous War.*

64 Razack, *Dark Threats and White Knights*, 26.

65 Dallaire, *Shake Hands with the Devil*, 6.

66 Razack, "Stealing the Pain of Others," 382. Razack is extending Susan Sontag's analysis in "Regarding the Pain of Others."

67 Ibid., 389.

68 Razack, *Dark Threats and White Knights*, 13–14.

69 Ibid., 47.

70 Dallaire, *Shake Hands with the Devil*, 43.

71 Razack, *Dark Threats and White Knights*, 22.

72 Razack, "Stealing the Pain of Others," 384–85.

73 Like Conrad's *Heart of Darkness*, Rudyard Kipling's poem "The White Man's Burden" was published in 1899. Razack draws parallels between these turn-of-the-twentieth-century colonial cultural productions and contemporary Canadian peacekeeping narratives (*Dark Threats and White Knights*).

74 Razack, *Dark Threats and White Knights*, 5.

75 See Taylor, *Disappearing Acts*. I am drawing on Taylor's theorization of percepticide as a process in which a national population blinds itself to state violence.

76 McKay and Swift, *Warrior Nation*, 199.

77 Ibid., 200.

78 Payne, "War, Unvarnished."

79 Royal Canadian Legion, "Paintings in War Museum Anger Veterans Group."

80 Matthews, "'The Trophies of Their Wars,'" 282.

81 Andrew Burtch, email message to author, 20 October 2014.

82 Scott, *American War Machine.*

83 For a detailed history of Canada's war art collection and a nuanced analysis of the complex relationship between institutional military memory stakeholders in managing Canada's war art, see *Art or Memorial?*,by the Canadian War Museum's war art curator, Laura Brandon. Brandon also curated *A Brush with War: Military Art from Korea to Afghanistan*, a War Museum exhibit that travelled across Canada from December 2010 through March 2011.

84 Asad, *On Suicide Bombing.*

85 See Carr, "War, History, and the Education of (Canadian) Memory," for a discussion of the role of Veterans Affairs Canada in the development Remembrance Day school curricula. Carr also notes that the Department of Canadian Heritage collaborates with the Royal Canadian Legion to produce CD-ROMs for Canadian schools (68). The Canadian War Museum also writes its own teaching guides. See also Fournier et al., "Learning to Commemorate," for a critical analysis of how Ontario

schoolchildren are taught to remember past and current wars, through Remembrance Day curriculum documents and national government guides.

CHAPTER 3: UNBECOMING CANADIAN MILITARISM'S FORGETFUL NARRATIVES: UNRAVELLING THE UNIFORM'S AMBIGUOUS MEANINGS

1 This chapter is an elaboration of two previously published articles: Vosters, "Beyond Heroism and towards Shared Vulnerability: Re-Imagining Canada's Affective Deployments of Mourning in Response to Afghan War Deaths"; and Vosters, "Between Worlds: Reflections on a Year of Falling."

2 Quoted by Clare Bayley in "A Very Angry Young Woman."

3 A version of this opening italicized section appeared on my *Impact Afghanistan War* blog.

4 Rankin and Contenta, "A Depraved Double Life." The *Star* did not invent this code. In fact, the effectiveness of the trope of queerness as an indicator of violent sexual pathologies relies on its prolific circulation throughout popular culture mediums.

5 See Salbi, *The Other Side of War.*

6 When I wrote this journal/blog entry, the official number of missing and murdered Indigenous women was 500. A Royal Canadian Mounted Police report, "Murdered Aboriginal Women," released on 16 May 2014, placed the official number at 1,181. The report came after decades of sustained and painstaking labour on the part of an assemblage of Indigenous (and ally) community activists, artists, and scholars who worked to bring the issue of Canada's murdered and missing Indigenous women to the arena of public discourse and consciousness. Because of a lack of data there is still no accurate accounting of the missing and murdered, but activists place the number as high as 4,000 (see Tasker, "Confusion Reigns over Number of Missing, Murdered Indigenous Women").

7 In addition to the torture-rape-murders of Lloyd and Comeau, Williams was convicted of eighty-two fetish break-and-enters and thefts and two sexual assaults. During the break-ins Williams took photos of himself dressed in the underwear belonging to the women and girls whose homes and rooms he violated. During the two sexual assaults he was convicted of, Williams held his victims blindfolded and captive for hours as he directed them to pose for photos. Laurie Massicotte, then a neighbour of Williams, was one of his victims. According to Massicotte, the police did not believe her account of the assault and treated her case as a faked copycat of a previous sexual assault that had been perpetrated in the neighbourhood. Williams eventually confessed to both assaults, the one he perpetrated on Massicotte and the one she was presumed to be basing her "copycat" assault on. *Huffington Post Canada*, "Victim Sues Russell Williams, Ontario Police for $7M."

8 Appleby, "The Tire Track That Broke the Case Wide Open."

9 Levin, *Performing Ground*, 4–5.

10 During the Afghan war a significant number of the Canadian Armed Forces casualties who were assimilated into the "heroic" fallen warrior discourse were actually killed in training accidents or other non-combat-related incidents. In addition to bolstering the homogenizing "fallen soldiers" narrative, this kind of assimilation of the dead shields the Canadian Forces from criticism of its overarching training practices and their effects on enlisted personnel. See Wetselaar and Declerq, "Soldier Killed at CFB Petawawa."

11 Barber, *Women's Work*, 30.

12 Ibid.

13 Hale and Wills, *Threads of Labour*, 4.

14 Connell, "Globalization, Imperialism, and Masculinities."

15 Developed by the U.S. military as a promotional, recruitment, and education tool, the popular online first-person shooter game America's Army premiered on 4 July 2002 and is distributed via free download. The "game" is the brainchild of Colonel Casey Wardynski. On a Best Buy games-buying expedition with his two sons, the colonel was "amazed to discover that about 60 percent of the games available involved something that looked like an army." Quoted in Brady, *Performance, Politics, and the War on Terror*, 86. Wardynski saw in the virtual war game an opportunity to supply the real U.S. Army with "a better prepared customer" (87).

16 Fusco, *A Field Guide for Female Interrogators*.

17 Ibid., 55.

18 Ibid., 51.

19 Ibid., 54.

20 Stemple, "Male Rape and Human Rights," 618.

21 Taylor, *Disappearing Acts*, 152.

22 Ibid., 5.

23 Ibid., 20.

24 Stemple, "Male Rape and Human Rights," 632.

25 Ibid., 633.

26 Ibid., 624.

27 Canadian War Museum, display panel.

28 Stemple, "Male Rape and Human Rights," 614.

29 Razack, *Dark Threats and White Knights*, 97.

30 Connell, "Globalization, Imperialism, and Masculinities."

31 See Canada, Government of Canada, National Defence and the Canadian Armed Forces, "Recent Fallen Canadians."

32 Kristeva, *Black Sun*, 97. The "Thing" Kristeva references in her psychoanalytic analysis is the abject experience that exceeds language's capacity for symbolic representation and, therefore, requires literary innovation to communicate its true meaning.

33 Bennett, *Vibrant Matter*, 121.

34 Bruno Latour, quoted in Bennett, *Vibrant Matter*, 9.

35 Bennett, *Vibrant Matter*, xvi.

36 Ibid., 104.

37 Taylor, *The Archive and the Repertoire*, 64.

38 Quoted in Bassir, *An Anthology of West African Verse*, 24. Every effort has been made to obtain permission to include the lines of Diop's poem in this publication.

39 Bennett, *Vibrant Matter*, xvi.

40 Mbembe, "Necropolitics," 11, 21.

41 Ibid., 21. Emphasis is Mbembe's.

42 Chare, *Auschwitz and Afterimages*, 107. Extending Kristeva's theorizations of the abject through an analysis of literary and visual accounts of the Holocaust, Chare argues that for survivors of Auschwitz, memory is a dangerous "threat to self" and that through the process of recollection, the self collapses

into the abject horror of the experience, producing a state of "semiotic excess" in which the experience overwhelms language's symbolic capacities. Chare argues that it is only through the use of stylistic innovations that language is able to transcend its limitation as a medium of purely symbolic or "efficient" communication and therefore to facilitate the transmission of the true meaning of trauma's abject horror.

43 Mbembe, "Necropolitics," 22.

44 Roach, *Cities of the Dead*, 4.

45 Ibid., 11.

46 Cheadle, "Canada's Libya Mission."

47 Ahmed, "Happy Objects," 30.

48 Ibid.

49 Brady, *Performance, Politics, and the War on Terror*.

50 Connell, *The Men and the Boys*, 40–41.

51 Ibid., 41.

52 Quoted in Robertson, "Rebellious Doilies and Subversive Stitches," 191.

53 Ibid., 198.

54 Roberts, "Put Your Thing Down, Flip It, and Reverse It," 245–46.

55 Ibid., 247–48.

56 Quoted in Black and Burisch, "Craft Hard Die Free," 210.

57 Ibid., 207.

58 Roberts, "Put Your Thing Down, Flip It, and Reverse It," 253.

59 Ibid., 251–53.

60 Quoted in Black and Burisch, "Craft Hard Die Free," 209.

61 Roberts, "Put Your Thing Down, Flip It, and Reverse It," 253.

62 Schneider, *Performing Remains*, 2. Emphasis is Schneider's.

63 Ibid., 174. Emphasis is Schneider's.

64 Katja Čičigoj, email message to author, 21 October 2012.

65 Ibid.

66 Ibid.

CHAPTER 4: THE CANADIAN MUSEUM FOR HUMAN RIGHTS: COLLISIONAL ENCOUNTERS OF UNBECOMING CANADIAN NATIONALISMS

1 Newman and Levine, *Miracle at the Forks*, 1. *Miracle* is as much a tribute to the late Izzy Asper and his family as it is to the museum itself. Much of the book reads like a political fundraising thriller, with stories of million-dollar handshakes and Izzy and his "lieutenants" steadfastly ushering the museum through changing municipal, provincial, and federal administrations.

2 Shoal Lake 40 First Nation, "Shoal Lake 40 Launches the Museum *for* Canadian Human Rights Violations."

3 Predock, "Canadian Museum for Human Rights." Note: When I returned to Predock's website on 26 April 2018, to recheck this quote prior to publication, Predock's assertion that "the First Nations sacred relationship to water is honoured" had been removed.

4 Shoal Lake 40 First Nation, "Shoal Lake 40 Launches the Museum *for* Canadian Human Rights Violations."

5 Ibid. Emphasis in original.

6 CBC, CBC News/Thunder Bay, "First Nation Offended by Canadian Museum for Human Rights."

7 Shoal Lake 40 First Nation, "Shoal Lake 40 Launches the Museum *for* Canadian Human Rights Violations."

8 Tuck and Yang, "Decolonization Is Not a Metaphor," 1.

9 Ibid., 35.

10 Kulchyski, *Aboriginal Rights Are Not Human Rights*, 20–21.

11 Ibid., 64.

12 Tuck and Yang, "Decolonization Is Not a Metaphor," 35. As a project of reparation and redress, Tuck and Yang assert that decolonization calls upon settler populations to adopt an "ethic of incommensurability" on the road to an unsettled future.

13 Windigo, "Human Rights Watch Cries Foul on First Nation Water Crisis."

14 Quoted in Newman and Levine, *Miracle at the Forks*, 26. Emphasis is mine. In addition to their use of a scenario discovery, Newman and Levine also deploy a language of militaristic conquest throughout *Miracle*.

15 The gathering place narrative has become so much a part of museum's brand that it is even used in the promotion of their ERA Bistro, which the display panel at the museum's ticket counter advertises as "a gathering place for good food, sharing, and reflection."

16 See Puar, *Terrorist Assemblages*.

17 Taylor, *The Archive and the Repertoire*, 3.

18 "Sandra" is a pseudonym.

19 These quotes are gleaned from an illuminated display located at the museum's ticket counter.

20 Canadian Museum for Human Rights, Discover the Building tour, 17 January 2016.

21 Martin, "Teachers' Union Willing to Pay to Name Class."

22 Canadian Museum for Human Rights, video display.

23 Ibid.

24 Wong, "Human Rights Hypocrisy."

25 Schneider, *Performing Remains*.

26 Logan, "National Memory and Museums."

27 Busby, Muller, and Woolford, introduction to *The Idea of a Human Rights Museum*, 13.

28 Logan, "National Memory and Museums," 120.

29 Fallding, "Toward Radical Transparency at the Canadian Museum for Human Rights," 71.

30 Ibid., 80.

31 Taylor, *The Archive and the Repertoire*, 36.

32 Newman and Levine, *Miracle at the Forks*, 44.

33 Bozikovic, "Canadian Museum for Human Rights."

34 Newman and Levine, *Miracle at the Forks*, 105.

35 RBC Media Newsroom, "Reaching for the Stars."

36 Newman and Levine, *Miracle at the Forks*, 43.

37 *Ukrainian Weekly*, "Canadians for Genocide Museum Protest the Prime Minister's Stance."

38 Weder, "Faulty Tower."

39 Ibid.

40 Bozikovic, "Canadian Museum for Human Rights."

41 Wodtke, "A Lovely Building for Difficult Knowledge," 107.

42 See Smith, "The Architecture of Aftermath." Smith uses the term "iconomy" to describe the "central importance to human affairs of the image economy, that is, the symbolic exchanges between people, things, ideas, interest groups and cultures that take predominantly visual form" (37). See also Wodtke, "A Lovely Building for Difficult Knowledge."

43 Vosters, "Sochi Olympics 2014, Canadian Truth and Reconciliation, and the Haunting Ghouls of Canadian Nationalism."

44 Schneider, *Performing Remains*, 174. Emphasis is Schneider's.

45 Gordon, *Ghostly Matters*, xvi.

46 Belmore, "In a Wilderness Garden," 93.

47 Ibid.

48 Ibid.

49 Ibid.

50 Fusco, "The Other History of Intercultural Performance," 41. See also Taylor, *The Archive and the Repertoire*.

51 Fusco, "The Other History of Intercultural Performance," 41.

52 Ritter, "The Reclining Figure and Other Provocations," 55.

53 Emberley, *The Testimonial Uncanny*.

54 Belmore quoted in Sandals, "Rebecca Belmore to Make Major Human Rights Museum Piece."

55 Quoted in ibid.

56 Another piece that affectively haunts the museum through its silent or non-logocentric performance of absence is *The REDress Project* by Métis artist Jaime Black.

57 Quoted in Augaitis, "Ayum-ee-aawach Oomama-mowan," 46.

58 Canadian Museum for Human Rights, display.

59 University of Winnipeg, "Bead Making Workshop."

60 Burgess, "The Imagined Geographies of Rebecca Belmore."

61 CBC, CBC News/Indigenous, "First Nations Artist Rebecca Belmore Creates a Blanket of Beads."

62 Failler, "Hope without Consolation," 246.

63 Canadian Museum for Human Rights, "From Darkness to Light."

64 *Ukrainian Weekly*, "Canadians for Genocide Museum Protest the Prime Minister's Stance."

65 Rothberg, "From Gaza to Warsaw," 523.

66 Logan, "National Memory and Museums," 124.

67 Coulthard, "Beyond Recognition," 188–89.

68 Indigenous communities fighting to protect their land and resources are waging similar campaigns across Canada. In Manitoba, hydro-affected communities are organizing to demand redress for damaged lands, to halt the building of future mega-dam projects and/or to renegotiate the terms of these projects. As with Shoal Lake 40's Museum *for* Canadian Human Rights Violations, a critical component of these campaigns is exposing the hypocrisy of the purifying institutional and governmental narratives that mask the material effects of resource extraction.

69 While the City of Winnipeg and the Province of Manitoba had each committed to pay one third of the project, then prime minister Stephen Harper refused to commit to pay the federal government's share. During the 2015 election campaign that led to his becoming prime minster, Justin Trudeau made a number of commitments to Indigenous communities, including funding Freedom Road and launching a public inquiry into the missing and murdered Aboriginal women and girls in Canada.

70 Puar, Pitcher, and Gunkel, "Q&A with Jasbir Puar," 3.

71 Robinson, "Feeling Reconciliation, Remaining Settled." Robinson asserts that while settler Canadians conflate their audience experience of shared affect with the positive affect of reconciliation, the shared affective experience generated through performance "may have strikingly different efficacies for Indigenous and settler audience members" (278).

CHAPTER 5: UNBECOMING CANADA 150: BY MANY MEANS NECESSARY

1 Simpson, *Mohawk Interruptus*, 177.

2 The 2017 Starts Now project was produced in partnership with VIA Rail and Community Foundations of Canada. CBC, CBC 20!7 Canada 150, *What's Your Story?*

3 CBC, CBC 20!7 Canada 150, *Canada: The Story of Us.*

4 CBC, CBC 20!7 Canada 150, *We Are Canada.*

5 CBC, CBC 20!7 Canada 150, *Becoming Canadian.*

6 CBC, CBC 20!7 Canada 150, *We Are the Best.*

7 CBC, CBC 20!7 Canada 150, *CBC Short Docs: Indigenous.*

8 Truth and Reconciliation Commission of Canada, *Final Report: Honouring the Truth, Reconciling the Future*, vol. 1, 327. The full text of Call to Action 47 reads: "We call upon federal, provincial, territorial, and municipal governments to repudiate concepts used to justify European sovereignty over Indigenous peoples and lands, such as the Doctrine of Discovery and *terra nullius* and to reform those laws, government policies, and litigation strategies that continue to rely on such concepts."

9 Belcourt, in CBC, CBC Arts, AGO Creative Minds at Massey Hall: "Art and Nationhood."

10 Ibid.

11 Monkman, *Shame and Prejudice*, exhibition brochure.

12 Ibid.

13 CBC, CBC Radio "Kent Monkman Puts the Indigenous Experience into Art History."

14 Ibid.

15 Martin, "The Robert Harris Group Portrait."

16 Monkman, *Curator's Tour with Kent Monkman* (video), 28:00–28:30.

17 Elston, "Subverting Visual Discourses of Gender and Geography," 182.

18 Schneider, *The Explicit Body in Performance*, 13.

19 Elston, "Subverting Visual Discourses of Gender and Geography," 184.

20 Ibid., 186.

21 Ibid., 181.

22 Monkman, *Shame and Prejudice*, exhibition brochure, 22.

23 Ibid., 13.

24 Simpson, *Mohawk Interruptus*,112.

25 Belcourt, "Nationhood, Reconciliation, Art."

26 Butler, *Precarious Life*, 37.

27 Palmater, "Canada 150 Is a Celebration of Indigenous Genocide."

28 Belcourt, "Starting this coming May . . ."

29 Belcourt, "Nationhood, Reconciliation, Art."

30 Onaman Collective.

31 Onaman Collective, "Nimkii Aazhibikong."

32 Commanda, "Introducing Nimkii Aazhabikong: Culture Camp Forever."

33 Coulthard, *Red Skin, White Masks*. Coulthard is not speaking directly about Belcourt or the Onaman Collective. Rather, he is addressing how forms of Indigenous resistance engage oppositional acts while simultaneously performing "affirmative *enactment*[s]," 169.

34 Simpson, *Mohawk Interruptus*, 22.

35 Elliot, "Christi Belcourt Says Indigenous Resistance Didn't Start with Canada 150."

36 As quoted in Commanda, "Introducing Nimkii Aazhabikong: Culture Camp Forever."

37 Palmater, "Canada 150 Is a Celebration of Indigenous Genocide."

38 Simpson, "Our Elder Brothers," 77.

39 Coulthard, *Red Skin, White Masks*, 166.

40 Belcourt, "Canada, I can cite for you, 150."

41 Ibid.

42 Simpson, *Lighting the Eighth Fire*, 13.

43 Ibid., 14.

44 Ibid., 16.

45 Alfred, *Peace, Power, Righteousness*, 56.

46 Simpson, "Fish Broth and Fasting."

47 Brewster, "Canada's Arms Deal with Saudi Arabia Includes 'Heavy Assault' Vehicles."

48 Nguyen, *Nothing Ever Dies*, 4.

49 Forsey, "Dominion of Canada."

50 Archaic fifteenth-century English term meaning "so it must be."

51 These phrases are subtitles for the first two sections of Steele and Tomczak's video.

52 Nguyen, *Nothing Ever Dies*, 19.

53 Alexander and Margarete Mitscherlich, as quoted in Gilroy, *Postcolonial Melancholia*, 99.

54 CBC News/Windsor, "Windsor Law Professor Calls on Senator Beyak to Educate Herself."

55 Tasker, "Conservative Senator Defends 'Well-Intentioned' Residential School System."

56 Robinson, "Feeling Reconciliation, Remaining Settled," 278.

57 Wente, "Canada Can't Look Away after 2017. We Won't Let It."

BIBLIOGRAPHY

Abma, Sandra. "Budget Boosts Funding to Canada Council, CBC: Government to Invest $1.9B in the Arts Over the Next Five Years—Including $675 Million for CBC." *CBC News*, 22 March 2016. http://www.cbc.ca/news/canada/ottawa/arts-federal-budget-canada-council-heritage-1.3501480.

Ahmed, Sara. "Happy Objects." In *The Affect Theory Reader*, edited by Melissa Gregg and Gregory Seigworth, 29–51. London: Duke University Press, 2010.

Alfred, Gerald R. (Taiaiake). *Peace, Power, Righteousness: An Indigenous Manifesto*. 2nd ed. Don Mills, ON: Oxford University Press, 2008.

Althusser, Louis. "Ideology and Ideological State Apparatuses (Notes towards an Investigation)." In *Lenin and Philosophy and other Essays*. London: Monthly Review Press. 1971, 85–126.

America's Army. Fact Sheet. America's Army, Press Resources, n.d. https://www.americasarmy.com/press.

Anderson, Benedict. *Imagined Communities*. London: Verso, 1991.

Appleby, Timothy. "The Tire Track That Broke the Case Wide Open." *Globe and Mail*, 10 February 2010.

Art Gallery of Ontario. *Every. Now. Then. Reframing Nationhood*. Exhibition curated by Andrew Hunter. Toronto, 2017.

Asad, Talal. *On Suicide Bombing*. New York: Columbia University Press, 2007.

Asch, Michael. *On Being Here to Stay: Treaties and Aboriginal Rights in Canada*. Toronto: University of Toronto Press, 2014.

Augaitis, Daina. "Ayum-ee-aawach Oomama-mowan: Speaking to Their Mother: Daina Augaitis and Rebecca Belmore in Conversation." In *Rebecca Belmore: Rising to the Occasion*, edited by Daina Augiatis and Kathleen Ritter, 41–47. Vancouver: Vancouver Art Gallery, 2008.

Ball, David P. "Waterless Reserve Celebrates New 'Freedom Road' Funding." *Tyee*, 17 December 2015. https://thetyee.ca/News/2015/12/17/Waterless-Reserve-Celebrates-New-Freedom-Road-Funding/.

Barber, Elisabeth Wayland. *Women's Work: The First 20,000 Years*. New York: W.W. Norton, 1994.

Bassir, Olumbe. *An Anthology of West African Verse*. Ibadan, Nigeria: Ibadan University Press, 1957.

Bayley, Clare. "A Very Angry Young Woman." *Independent*, 23 January 1995. http://www.independent.co.uk/arts-entertainment/a-very-angry-young-woman-1569281.html.

Belcourt, Christi. "Canada, I can cite for you, 150." 5 January 2017. http://christibelcourt.com/canada-i-can-cite-for-you-150/.

———. "Starting this coming May . . ." Facebook. 27 March 2017. https://www.facebook.com/christibelcourt/posts/10154926450820272.

Belmore, Rebecca. *Ayumm-ee-aawach Oomama-mowan: Speaking to Their Mother*. Sound installation. Various locations throughout Canada and the United States, 1991, 1992, 1996.

———. *The Blanket.* Video installation. Plug In Institute of Contemporary Art, Winnipeg, 2011.

———.*a blanket for Sarah*. Installation. Vancouver, Vancouver Art Gallery, 1994.

———.*Blood on the Snow*. Installation. Vancouver, Morris and Helen Belkin Gallery, 2002.

———."In a Wilderness Garden." In *Rebecca Belmore: Rising to the Occasion*, edited by Daina Augiatis and Kathleen Ritter, 93–94. Vancouver: Vancouver Art Gallery, 2008.

———. *Trace.* Installation. Canadian Museum for Human Rights, Winnipeg, 2014.

Bennett, Jane. *Vibrant Matter: A Political Ecology of Things*. London: Duke University Press, 2010.

Bergen, Robert. *Censorship; the Canadian News Media and Afghanistan: A Historical Comparison with Case Studies*. Calgary Papers in Military and Strategic Studies, 2009.

Berland, Jody, and Blake Fitzpatrick, eds. *Cultures of Militarization*. Special issue of *Topia: Canadian Journal of Cultural Studies* Number 23–24 (2010).

Black, Anthea, and Nicole Burisch. "Craft Hard Die Free: Radical Curatorial Strategies for Craftivism." In *Extra/Ordinary: Craft and Contemporary Art*, edited by Maria Elena Buszek, 204–21. Durham, NC: Duke University Press, 2011.

Black, Jaime. *The REDress Project*. Installation. Canadian Museum for Human Rights, Winnipeg. 2010.

Boast, Robin. "Neocolonial Collaboration: Museum as Contact Zone Revisited." *Museum Anthropology* 34, no. 1 (2011): 56–70.

Bourke, Angela. "The Irish Traditional Lament and the Grieving Process." *Women's Studies International Forum* 11, no. 4 (1988): 287–91.

———. "More in Anger Than in Sorrow: Irish Women's Lament Poetry." In *Feminist Messages: Coding in Women's Folk Culture*, edited by J.N. Radner, 160–82. Urbana: University of Illinois Press, 1993.

Bozikovic, Alex. "Canadian Museum for Human Rights: An Anticipated Work of Architecture, but Not One of Our Best." *Globe and Mail*, 26 September 2014. http://www.theglobeandmail.com/arts/art-and-architecture/canadian-museum-for-human-rights-an-anticipated-work-of-architecture-but-not-one-of-our-best/article20801763/.

———. "National Holocaust Monument Design Unveiled." *Globe and Mail*, 12 May 2014. http://www.theglobeandmail.com/life/home-and-garden/architecture/national-holocaust-monument-design-unveiled/article18613725/.

Bradshaw, James. "Study Reveals Erosion in Arts Funding." *Globe and Mail*, 20 September 2008. http://www.theglobeandmail.com/arts/study-reveals-erosion-in-arts-funding/article659813/.

Brady, Sara. *Performance, Politics, and the War on Terror: "Whatever It Takes."* New York: Palgrave Macmillan, 2012.

Brandon, Laura. *Art and War*. London: I.B. Tauris, 2007.

———.*Art or Memorial?: The Forgotten History of Canada's War Art*. Calgary: University of Calgary Press, 2006.

———.*A Brush with War: Military Art from Korea to Afghanistan*. Canadian War Museum. Gatineau, QC: Canadian Museum of Civilization, 2009. Exhibition guide.

Brewster, Murray. "Canada's Arms Deal with Saudi Arabia Includes 'Heavy Assault' Vehicles." *CBC News*, 19 March 2018. http://www.cbc.ca/news/politics/canada-saudi-arms-deal-1.4579772.

Burgess, Marilyn. "The Imagined Geographies of Rebecca Belmore." In *Rebecca Belmore: Rising to the Occasion*, edited by Daina Augiatis and Kathleen Ritter. Vancouver: Vancouver Art Gallery, 2008.

Busby, Karen, Adam Muller, and Andrew Woolford, eds. *The Idea of a Human Rights Museum*. Winnipeg: University of Manitoba Press, 2015.

Butler, Don. "New Year's Eve Twin Fireworks Display to Cost More Than $200K." *Ottawa Citizen*, 13 September 2016. http://ottawacitizen.com/news/local-news/new-years-eve-twin-fireworks-display-to-cost-more-than-200k.

Butler, Judith. *Frames of War: When Is Life Grievable?* New York: Verso, 2010.

———.*Precarious Life: The Powers of Mourning and Violence*. New York: Verso, 2006.

———."Violence, Mourning, Politics." *Studies in Gender and Sexuality* 4, no. 1 (2003): 9–37.

Canada. Government of Canada. Canada 150 Fund. http://canada.pch.gc.ca/eng/1424795454758/1434974349768.

———. Government of Canada. Ken McDonald, MP. "Canada 150—Join the Celebration!" 14 March 2016. https://kmcdonald.liberal.ca/news-nouvelles/canada-150-join-the-celebration/.

———. Government of Canada. National Defence and the Canadian Armed Forces. "Recent Fallen Canadians." http://www.forces.gc.ca/en/honours-history-fallen-canadians/index.page.

———. Government of Canada. National Defence and the Canadian Armed Forces. "The Canadian Armed Forces in Afghanistan. http://www.forces.gc.ca/en/ndoh/canadian-forces-in-afghanistan.page.

———. Government of Canada. National Defence and the Canadian Armed Forces. "Russell Williams' Release from the Canadian Forces Complete." News Release, 10 December 2010. https://www.canada.ca/en/news/archive/2010/12/russell-williams-release-canadian-forces-complete.html?=undefined&wbdisable=true.

———. Government of Canada. Veterans Affairs Canada. "Civilian Shoes to Combat Boots." N.d. http://www.veterans.gc.ca/eng/remembrance/information-for/educators/learning-modules/vimy-ridge/civilian-shoes-to-combat-boots.

———. Government of Canada. Video of Canada 150 Celebrations.http://canada.pch.gc.ca/eng/1482412398587.

———. Parliament. *Guarding History: A Study into the Future, Funding, and Independence of the Canadian War Museum*. Report of the Subcommittee on Veterans Affairs of the Standing Senate Committee on Social Affairs, Science and Technology, Ottawa, 1998.

———. Parliament. Senate. *The Valour and the Horror: Report of the Standing Committee on Social Affairs, Science and Technology*. Ottawa, 1993.

———. Royal Commission on National Development in the Arts, Letters and Sciences 1941–1951. *Report of the Royal Commission on National Development in the Arts, Letters and Sciences 1941–1951*. (Massey Report). Ottawa: Edmond Cloutier, 1951.

Canada Post. "Canada Post Celebrates Opening of the Canadian Museum for Human Rights with New Stamp." News Release, 20 August 2014. https://www.canadapost.ca/web/en/blogs/announcements/details.page?article=2014/08/20/canada_post_celebrat&cattype=announcements&cat=newsreleases.

CBC (Canadian Broadcasting Corporation). CBC 20!7 Canada 150. *Becoming Canadian*. http://2017guide.cbc.ca/item/becoming-canadian/.

———. CBC 20!7 Canada 150. *Canada: The Story of Us.* http://2017guide.cbc.ca/item/canada-the-story-of-us/.

———. CBC 20!7 Canada 150. *CBC Short Docs: Indigenous.* http://2017guide.cbc.ca/item/cbc-short-docs-indigenous/.

———. CBC 20!7 Canada 150. *We Are Canada.* http://2017guide.cbc.ca/item/we-are-canada/.

———. CBC 20!7 Canada 150. *We Are the Best.* http://2017guide.cbc.ca/item/we-are-the-best/.

———. CBC 20!7 Canada 150. *What's Your Story? Here's How You Can Share Your Canadian Stories with Us.* Updated 2 March 2017. http://www.cbc.ca/2017/whatsyourstory/what-s-your-story-here-s-how-you-can-share-your-canadian-stories-with-us-1.3986330.

———. CBC Arts. AGO Creative Minds at Massey Hall: "Art and Nationhood." Host Matt Galloway. Guests David Adjaye, Christi Belcourt, Junot Diaz, and Paul Gross. 21 April 2017. https://www.facebook.com/CBCArts/videos/1508645642492632/.

———. CBC News. "Senator Murray Sinclair Responds to Lynn Beyak's Defence of Residential Schools." 29 March 2017. http://www.cbc.ca/news/politics/murray-sinclair-lynn-beyak-residential-schools-1.4045465.

———. CBC News/Canada. "War Museum's Paintings Anger Veterans Groups." cbc.ca, 4 May 2005. http://www.cbc.ca/news/canada/war-museum-s-paintings-anger-veterans-group-1.552891.

———. CBC News/Indigenous. "First Nations Artist Rebecca Belmore Creates a Blanket of Beads: Art Work Challenges Colonial History, Commissioned by Canadian Museum for Human Rights." 15 March 2014. http://www.cbc.ca/news/indigenous/first-nations-artist-rebecca-belmore-creates-a-blanket-of-beads-1.2571509.

———. CBC News/Manitoba. "Shoal Lake 40 First Nation's Freedom Road a Path to Reconciliation: Chief." 17 December 2015. http://www.cbc.ca/news/canada/manitoba/shoal-lake-40-first-nation-s-freedom-road-a-path-to-reconciliation-chief-1.3369622.

———. CBC News/Manitoba. "A Tribe Called Red Cancels Performance at Human Rights Museum." cbc.ca, 18 September 2014. http://www.cbc.ca/news/canada/manitoba/a-tribe-called-red-cancels-performance-at-human-rights-museum-1.2771222.

———. CBC News/Thunder Bay. "First Nation Offended by Canadian Museum for Human Rights." 3 June 2014. http://www.cbc.ca/news/canada/thunder-bay/first-nation-offended-by-canadian-museum-for-human-rights-1.2662256.

———. CBC News/Windsor. "Windsor Law Professor Calls on Senator Beyak to Educate Herself about Residential Schools." 3 April 2017. http://www.cbc.ca/news/canada/windsor/windsor-law-professor-calls-on-senator-beyak-to-educate-herself-about-residential-schools-1.4052440.

———. CBC News/World. "Canadian Soldier Killed in Afghanistan." cbcbooks.ca, 11 April 2010. http://www.cbc.ca/news/world/canadian-soldier-killed-in-afghanistan-1.922097.

———. CBC News/World. "Canadian Soldier Killed in Afghanistan." cbcbooks.ca, 20 July 2010. http://www.cbc.ca/news/world/canadian-soldier-killed-in-afghanistan-1.883433.

———. CBC Radio. "What Does Canada 150 Mean for Indigenous Communities?" *The Current*, 16 March 2017. http://www.cbc.ca/radio/thecurrent/the-current-for-march-16-2017-1.4026463/what-does-canada-150-mean-for-indigenous-communities-1.4027484.

———. CBC Radio. "Kent Monkman Puts the Indigenous Experience into Art History." *Unreserved*, 29 January 2017. http://www.cbc.ca/radio/unreserved/art-representation-and-why-it-matters-1.3953926/kent-monkman-puts-the-indigenous-experience-into-art-history-1.3958514.

CBC Television. "The Unseen Scars: Post Traumatic Stress Disorder." *National Affairs Program.* 1998.

Canadian Conference of the Arts, Canadian Arts Coalition, and Saskatchewan Arts Alliance. "Budget 2015: Culture and Arts, Still A Low Priority for the Government." Report prepared on behalf of the Canadian Conference of the Arts, Canadian Arts Coalition, and Saskatchewan Arts Alliance, 15 September 2015. http://ccarts.ca/wp-content/uploads/2015/09/Budget_Analysis_2015_en-1.pdf.

Canadian Museum for Human Rights. Discover the Building tour, 17 January 2016.

———. "From Darkness to Light." https://humanrights.ca/blog/darkness-light.

Canadian Museum of History, Canadian War Museum. "Summary of the Corporate Plan of the Canadian Museum of History 2014–2015 to 2018–2019." n.d. https://ace-notebook.com/summary-of-the-corporate-plan-2015-to-2019-free-related-pdf.html.

Canadian Newswire. "Government of Canada to Mark 100th Anniversary of the Battle of Vimy Ridge." 24 March 2017. http://www.newswire.ca/news-releases/government-of-canada-to-mark-100th-anniversary-of-the-battle-of-vimy-ridge-617034494.html.

Canadian War Museum. *1812: Virtual Exhibition*. http://www.warmuseum.ca/war-of-1812/.

Carr, Graham. "War, History, and the Education of (Canadian) Memory." In *Contested Pasts: The Politics of Memory*, edited by Katherine Hodgkin and Susannah Radston, 57–78. London: Routledge, 2003.

Chare, Nicholas. *Auschwitz and Afterimages: Abjection, Witnessing and Representation*. New York: I.B. Tauris, 2011.

Chase, Steven. "Ottawa Spends More on Military History amid Criticism over Support for Veterans." *Globe and Mail*, 16 June 2014. http://www.theglobeandmail.com/news/politics/ottawa-commemorates-military-history-while-under-fire-for-veteran-support/article19176795/.

Cheadle, Bruce. "Canada's Libya Mission: Military Honoured for Role in Campaign." Canadian Press, *HuffPost Canada*, 24 November 2011. https://www.huffingtonpost.ca/2011/11/24/canada-libya-mission-military-honoured_n_1111880.html.

Commanda, Erica. "Introducing Nimkii Aazhabikong: Culture Camp Forever." *Muskrat Magazine*, 21 June 2017. http://muskratmagazine.com/introducing-nimkii-aazhabikong-culture-camp-forever/.

Connell, R.W. "Globalization, Imperialism, and Masculinities." In *Handbook of Studies on Men and Masculinities*, edited by Michael S. Kimmel, Jeff Hearn, and R.W. Connell, 71–89. Thousand Oaks, CA: Sage Publications, 2005.

———. *The Men and the Boys*. Berkeley: University of California Press, 2000.

Connerton, Paul. *The Spirit of Mourning: History, Memory and the Body*. Cambridge: Cambridge University Press, 2011.

Conrad, Joseph. *Heart of Darkness*. New York: Dover, 1990.

Coppola, Francis Ford, dir. *Apocalypse Now*. Paramount Studios, 1979. DVD, 153 min.

Coulon, Jocelyn, and Michel Liégeois. *Whatever Happened to Peacekeeping? The Future of a Tradition*. Canadian Defence and Foreign Affairs Institute, 2010.

Coulthard, Glen Sean. "Beyond Recognition: Indigenous Self-Determination as Prefigurative Practice." In *Lighting the Eighth Fire: The Liberation, Resurgence and Protection of Indigenous Nations*, edited by Leanne Simpson, 187–204. Winnipeg: Arbeiter Ring Publishing, 2008.

———. *Red Skin, White Masks: Rejecting the Colonial Politics of Recognition*. Minneapolis: University of Minnesota Press, 2014.

Craps, Stef. *Postcolonial Witnessing: Trauma Out of Bounds*. New York: Palgrave, 2013.

CTV News/Kitchener. "Canada in Afghanistan: From Digging Trenches to Digging Mines?" 14 March 2014. http://kitchener.ctvnews.ca/canada-in-afghanistan-from-digging-trenches-to-digging-mines-1.1729146.

Dallaire, Roméo. *Shake Hands with the Devil: The Failure of Humanity in Rwanda.* Toronto: Random House Canada, 2003.

Der Derian, James. *Virtuous War: Mapping the Military-Industrial-Media-Entertainment Network.* New York: Routledge, 2009.

Dettloff, Claude P. *Wait for Me, Daddy.* 1940. Photograph. *Life Magazine* 21 October 1940. Reproduced by the Canadian War Museum, Ottawa.

Diop, Birago. "Souffles (Breaths)" in Olumbe Bassir, *An Anthology of West African Verse,* Ibadan University Press, 1957, 24–25.

Elliot, Alicia. "Christi Belcourt Says Indigenous Resistance Didn't Start with Canada 150." CBC/20!7 Canada150, 22 February 2017. http://www.cbc.ca/2017/resistance150-christi-belcourt-on-indigenous-history-resilience-and-resurgence-1.3992226.

Elston, M. Melissa. "Subverting Visual Discourses of Gender and Geography: Kent Monkman's Revised Iconography of the American West." *Journal of American Culture* 35, no. 2 (2012): 181–90.

Emberley, Julia V. *The Testimonial Uncanny: Indigenous Storytelling, Knowledge, and Reparative Practices.* Albany, NY: SUNY Press.

Engler, Yves. "A Propaganda System: How Canada's Government, Corporations, Media and Academia Sell War and Exploitation." Lecture at the University of Winnipeg, 2 November 2016. Sponsored by Peace Alliance Winnipeg: Council of Canadians, Winnipeg; *Canadian Dimension Magazine*, and CKUW-FM 95.9, Winnipeg. https://canadiandimension.com/articles/view/yves-engler-a-propaganda-system.

Evans, Lara E. "The Scout Series." *Not Artomatic: A Blog Wrestling with Art*, 3 March 2010. https://notartomatic.wordpress.com/2010/03/03/oka-crisis-the-champlain-monument-and-the-art-of-acting-out-change-without-erasing-the-past/.

Failler, Angela. "Hope without Consolation: Prospects for Critical Learning at the Canadian Museum for Human Rights." *Review of Education, Pedagogy, and Cultural Studies* 37, no. 2 (2015): 227–50.

Fallding, Helen. "Toward Radical Transparency at the Canadian Museum for Human Rights: Lessons from Media Coverage during Construction." In *The Idea of a Human Rights Museum*, edited by Karen Busby, Adam Muller, and Andrew Woolford, 70–86. Winnipeg: University of Manitoba Press, 2015.

Feldman, Allen. "Memory Theatres, Virtual Witnessing, and the Trauma-Aesthetic." *Biography* 27, no.1 (2004): 163–202.

Filewod, Alan. "National Theatre, National Obsession." In *Canadian Theatre History: Selected Readings*, edited by Don Rubin, 407–20. Toronto: Playwrights Canada Press, 1996.

Findlay, Len. "Redress Rehearsals: Legal Warrior, COSMOSQUAW, and the National Aboriginal Achievement Awards." In *Reconciling Canada: Critical Perspectives on the Culture of Redress*, edited by Jennifer Henderson and Pauline Wakeham, 217–35. Toronto: University of Toronto Press, 2013.

Fisher, Pete. *Highway of Heroes: True Patriot Love.* Toronto: Dundurn Press, 2011.

Forsey, Eugene A. "Dominion of Canada." In *The Canadian Encyclopedia.* Historica Canada. 2 July 2006. http://www.thecanadianencyclopedia.ca/en/article/dominion/.

Forsythe, James. *Safer Ground?* Directed by Julia Ainsworth. Teesri Duniya Theatre, Montreal, 8 November 2012. Performance.

Fournier, Gillian, et al. "Learning to Commemorate: Challenging Prescribed Collective Memories of War." *Social Alternatives* 31, no. 2 (2012): 41–45.

Fremeth, Howard. "Searching for the Militarization of Canadian Culture: The Rise of a Military-Cultural Memory Network." In *Cultures of Militarization,* edited by Jody Berland and Blake Fitzpatrick, special issue of *Topia: Canadian Journal of Cultural Studies* 23–24 (2010): 52–76.

Freud, Sigmund. "Mourning and Melancholia." In *General Psychological Theory*, edited by Philip Rieff. New York: Collier Publishing, 1963.

Fusco, Coco. *A Field Guide for Female Interrogators*. New York: Seven Stories Press, 2008.

———. "The Other History of Intercultural Performance." In *English Is Broken Here: Notes on Cultural Fusion in the Americas*, edited by Coco Fusco, 37–63. New York: New Press, 1995.

Garneau, David. "Imaginary Spaces of Conciliation and Reconciliation." In *Arts of Engagement: Taking Aesthetic Action in and beyond the Truth and Reconciliation Commission of Canada*, edited by Dylan Robinson and Keavy Martin, 21–41. Waterloo, ON: Wilfrid Laurier University Press, 2016.

Gilroy, Paul. *Postcolonial Melancholia*. New York: Columbia University Press, 2005.

Gordon, Avery F. *Ghostly Matters: Haunting the Sociological Imagination*. Minneapolis: University of Minnesota Press, 1997.

Gorer, Geoffrey. *Death, Grief and Mourning*. New York: Anchor Books, 1965.

Greenberg, Reesa. "Constructing the Canadian War Museum/Constructing the Landscape of a Canadian Identity." In *(Re) Visualizing National History: Museums and National Identities in Europe in the New Millennium*, edited by Robin Ostow, 183–99. Toronto: University of Toronto Press, 2008.

Gross, Paul, dir. *Passchendaele*. Damberger Film and Cattle Rhombus Media Whizbang Films, 2008. Film.

———. *Hyena Road*. Elevation Pictures and WTFilms. Produced by Niv Fichman and Paul Gross. 2016. Film.

Guardian. "Canada to Boost Military Budget by 70% after Pressure from US to Spend More." 7 June 2017. https://www.theguardian.com/world/2017/jun/07/canada-increase-military-spending-nato.

Hale, Angela, and Jane Wills. *Threads of Labour: Garment Industry Supply Chains from the Workers' Perspective*. Oxford: Blackwell Publishing, 2005.

Hanieh, Adam. "A 'Single War': The Political Economy of Intervention in the Middle East and Central Asia." In *Empire's Ally: Canada and the War in Afghanistan*, edited by Jerome Klassen and Greg Albo, 74–105. Toronto: University of Toronto Press, 2013.

Henderson, Jennifer, and Pauline Wakeham. *Reconciling Canada: Critical Perspectives on the Culture of Redress*. Toronto: University of Toronto Press, 2013.

Hill, Richard William. "Jeff Thomas: Working Histories." In *Jeff Thomas: A Study in Indianness*, 8–17. Toronto: Gallery 44, 2004. Exhibition catalogue.

Hockey, Jenny. "Women in Grief: Cultural Representation and Social Practice." In *Death, Gender and Ethnicity*, edited by David Field, Jenny Hockey, and Neil Small, 89–109. New York: Routledge, 1997.

Holst-Warhaft, Gail. *The Cue for Passion: Grief and Its Political Uses*. London: Harvard University Press, 2000.

———. *Dangerous Voices: Women's Laments and Greek Literature*. New York: Routledge, 1992.

HuffPost Canada. "Victim Sues Russell Williams, Ontario Police for $7M." 25 September 2011. http://www.huffingtonpost.ca/2011/09/25/victim-sues-russell-williams-ontario-police_n_979926.html.

Hunter, Andrew, ed. *Every. Now. Then. Reframing Nationhood*. Toronto: Art Gallery of Toronto, 2017. Exhibition catalogue.

Isaac, Jaimie, and Julie Nagam. "Reverberations, Vibrations, Echoes That Invigorate the Stone Fortress." In *INSURGENCE/RESURGENCE*, edited by Jaimie Isaac and Julie Nagam, 12–21. Winnipeg: Winnipeg Art Gallery, 2017. Exhibition catalogue.

Jago, Robert. "Why Is Senator Lynn Beyak Publishing Racist Letters on Her Website?" *Walrus*, 3 January 2018. https://thewalrus.ca/why-is-senator-lynn-beyak-publishing-racist-letters-on-her-website/.

Jenkins, Barbara. "Cultural Spending in Ontario, Canada: Trends in Public and Private Funding." *International Journal of Cultural Policy* 15, no. 3 (2009): 14.

Joly, Mélanie. "Canada 150: Kick-Off Celebrations," Canadian Heritage, 31 December 2016. https://www.youtube.com/watch?v=opJP8riKEgk.

Joya, Angela. "Failed States and Canada's 3D Policy in Afghanistan." In *Empire's Ally: Canada and the War in Afghanistan*, edited by Jerome Klassen and Greg Albo, 277–305. Toronto: University of Toronto Press, 2013.

Kadi, Joanna. *Thinking Class: Sketches from a Cultural Worker*. New York: South End Press, 1996.

Kane, Sarah. *Blasted*. Directed by Brendan Healy. Buddies in Bad Times Theatre, Toronto, October 2010. Performance.

Kariouk, Paul duBellet. "Capital Improvement: The New Canadian War Museum Revitalizes Ottawa's Lebreton Flats, Acknowledges the Parliament Buildings and Provides a Welcome Addition to the Institutional Importance of the Nation's Capital." *Canadian Architecture* 50, no. 9 (2005): 32–38.

Kearns, Gertrude. Artist Statement for *UNdone: Dallaire/Rwanda* exhibition, Propeller Visual Arts Centre in Toronto, October 2002.

———. *Dallaire #6*. 2002. Enamel, oil on nylon. War Art Collection, Canadian War Museum, Ottawa, ON.

———. *Somalia #2, Without Conscience*. 1996. Acrylic on canvas. Beaverbrook Collection of War Art, Canadian War Museum, Ottawa.

Klassen, Jerome, and Greg Albo, eds. *Empire's Ally: Canada and the War in Afghanistan*. Toronto: University of Toronto Press, 2013.

Kristeva, Julia. *Black Sun: Depression and Melancholia*. Translated by Leaon S. Roudiez. New York: Columbia University, 1989.

Kuglin, Ernst. "Williams Stripped of Rank, Says General." *Kingston Whig-Standard*, 21 October 2010. http://www.thewhig.com/2010/10/21/williams-stripped-of-rank-says-general.

Kulchyski, Peter. *Aboriginal Rights Are Not Human Rights: In Defence of Indigenous Struggles*. Winnipeg: ARP Books, 2013.

Leblanc, Daniel, and Steven Chase. "Ottawa Lays Out $62-Billion in New Military Spending over 20 Years." *Globe and Mail*, 7 June 2017. https://www.theglobeandmail.com/news/politics/ottawa-lays-out-62-billion-in-new-military-spending-over-20-years/article35231311/.

Levin, Laura. *Performing Ground: Space, Camouflage and the Art of Blending In*. New York: Palgrave Macmillan, 2014.

Levinas, Emmanuel. "Cities of Refuge." In *Beyond the Verse: Talmudic Readings and Lectures*, 34–52. Bloomington: Indiana University Press, 1994.

Logan, Tricia. "National Memory and Museums: Remembering Settler Colonial Genocide of Indigenous Peoples in Canada." In *Remembering Genocide*, edited by Nigel Eltringham and Pam MacLean, 112–30. New York: Routledge, 2014.

Lonetree, Amy. *Decolonizing Museums: Representing Native America in National and Tribal Museums*. Chapel Hill: University of North Carolina Press, 2012.

MacKay, Allan Harding. *Canadian (UN) Armoured Personnel Carrier, Somalia*. 1993. Charcoal Sketch. Beaverbrook Collection of War Art, Canadian War Museum, Ottawa.

Martin, Ged. "The Robert Harris Group Portrait." ActiveHistory.ca, 10 July 2016. http://activehistory.ca/2016/07/the-robert-harris-group-portrait/.

Martin, Nick. "Teachers' Union Willing to Pay to Name Class." *Winnipeg Free Press*, 2 June 2013. http://www.winnipegfreepress.com/local/teachers-union-willing-to-pay-to-name-class-189967501.html.

Massumi, Brian. "Fear (the Spectrum Said)." *positions* 13, no. 1 (2005): 31–48.

———. "The Future Birth of the Affective Fact: The Political Ontology of Threat." In *The Affect Theory Reader*, edited by Melissa Gregg and Gregory J. Seigworth, 52–70. Durham, NC: Duke University Press, 2007.

Matthews, Sara. "'The Trophies of Their Wars': Affect and Encounter at the Canadian War Museum." *Museum Management and Curatorship* 28, no. 3 (2013): 272–87.

Mbembe, Achille. "Necropolitics." *Public Culture* 15, no. 1 (2003): 11–40.

McCrae, John. "In Flanders Fields." In *In Flanders Fields: and Other Poems by John McCrae*. Toronto: W. Briggs, 1919.

McCready, A.L. "Tie a Yellow Ribbon 'Round Public Discourse, National Identity and the War: Neoliberal Militarization and the Yellow Ribbon Campaign in Canada." In *Cultures of Militarization*, edited by Jody Berland and Blake Fitzpatrick, special issue of *Topia: Canadian Journal of Cultural Studies* 23–34 (2010): 28–51.

———. *Yellow Ribbons: The Militarization of Identity in Canada*. Winnipeg: Fernwood, 2013.

McKay, Ian, and Jamie Swift. *Warrior Nation: Rebranding Canada in an Age of Anxiety*. Toronto: Between the Lines, 2012.

McKenna, Brian, and Terrence McKenna. *The Valour and the Horror*. Directed by Brian McKenna. National Film Board and Canadian Broadcasting Corporation, 1992. Film. 312 min.

Mercier, Noémi, and Alec Castonguay. "Our Military's Disgrace." *Maclean's*, 16 May 2014. http://www.macleans.ca/news/canada/our-militarys-disgrace/.

Monkman, Kent. *Curator's Tour with Kent Monkman – Shame and Prejudice: A Story of Resilience*. Art Museum of Toronto, 4 February 2017. Video. https://vimeo.com/209447083.

———. *Shame and Prejudice: A Story of Resilience*. Exhibition. Art Gallery at the University of Toronto, 2017.

———. *Shame and Prejudice: A Story of Resilience*. Art Gallery at the University of Toronto, 2017. Exhibition brochure.

Moriyama, Raymond. *In Search of a Soul: Designing and Realizing the New Canadian War Museum*. Vancouver: Douglas and McIntyre, 2006.

Mukta, Parita. "The 'Civilizing Mission': The Regulation of Mourning in Colonial India." *Feminist Review* 63 (1999): 25–47.

Muñoz, José Esteban. *Disidentifications: Queers of Color and the Performance of Politics*. Minneapolis: University of Minnesota Press, 1999.

National Geographic. "Winnipeg, Canada: Little Spark on the Prairie." Best Trips 2016. http://documentslide.com/documents/ng-traveler-dec-15.html.

NBC. "A Hard Road: The Highway of Heroes." *Nightly News*, 11 November 2008. http://www.nbcnews.com/video/nightly-news/27651384#27651384.

Newman, Peter C., and Allan Levine. *Miracle at the Forks: The Museum That Dares Make a Difference*. Vancouver: Figure 1 Publishing, 2014.

Nguyen, Viet Thanh. *Nothing Ever Dies: Vietnam and the Memory of War*. Cambridge, MA: Harvard University Press, 2016.

Onaman Collective. http://onamancollective.com.

Orr, Jackie. "The Militarization of Inner Space." *Critical Sociology* 30, no. 2 (2004): 451–81.

———. *Panic Diaries: A Genealogy of Panic Disorder*. Durham, NC: Duke University Press, 2006.

Ouzounian, Richard. "Blasted: Sarah Kane's Uniquely Twisted View of the World." *Star*, 29 September 2010. https://www.thestar.com/entertainment/stage/2010/09/29/blasted_sarah_kanes_uniquely_twisted_view_of_the_world.html.

Palmater, Pamela. "Canada 150 Is a Celebration of Indigenous Genocide." *Now Magazine*, 29 March 2017.

———. "Trans Mountain Pipeline Crisis Is a Watershed Moment for Trudeau–First Nations Relations." *Now Magazine*, 26 April 2018. https://nowtoronto.com/news/trans-mountain-trudeau-first-nations/.

Patraka, Vivian M. *Spectacular Suffering: Theatre, Fascism, and the Holocaust*. Bloomington: Indiana University Press, 1999.

Payne, Elizabeth. "War, Unvarnished: One of the First Images to Confront Visitors When They Enter the New Canadian War Museum Is Not about War but about Shame." *Ottawa Citizen*, 1 May 2005.

Pearce, Maryanne. "An Awkward Silence: Missing and Murdered Vulnerable Women and the Canadian Justice System." PhD diss., University of Ottawa, 2013.

Phillips, Ruth. "Re-Placing Objects: Historical Practices for the Second Museum Age." *Canadian Historical Review* 86, no. 1 (2005): 83–110.

———. "Settler Monuments, Indigenous Memory." In *Settling and Unsettling Memories: Essays in Canadian Public History*, edited by Nicole Neatby and Peter Hodgins, 340–68. University of Toronto Press, 2012.

Predock, Antoine. "Canadian Museum for Human Rights." Antoine Predock Architect PC website. http://www.predock.com/CMHR/CMHR.html.

Puar, Jasbir, Ben Pitcher, and Henriette Gunkel. "Q&A with Jasbir Puar." *Darkmatter*, 2 May 2008. http://www.darkmatter101.org/site/2008/05/02/qa-with-jasbir-puar/.

———. *Terrorist Assemblages: Homonationalism in Queer Times*. Durham, NC: Duke University Press, 2007.

Rankin, Jim, and Sandro Contenta. "A Depraved Double Life." *Toronto Star*, 19 October 2010.

Raymont, Peter, dir. *Shake Hands with the Devil: The Journey of Roméo Dallaire*. Canadian Broadcasting Corporation, 2004. 91 min.

Razack, Sherene. *Dark Threats and White Knights: The Somalia Affair, Peacekeeping and the New Imperialism*. Toronto: University of Toronto Press, 2004.

———. "Introduction: When Place Becomes Race." In *Race, Space, and Law: Unmapping a White Settler Society*, 1–20. Toronto: Between the Lines, 2002.

———. "Stealing the Pain of Others: Reflections on Canadian Humanitarian Responses." *Review of Education, Pedagogy, and Cultural Studies* 29, no. 4 (2007): 375–94.

Razack, Sherene, Malinda Smith, and Sunera Thobani. Introduction to *States of Race: Critical Race Feminism for the 21st Century*, edited by Sherene Razack, Malinda Smith, and Sunera Thobani, 1–19. Toronto: Between the Lines, 2010.

RBC Media Newsroom. "Reaching for the Stars: Creating the Canadian Brand for Human Rights Leadership." 19 October 2005. http://www.rbc.com/newsroom/speeches/20051019coffey.html.

Ritter, Kathleen. "The Reclining Figure and Other Provocations." In *Rebecca Belmore: Rising to the Occasion*, edited by Daina Augiatis and Kathleen Ritter, 53–65. Vancouver: Vancouver Art Gallery, 2008.

Roach, Joseph. *Cities of the Dead: Circum-Atlantic Performance*. New York: Columbia University Press, 1996.

Roberts, Lacey Jane. "Put Your Thing Down, Flip It, and Reverse It: Reimagining Craft Identities Using Tactics of Queer Theory." In *Extra/Ordinary: Craft and Contemporary Art*, edited by Maria Elena Buszek, 243–59. Durham, NC: Duke University Press, 2011.

Robertson, Kristy. "Rebellious Doilies and Subversive Stitches: Writing a Craftivist History." In *Extra/Ordinary: Craft and Contemporary Art*, edited by Maria Elena Buszek, 184–203. Durham, NC: Duke University Press, 2011.

Robinson, Dylan. "Feeling Reconciliation, Remaining Settled." In *Theatres of Affect: New Essays on Canadian Theatre*, vol. 4, edited by Erin Hurley, 275–306. Toronto: Playwrights Canada Press, 2014.

Rothberg, Michael. "From Gaza to Warsaw: Mapping Multidirectional Memory." *Criticism* 53, no. 4 (2011): 523–48.

Royal Canadian Legion. "Paintings in War Museum Anger Veterans Group." *Hunter News*, July/Aug. 2005. Royal Canadian Legion Branch 322 Ajax, Ontario.

———. "Teachers Guide." 29 August 2012. http://www.legion.ca/youth/teaching-guide/.

Royal Canadian Mounted Police. "Murdered Aboriginal Women: A National Operational Overview." Royal Canadian Mounted Police, 16 May 2014. http://www.rcmp-grc.gc.ca/en/missing-and-murdered-aboriginal-women-national-operational-overview.

Ruddick, Sara. "The Rationality of Care." In *Women, Militarism, and War: Essays in History, Politics, and Social Theory*, edited by Jean Bethke Elshtain and Sheila Tobias, 229–54. Totowa, NJ: Rowman and Littlefield, 1990.

Rukszto, Katarzyna. "Haunted Spaces, Ghostly Memories: The Canadian War Museum." *Third Text* 22, no. 6 (2008): 743–54.

Saint John, Michelle, dir. *Colonization Road.* Decolonization Road Production Inc. in association with The Breath Films, 2016. Film.

Salbi, Zainab. *The Other Side of War: Women's Stories of Survival and Hope*. Washington, DC: National Geographic, 2006.

Sandals, Leah. "Rebecca Belmore to Make Major Human Rights Museum Piece." *Canadian Art*, 24 January 2014. canadianart.ca/news/rebecca-belmore-2/.

Schechner, Richard. *Performance Studies: An Introduction*. New York: Routledge, 2006.

Schneider, Rebecca. *The Explicit Body in Performance*. New York: Routledge, 1997.

———. *Performing Remains: Art and War in Times of Theatrical Reenactment*. New York: Routledge, 2011.

Scott, Peter Dale. *American War Machine: Deep Politics, the CIA Global Drug Connection, and the Road to Afghanistan*. Lanham, MD: Rowman and Littlefield, 2010.

Seremetakis, C. Nadia. *The Last Word: Women, Death, and Divination in Inner Mani*. Chicago: University of Chicago Press, 1991.

Seth. *Dominion* (2001–ongoing). Installation. At *Every. Now. Then. Reframing Nationhood* exhibition, Art Gallery of Ontario, Toronto, 2017.

Shoal Lake 40 First Nation. "Shoal Lake 40 Launches the Museum *for* Canadian Human Rights Violations." Press release, 16 September 2014. https://intercontinentalcry.org/shoal-lake-40-launches-museum-canadian-human-rights-violations-25572/.

———. "Use of Shoal Lake Water Makes Museum 'A Shrine to Canadian Hypocrisy.'" Press release, 27 March 2014. http://www.sl40.ca/docs/letter_to_predock_museum_for_human_rights_architect.pdf.

Silver, Steven, dir. *The Last Just Man*. Barna-Alper Productions, 2001. Film. 70 min.

Simon, Roger, Sharon Rosenberg, and Claudia Eppert, eds. Introduction to *Between Hope and Despair: Pedagogy and the Remembrance of Historical Trauma*, edited by Roger I. Simon, Sharon Rosenberg, and Claudia Eppert, 1–8. Lanham, MD: Rowman and Littlefield, 2000.

Simpson, Audra. *Mohawk Interruptus: Political Life across the Borders of Settler States*. Durham, NC: Duke University Press, 2014.

Simpson, Leanne. "Fish Broth and Fasting." Blog, 13 January 2013. https://morphicenergies.wordpress.com/2013/01/19/fish-broth-fasting/.

———, ed. *Lighting the Eighth Fire: The Liberation, Resurgence, and Protection of Indigenous Nations*. Winnipeg: Arbeiter Ring, 2008.

———. "Our Elder Brothers: The Lifeblood of Resurgence." In *Lighting the Eighth Fire: The Liberation, Resurgence, and Protection of Indigenous Nations*, edited by Leanne Simpson, 73–88. Winnipeg: Arbeiter Ring Publishing, 2008.

Skinner, Michael. "Canadian Mining Companies Make the Big Move into Afghanistan." Global Research: Centre for Research on Globalization, 13 December 2011. https://www.globalresearch.ca/canadian-mining-companies-make-the-big-move-into-afghanistan/28187.

———. "The Empire of Capital and the Latest Inning of the Great Game." In *Empire's Ally: Canada and the War in Afghanistan*, edited by Jerome Klassen and Greg Albo, 106–38. Toronto: University of Toronto Press, 2013.

Smith, Linda Tuhiwai. *Decolonizing Methodologies: Research and Indigenous Peoples*. London, UK: Zed Books, 1999.

Smith, Terry. "The Architecture of Aftermath: Iconomy and Contemporaneity." *Bulletin of the Institute of Humanity, Human and Social Sciences* 88 (2007): 33–47.

Sontag, Susan. *Regarding the Pain of Others*. New York: Farrar, Straus and Giroux, 2003.

Spivak, Gayatri Chakravorty. "Nationalism and the Imagination." *Lectora 15* (2009): 75–98.

Spottiswoode, Roger, dir. *Shake Hands with the Devil.* Barna-Alper Productions and Halifax Film Company, 2007. 112 min.

Star. "Top General's Comments Anger Liberals." 16 February 2007. https://www.thestar.com/news/2007/02/16/top_generals_comments_anger_liberals.html.

Steele, Lisa, and Kim Tomczak. *The Afternoon Knows What the Morning Never Suspected.* Three-channel video installation. At *Every. Now. Then. Reframing Nationhood* exhibition, Art Gallery of Ontario, Toronto, 2017.

Stemple, Lara. "Male Rape and Human Rights." *Hastings Law Journal* 60, no. 3 (2008–9): 605–46.

Stewart, J., and Helmut Kallmann. "Massey Commission." In *The Canadian Encyclopedia.* Historica Canada. 6 February 2006. https://www.thecanadianencyclopedia.ca/en/article/massey-commission-emc.

Sweet Honey in the Rock. *Breaths.* Flying Fish Label, 1981. Sound recording.

Tasker, John Paul. "Confusion Reigns over Number of Missing, Murdered Indigenous Women". CBC News/Politics, 16 February 2016. http://www.cbc.ca/news/politics/mmiw-4000-hajdu-1.3450237.

———. "Conservative Senator Defends 'Well-Intentioned' Residential School System." CBCNews/Politics, 8 March 2017. http://www.cbc.ca/news/politics/residential-school-system-well-intentioned-conservative-senator-1.4015115/.

———. "Senator Lynn Beyak Says She Has 'Suffered' with Residential School Survivors." CBCNews/Politics, 27 March 2017. http://www.cbc.ca/news/politics/senator-lynn-beyak-suffered-residential-schools-1.4042627.

Taylor, Diana. *The Archive and the Repertoire: Performing Cultural Memory in the Americas.* Durham, NC: Duke University Press, 2003.

———. *Disappearing Acts: Spectacle of Gender and Nationalism in Argentina's "Dirty War."* Durham, NC: Duke University Press, 1997.

Teigrob, Robert. *Living with War: Twentieth-Century Conflict in Canadian and American History and Memory.* Toronto: University of Toronto Press. 2016.

Thobani, Sunera. "White Innocence, Western Supremacy: The Role of Western Feminism in the 'War on Terror.'" In *States of Race: Critical Race Feminism for the 21st Century*, edited by Sherene Razack, Malinda Smith, and Sunera Thobani, 127–46. Toronto: Between the Lines, 2010.

Thomas, David Gordon. *Circle Element.* Installation. At *Ancestral Land* exhibit, Buhler Hall, Canadian Museum for Human Rights, Winnipeg.

Thomas, Jeff. *F.B.I.*. Photograph. Ottawa, 1998.

———. Champlain Series: 2000–2011. http://jeff-thomas.ca/2014/06/champlain-2000-2005/.

———. *Seize the Space: Greg Hill in His Canoe.* Photograph. Nepean Point, Ottawa, 2000.

Thompson, Mark. "Should the Military Return to Counting Bodies?" *Time*, 2 June 2009. http://content.time.com/time/nation/article/0,8599,1902274,00.html.

Townsend-Gault, Charlotte. "Rebecca Belmore and James Luna on Location at Venice: The Allegorical Indian Redux." *Art History* 29, no. 4 (2006): 721–55.

Truth and Reconciliation Commission of Canada. *Final Report of the Truth and Reconciliation Commission of Canada: Honouring the Truth, Reconciling the Future,* Vol.1, *Summary*. Toronto: James Lorimer, 2015.

Tuck, Eve, and K. Wayne Yang. "Decolonization Is Not a Metaphor." *Decolonization: Indigeneity, Education, and Society* 1, no. 1 (2012): 1–40.

Ukrainian Weekly. "Canadians for Genocide Museum Protest the Prime Minister's Stance." Vol. 74, no. 19 (7 May 2006). http://www.ukrweekly.com/old/archive/2006/190615.shtml.

University of Winnipeg. "Bead Making Workshop." Cultural Studies Research Group, 8 March 2014. http://uwinnipeg.ca/csrg/news-and-events/2014/03/Bead%20Making%20Workshop.html.

Veterans Affairs Canada. "Civilian Shoes to Combat Boots." http://www.veterans.gc.ca/eng/remembrance/information-for/educators/learning-modules/vimy-ridge/civilian-shoes-to-combat-boots.

———. "Remembrance Day 2014 Teacher's Guide." 24 October 2014.

Vosters, Helene. "Between Worlds: Reflections on a Year of Falling." In *Theatre of Affect* (Essays), edited by Erin Hurley, 263–74. New Essays on Canadian Theatre vol. 4, general editor Ric Knowles. Toronto: Playwrights Canada Press, 2014.

———. "Beyond Heroism and towards Shared Vulnerability: Re-Imagining Canada's Affective Deployments of Mourning in Response to Afghan War Deaths." *FRAKCIJA* 58/59 (2012): 51–59.

———. *Flag of Tears: Lament for the Stains of a Nation*. Installation and participatory embroidery circle. FAC presents: *You're Not Here*, Daniels Spectrum, Toronto, 3–31 March, 2015.

———. *Impact Afghanistan War*. Public memorial performed daily in locations throughout Canada, United States, and Europe. Canada Day 2010–Canada Day 2011.

———. "Military Memorialization and Its Object(s) of Period Purification." In *Performing Objects and Theatrical Things*, edited by Joanne Zerdy and Marlis Schweitzer, 104–17. Palgrave McMillan: London, 2014.

———. "Piece/Peace Work: Engendering 'Rationalities of Care' through a *Thread-by-Thread* Deconstruction of Militarism." *Performance Research* 18, no. 2 (2013): 4–14.

———. "Sochi Olympics 2014, Canadian Truth and Reconciliation, and the Haunting Ghouls of Canadian Nationalism." In *Performance Studies and Canadian Culture* edited by Laura Levin and Marlis Schweitzer, 184–209. Montreal and Kingston: McGill-Queen's Press, 2014.

———. Stitch-by-Stitch. (2016 – ongoing). Participatory TRC sewing circle and reading group. Multiple locations and dates.

———. *Thread-by-Thread: A Participatory Deconstructing Militarism (Un)Sewing Circle*. 2012. Installation and participatory (un)sewing circle. Performance Studies International #18 and Ludus Festival, Armley Mills, UK, 28–30 June 2012.

———. *Unravel: A Meditation on the Warp and Weft of Militarism*. 2011–14. Visualeyez Performance Art Festival, Edmonton, 2011; Festival of Original Theatre, Toronto, 2012; Feminist Art Conference, Toronto, 2013; Culture Days, Walnut Contemporary Gallery, Toronto, 2013; WIAprojects: Babble/Babel, Toronto, 2013; and *Cross Section Art Exhibition*, Ryerson University, Toronto 2014.

Ward, John. "War Museum, Vets Reach Compromise." *Star*, 10 October 2007. https://www.thestar.com/news/canada/2007/10/10/war_museum_vets_reach_compromise.html.

Weder, Adele. "Faulty Tower: The Canadian Museum for Human Rights as Tourist Trap, Failed Memorial, and White Elephant." *Walrus*, 29 October 2014. https://thewalrus.ca/faulty-tower/.

Wente, Jesse. "Canada Can't Look Away after 2017. We Won't Let It." CBC, 27 December 2017. http://www.cbc.ca/2017/canada-can-t-look-away-after-2017-we-won-t-let-it-1.4350376.

Wetselaar, Sean, and Katherine Declerq. "Soldier Killed at CFB Petawawa." *Star*, 22 November 2014. https://www.thestar.com/news/gta/2014/11/22/soldier_killed_at_cfb_petawawa_reports_say.html.

Windigo, Delaney. "Human Rights Watch Cries Foul on First Nation Water Crisis. APTN (Aboriginal Peoples Television Network) National News, 7 June 2016. http://aptnnews.ca/2016/06/07/human-rights-watch-cries-foul-on-first-nation-water-crisis/.

Winnipeg Art Gallery. *INSURGENCE/RESURGENCE*. Exhibition curated by Jaimie Isaac and Julie Nagam. Winnipeg, 2017.

Withers, Denise, dir. *Roméo Dallaire: Witness the Evil.* Canadian Department of National Defence, 1998. Film.

Wodke, Larissa. "A Lovely Building for Difficult Knowledge: The Architecture of the Canadian Museum for Human Rights." *Review of Education, Pedagogy, and Cultural Studies* 37, nos. 2–3 (2015): 207–26.

Wong, Kimlee. "Human Rights Hypocrisy: The Canadian Museum for Human Rights." Global Research: Centre for Research on Globalization, 12 September 2014. http://www.globalresearch.ca/human-rights-hypocrisy-the-canadian-museum-for-human-rights/5401336.

INDEX

C

W

Y